N.Y. Board of trade Binghamton

Board of trade review of Binghamton, N.Y.

N.Y. Board of trade Binghamton

Board of trade review of Binghamton, N.Y.

ISBN/EAN: 9783744736008

Printed in Europe, USA, Canada, Australia, Japan

Cover: Foto ©Andreas Hilbeck / pixelio.de

More available books at **www.hansebooks.com**

BOARD OF TRADE REVIEW

—OF—

BINGHAMTON, N. Y.,

The Great Manufacturing City of Southern New York.

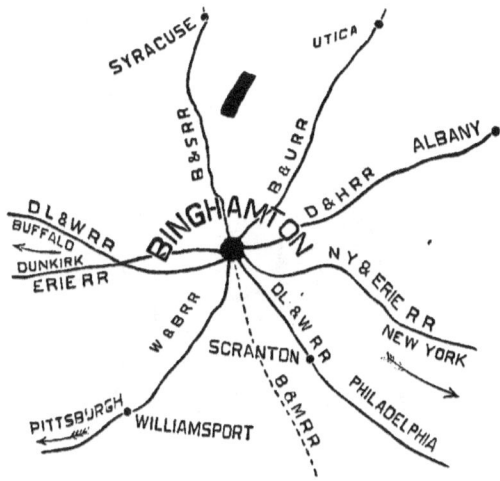

Its Magical Growth, Rapid Development, Wonderful Beauty, and Natural Attractions,

TOGETHER WITH AN ACCOUNT OF ITS

REPRESENTATIVE BUSINESS ENTERPRISES.

BINGHAMTON, N. Y.:
JAS. P. MCKINNEY, Publisher.
1892.

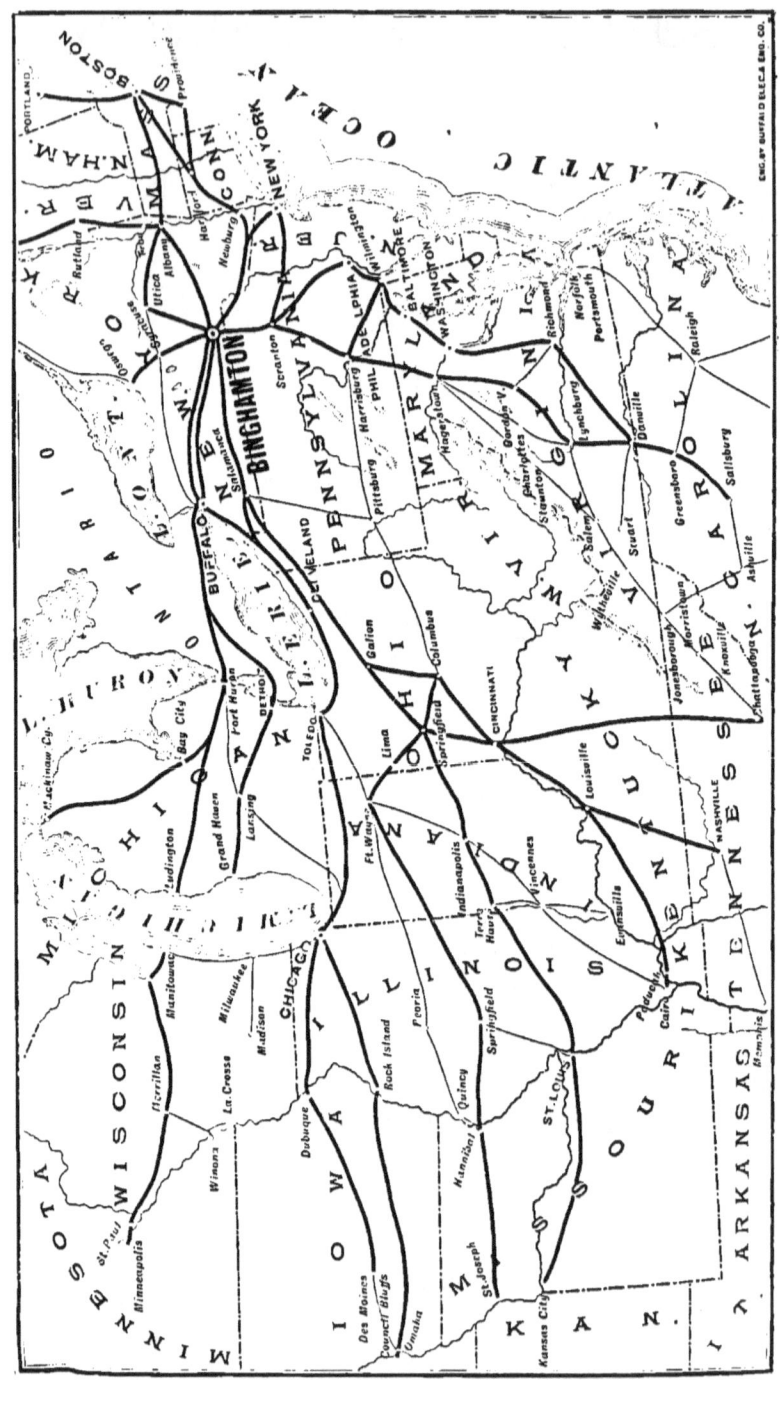

THE INDUSTRIAL ADVANTAGES

OF

BINGHAMTON, N. Y.

BY JAS. P. McKINNEY.

Inception and Development.

A large amount of matter has been collected and published with regard to the early history of Binghamton, which is doubtless highly interesting reading to those who by descent are naturally proud of the exploits of their forefathers. To the reader for whom this work is designed, such details, however, would prove of but little interest ; yet, while it is not our purpose to enter minutely into them, it is proper for us to embody, at the inception of this book, a few of the more notable facts in the development of this populous locality, from the trackless waste it once was.

The territory embraced within the present limits of Binghamton was granted, by royal patent, June 27, 1786, to William Bingham and others. Mr. Bingham was born in England and came to America when a young man. His residence and place of business was Philadelphia. He was well educated and had studied law in England, though on coming to America he adopted the pursuit of a merchant.

The first permanent settler within the territory was Captain Joseph Leonard, originally of Plymouth, Mass., who came with his family in 1787. A few weeks later came Colonel William Rose and his brother, traveling on foot from Connecticut. Other settlers followed, and within a year twenty families had located a mile or so above the confluence of the Chenango and Susquehanna rivers, the hamlet being known as "Chenang Pint."

In early times this region was covered with a dense growth of pine forest, and was, during the first stages of settlement, chiefly a lumber region. All business was then based upon this interest, it being regarded for many years as almost the only industry that would yield a return for labor in cash. The rivers furnished easy transit to market, and a raft of pine promised almost immediate results. So little attention did many of the early settlers pay to raising their own bread, that they went abroad even for their garden vegetables.

Previous to the year 1799 no village had been thought of where the City of Binghamton stands. During that year a charter was granted for building a bridge across the Chenango, and the residents of the "Point," realizing the importance of such a structure, removed en masse to the more favored locality, the first house being erected at what is now the southeast corner of Court and Water streets.

Mr. Bingham's policy toward settlers fostered emigration to the new hamlet, which, being so eligibly situated, made a steady growth and soon became an important trading center under the name of Binghamton, so called from its benefactor.

The Village of Binghamton was incorporated by an act of the Legislature on May 3, 1834. By this act the corporate limits were fixed and the Village divided into five wards.

During the year 1834 the construction of the Chenango canal was begun. It was finished in the spring of 1837 and gave Binghamton water connection with the Erie canal at Utica. This canal built up the interests of Binghamton rapidly. Simultaneously with the excitement throughout the State over the construction of canals, agitation of the subject of railroad building began. In 1849 the Erie railroad was completed from New York to Binghamton. The opening of this road so greatly enlarged the commercial facilities of Binghamton that the natural advantages of its situation began to be more apparent. Projects for the building of other roads soon began to be entertained. From the south came the Lackawanna, furnishing an outlet for the Wyoming Valley and the rich coal fields of Northern Pennsylvania. Then came the Syracuse and Binghamton, the Albany and Binghamton, and later the Utica and Chenango Valley. In 1867 Binghamton had attained a population of about 11,000 inhabitants, and during that year assumed a City form of government.

Binghamton in 1892.

It has been somewhat irreverently said that "God made the country and man made the town." Were this true of other cities the saying has but a partial application to Binghamton, whose grand "umbrageous temples not made with hands" are the glory of the streets and avenues and the pride of the inhabitants. As a place of residence Binghamton is unsurpassed, if indeed equalled by any other city in New York. Its velvety lawns, fine river, valley and mountain drives, its shaded streets, its agreeable climate, the prevalence of thrift and comfort apparent even in the dwellings of the working people, and the numerous spacious and costly mansions of the rich, together with unsurpassed religious privileges and educational facilities combine to make this city one of the few spots on earth akin to Paradise.

BROOME COUNTY COURT HOUSE.

Binghamton is the capital of Broome County, one of the most thriving counties in the State of New York. It is beautifully situated at the confluence of the Susquehanna and Chenango rivers, about seven miles as the crow flies from the northern bounds of Pennsylvania. The city embraces an area of about four square miles. Beyond, and contiguous to the city lines, the territory is closely built, the suburbs containing a population of from 3,500 to 4,000 inhabitants who work in Binghamton and should be annexed. The site on which the city stands comprises not only the extended area of table land intervening between the converging rivers, but the valleys lying along the opposite banks, both of the Susquehanna and the Chenango. The latter river divides that portion of the city lying north of the Susquehanna in a northerly and southerly direction into two nearly equal parts. The different sections are connected together by substantial and convenient free bridges.

The city, except where the rivers enter and pass out, with valleys of greater or less width, is environed with hills. Those which lie upon the north, divided by the Chenango, and those upon the south, along the line of the Susquehanna, have a nearer proximity to the city than those which lie towards the other points of the compass. The hills do not reach the dignity of mountains, but their easy slopes and their rich and distinctive foliage give them a beautiful and picturesque appearance.

Divided into three parts by the Susquehanna and Chenango rivers, which here unite their waters, it forms a scene at once picturesque and beautiful, filling the beholder with admiration. Looking to the north, to the south, to the east, to the west, a scene of such rich and varied beauty is presented to the view that but little else could heighten its charms or add to its attractiveness.

Binghamton has had a healthy and a rapid growth during the last half-dozen years. In 1870 its population was 12,692; in 1875, 15,550, in 1880, 17,315, and in 1890, when the last general census was taken, 35,093. A careful census at the present time would probably show not less than 38,000.

A City of Homes.

This designation cannot be improved upon, for after admiring the splendid residences of the wealthy and the handsome houses of the well-to-do, the eye of the visitor will rest with infinite pleasure upon the houses of the mechanic, the clerk, the young business man and the laborer, miles and miles of streets being lined with neat but inexpensive houses, often surrounded by a plot of ground, and each owned by its occupant. Land has never been held at fancy prices, and the result is as has been stated. The reasonable prices at which the working classes have been able to obtain the great boon of owning their own domiciles has materially enhanced the welfare of the city, and apart from stimulating habits of thrift, has created a class of citizens who are content, and having a stake in the country are not so prone to become mixed up

RESIDENCE OF MR. GEORGE H. BARLOW, FRONT ST.

in labor troubles. The savings banks and numerous building and loan associations have done much good in this direction by loaning money at low rates of interest to mechanics and others, to enable them to own their own houses. Numerous capitalists also stand ready to build and sell houses, payment to be made in small weekly sums, out of the savings of wages, and no mechanic with steady employment and decent wages need be without a home of his own in Binghamton for any length of time if he desires to have one. Hundreds of houses have been built in this way in the past few years and the suburbs of Binghamton are rapidly filling up with neat and tasteful homes for the masses.

The Streets

Are almost always the first subject of remark by visitors to the city, and worthily so, both on account of their width, cleanliness and fine shade trees, with which they are almost universally lined. The streets of Binghamton are regularly and tastefully laid out, many of them being very wide and spacious. The streets belonging to the city approximate fifty miles in length. Court street is the principal business thoroughfare. Washington street is next in importance, followed by State, Water, Chenango, Collier and Wall. The streets in the business part of the city are well paved.

Walks and Drives.

The country surrounding Binghamton affords a great variety of delightful walks and drives, and presents many attractive and interesting views. Many of the drives, especially along the rivers, up or down, abound in romantic and picturesque scenery.

The Rivers.

The Susquehanna river, which forms so important an adjunct to Binghamton, takes its rise in Otsego Lake. It flows in graceful sweeps and curves in a southerly direction after entering the county of Broome, crosses the Pennsylvania line and makes a great bend in that State, re-enters New York State again, flowing in a northwesterly direction to Binghamton. Here it is joined by the Chenango and their united waters flow to the west border of the county in a direction a little south of west. The Chenango river has its rise in Oneida county.

These rivers, as viewed from the bridges—whether one looks up or down the Chenango, or up or down the Susquehanna—present a uniformly rapid current of about six miles an hour, with beautifully clean bottoms and banks, sparkling waters, and, in many places, shaded and well-kept lawns extending down to the water's edge. The scene presented is rather rural than commercial, but Binghamton derives much benefit from the rivers in beauty and recreation, pleasure boating being quite a feature, and the rapidity of the current, the purity and unobstructed condition of the stream being conducive to public health.

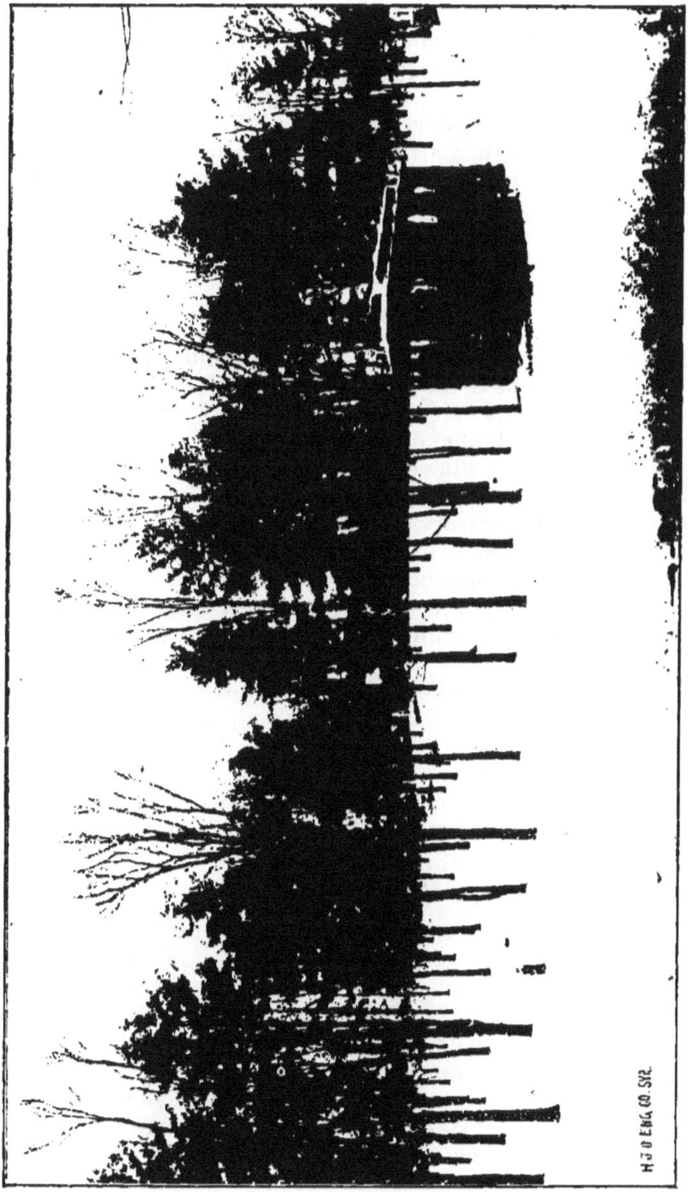

VIEW OF THE MOELLER ESTATE.

Bridges.

We have said that the different sections of Binghamton are connected by bridges. The bridges number five. The uppermost of these, crossing the Chenango river at Ferry street, is a fine suspension bridge, 360 feet in length between towers. The Court street bridge, crossing the Chenango lower down, is 358 feet long. The Rock-bottom bridge, an iron structure of fine workmanship, is the uppermost one on the Susquehanna, crossing at Carroll street, with a length between the shore abutments of 540 feet. The lower Susquehanna bridge, an iron structure, at the foot of Washington street, is about 700 feet long. A foot-bridge for the convenience of pedestrians also crosses the Susquehanna at the foot of Exchange street.

Climatic and Sanitary.

No consideration is more essential to the continued prosperity and happiness of a community than health. Statistics prove that Binghamton is one of the most healthful cities in the country. Its climate is pure and genial, the temperature being modified by the rivers. The City is elevated 850 feet above tide-water, giving the air a life-giving quality unsurpassed. The City is subject to no prevailing diseases, is well drained, and its sanitary condition is well regulated by an efficient board of health. In comparison with other cities the percentage of mortality in Binghamton is about the lowest in the State. The natural features of soil, climate and topography are conducive to health, and the natural drainage of locality has saved the tax-payers' pockets and preserved his health. With the introduction of water-works the necessary sewers followed to make perfect the sanitary system. A practical, well-built system of sewers drains the principal sections of the city, to which branch lines are annexed as required. Public improvements and regulations are constantly lowering the rate of mortality, while the population increases in defiance of the ordinary rule of nature. Typhoid fever, one of the direst enemies of large cities, is practically unknown here.

Water Works.

Binghamton has an excellent system of water works. The works are city property and are located in the east part of the city, the water being taken from wells sunk below the bed of the river and filtered through the sand and gravel of the naturally porous soil from a great depth, thus making it cool and pure. It is also abundant in quantity and may be increased to any extent required by additional wells or by the driving of tubes. The current of the water in these wells is from the hills toward the river, showing that pure mountain water is obtained. The works are equipped with two Holly pumping engines and four large boilers for generating power. The capacity is 18,000,000 gallons per twenty-four hours, which being far greater than the demand, the protection from fire is as completely assured as in any city in the

THE CITY OF BINGHAMTON.

SUSQUEHANNA VALLEY HOME FOR CHILDREN.

country. The efficiency of the water works is proven by the rates of fire insurance, which are from twenty to forty per cent. lower than in Syracuse, the nearest sister city.

Fire Department.

Among other good things Binghamton possesses an excellent fire department, which, though a volunteer department, is well organized and disciplined and has shown itself capable of most efficient service in arresting and preventing the spread of conflagrations. Most of the companies own their buildings. The department consists of two steamers, seven hose companies, two chemical engines, one hook and ladder company, a fire alarm telegraph system, 375 hydrants and other necessary apparatus of the latest improved character. The firemen are trained and expert, and the service is upon an efficient basis.

Police Department.

All parts of the city are well patrolled by a sturdy and experienced force of police, which, we are happy to say, owing to the orderly character of the community and the absence of that tough element, more notable in larger cities, has little occasion for extreme measures, though the vigilance of the department is in no wise neglected for these reasons.

Educational.

It may be taken for granted that a city of enterprise and intelligence, such as Binghamton, has considered matters of education of primary importance. No expense has been spared in perfecting and developing a complete system of public schools, and not content with this, several scholastic institutions of high rank have here found adequate support and management. Schools of the best order, freely accessible to the poorest child in the city, are in daily operation. Every child so far belongs to the State. Ignorance is more costly than schools, and no investment can be so uniformly productive of good returns to the State as that devoted to the culture of those who themselves are soon to be the State. Hence; the doors of the public schools are thrown wide open and the children are welcome without money or price, not from the parlors of the rich only, but also from the highways and ditches. In the matter of schools, the city has certainly little to ask for, and its citizens point with pardonable pride to its splendid system of public schools, with its high school, which is unsurpassed in the State, in respect either of the conveniences of the building or the completeness of its appointments for teaching the higher branches of a common school education. There are sixteen public schools in Binghamton employing 111 teachers; two ladies' seminaries, two business colleges, one school of stenography and one kindergarten.

St. Joseph's Academy.

This is a Catholic institution conducted by the Sisters of St. Joseph. The academy is beautifully located near the junction of the Chenango and Susquehanna rivers, and is an important feature in the educational department of Binghamton. It was established in 1862 and is one of the most flourishing institutions of learning in the State.

Susquehanna Valley Home.

This institution is pleasantly situated on high ground overlooking the city and its purpose is to provide a home for the friendless orphans and children of indigent parents. Its wards are gathered from the counties of Broome, Chenango, Cortland, Delaware, Tioga and Tomp-

RESIDENCE OF MR. C. A. WILKINSON, FRONT STREET.

kins. This institution is the pioneer in this country having for its primary object the removal of children from the county poor houses. Through its influence and example the law of 1876 was enacted, prohibiting the placing of children between the ages of three and sixteen years in the alms-houses of the State and providing for their care and education.

City School Library.

The City School Library was established in 1861, when the Board of Education purchased, as a nucleus, the library of the Y. M. C. A. Additions have been made to the library every year, and the whole number of volumes is now about 8,000. Residents of the city and non-resident pupils, on signing application and pledge to abide by the rules of the library, are entitled to free use of books. The library is open Mondays, Tuesdays, Wednesdays, Thursdays and Fridays, between the hours of 2 and 6, and Saturdays between the hours of 2 and 8 P. M., except legal holidays and at such time as it is closed by order of the Board of Education.

The Public Institutions

Of Binghamton are of great importance and usefulness, presenting very substantial evidence of the city's accumulating wealth and of its eminently thorough and practical character. Among them are the Y. M. C. A., which occupies a prominent place among the public organizations of the city; the Binghamton City Hospital, the Binghamton State Hospital, St. Mary's Orphan Home, the House of the Good Shepherd, the Public Library, etc.

Binghamton State Hospital.

Standing out in bold relief on the hill east of the city, like a grim and silent sentinel, is a magnificent granite pile, occupied by those poor unfortunates—the chronic insane. The institution was formerly a State Inebriate Asylum. The site comprises over 252 acres of land, and was presented by the citizens of Binghamton. The grounds are devoted to suitable walks and lawns, and to farming purposes. The main structure is 365 feet in length, three stories high, in the castellated Gothic style, with massive towers, turrets and buttresses, embattled at the top. Adjoining the hospital proper are numerous other buildings for various uses. The ceremonies of laying the corner-stone took place September 24, 1858. The hospital is located about two miles eastward from the Court House, some 240 feet above the water, and commands a view of the Susquehanna and Chenango rivers and valleys for eight or nine miles each way. From the hospital grounds the best views of the city can be obtained.

Binghamton City Hospital.

This worthy institution is located at the upper end of Court street, on the bank of the Susquehanna river. It was first opened March 1, 1888, and has twenty beds. The domestic affairs of the hospital are entrusted to a board of fifteen lady managers. The medical department is in charge of a medical director and a staff of eight physicians and surgeons.

House of the Good Shepherd.

This institution was originally an old ladies' home, and later a general hospital was added by the Church of the Good Shepherd. The general hospital was abolished on the organization of the City Hospital, but two wards are still retained for hospital uses.

St. Mary's Orphan Home.

This institution is located on College Hill, and has about 100 orphans in charge. The asylum occupies a building founded in 1854 and known as the Susquehanna Seminary.

Young Men's Christian Association.

The Young Men's Christian Association was organized in 1865, and it has steadily grown in public favor and usefulness until its many-sided work of to-day is looked upon as a necessity. The Association owns a valuable property, located at Nos. 7 and 9 Court street, and occupies about half of the building for its own use. The building contains a large reading room and library, lecture room, parlors, hall, office, rooms of

PERRY BLOCK.

the boys' department, etc. The Railroad Department, located at 60 Lewis street, is supported by the railroad companies centering here and is doing a valuable work among their employes. The building contains reading and amusement rooms, bath rooms, library, rest room, committee rooms, etc.

The Binghamton Board of Trade.

The Binghamton Board of Trade was incorporated February 15, 1887. Its membership numbers 200. The objects of the association are to inculcate just and equitable principles in trade; to establish and maintain uniformity in commercial usages; to acquire, preserve and disseminate valuable business information; to protect and foster the mercantile and manufacturing industries; to promote the commerce of the city of Binghamton, and its general prosperity, by the solicitation of manufacturers and business enterprises to locate within its boundaries and adjacent territory; the promulgation of the advantages possessed by Binghamton as a desirable place of residence and for the employment of capital; the use of all proper means to obtain legislation, National, State and Municipal, favorable to the interests of the city and its inhabitants; the extension of facilities of transportation, and the protection of the trade of the city from unjust discrimination in rates of freight and otherwise; and generally by uniform and well directed efforts to advance and extend the welfare and promote the commercial integrity of the business community.

By such organized efforts as the above it is hoped that the manufacturing interests of the city, which have already attained great commercial importance and stability, will be enlarged and quickened with new life. The membership of the Board of Trade, pledged to the promotion of these objects, affords a guarantee that every well devised plan and project to further it will be liberally backed and supported. Rapid as have been its strides within the past decade, the next generation will see an enlargement of Binghamton's manufacturing interests commensurate with its commercial importance.

The Board of Trade makes the following offers to manufacturers:

1st. Free building sites, with the finest locations on trunk lines of railways.

2d. To erect buildings and rent same for term of years for 6 per cent. net on cost of building.

3d. To give land free and 10 per cent. of cost of the buildings erected by manufacturers.

Concerning the opportunities for establishing business enterprises here, all inquiries addressed to F. Newell Gilbert, Sec'y Board of Trade, Binghamton, N. Y., will receive prompt attention.

Inducements to Manufacturers.

The right place to manufacture successfully is evidently at a point where the raw materials accumulate naturally, and where, at the same time, there is cheap power and advanced and ample facilities for marketing the product. Binghamton pre-eminently furnishes these conditions. Situated at a focal point of seven great railroads, connecting the city with the markets of the whole country, and the lumber and coal regions of the immediate vicinity, material necessarily accumulates here, and cheap power is amply provided and assured for all time. Opportunities can be obtained here by the manufacturer superior to those of larger cities, for the reason that while equal facilities are found here, at the same time the best positions are available at comparatively little cost. Excellent coal, iron, hard-wood lumber and other materials for manufacturing purposes are right at hand, and no city has better

THE CITY OF BINGHAMTON.

THE ARLINGTON.

facilities for distributing the product. The manufacturer who locates here will find everything at hand for the successful furtherance of his enterprise, and a friendly and helping hand will be offered him by every citizen of the community. In brief, some of the general advantages and attractions of Binghamton are:

1st. It is located in one of the most fertile and productive portions of New York State, and in one of the most thriving and prosperous agricultural counties of the State.

2d. It is an important railroad centre, with outlets in every direction.

3d. It therefore possesses the advantages of railway competition, all competing lines expressing and showing a liberal spirit toward all manufacturing enterprises.

4th. It is situated in close proximity to coal and iron fields, and has competing and direct railway lines thereto.

5th. It has competing railway lines to New York, to Boston, and to the West. It has direct rail communication with Lake Ontario.

6th. The government of the city is based on the strictest ideas of economy, consistent with safe and sure progress, and the spirit of the people is decidedly in favor of every measure intended to make the rate of taxation low.

7th. It is rich in capital, strong in credit, untrammeled by debt, with small taxation, light municipal expenses, and cheap real estate, destined to advance rapidly in value.

8th. Statistics show that it is one of the healthiest cities in the Union, subject to no contagious diseases, and free from prevailing sickness.

9th. Its public school system is one of the best in the State and affords excellent educational facilities.

10th. The cost of living is much less than in larger cities.

11th. Its social advantages are numerous, the tone of society healthy, and the morals of the community beyond dispute.

In fact, no city in the Union offers so many advantages to the small or large manufacturer as does Binghamton at the present day.

The business men who control the capital have been trained to other pursuits, and have made their money there, and many of them may not now be fitted for a change, hence the opening must be filled principally by incoming capitalists and manufacturers, who will find local capitalists ready to join hands with skillful and enterprising managers. The introduction of new manufacturing enterprises will increase the opportunities of the retail merchant to establish successful mercantile enterprises, and the general growth and development of the city will be stimulated. The question is frequently asked, What can be manufactured in Binghamton to the best advantage? The simplest answer and an absolutely true one is: *Everything*. A good idea of what can be done may be obtained by a glance at the prosperous and flourishing branches of manufacturing business now carried on here.

Our Products

Now include acids, ale, aerated beverages, agricultural implements, architectural iron work, awnings, black-boards, blind staples, blank books, boilers, boots and shoes, boxes, brass goods, brushes, bricks, biscuits, baking powder, baskets, bed springs, butter packages, buttons, beer, cabinet work, carriages, carriage and saddlery hardware, carriage trimmings, car trimmings, chairs, chemicals, cigars, cigar boxes, clothing, coffees and spices, combs, confectionery, corn meal, canned fruits and vegetables, cider, cooperage stock, crackers, curtain fixtures, cutlery, cutters and sleighs, dairy products, dental goods, doors, sash and blinds, edge tools, electrical supplies, electro-plating, electric light, elevators (grain), engines, extracts, flags, flexible shafts, flour and feed, foundry work, furniture, fruit extracts, fur garments, gas, galvanized iron work, grocers' supplies, glass bottles, gloves and mittens, gold and silver plating, granite monuments, grates, grass seed, hardware, harness, headings, hoes and tools, horse clothing, hoops, horse collars, hubs and spokes, iron work, jewelry, lager beer, lubricators, leather, lumber and lumber products, lithographs, machinery, mantels, marble monuments, medicines, mince meat, models and patterns, mouldings, nickel plating, oils, optical goods, organs, overalls, outing garments, pants and shirts, paper boxes, paper, patterns, pharmaceutical preparations, pork products, pumps, pianos, phosphates, pie preparations, picture frames, printing presses, provisions, roofing materials, rubber stamps, saddlery hardware, sash, doors and blinds, sausages, scales, shirts, shoes, sheet-iron work, society goods, staves, signs, sleds, soap, spices, stairs, staples, steam heating plants, stencils, stone work, tacks, tents, tinware, tools, tobacco, umbrellas, upholstered furniture and chairs, varnishes, wagons, violins, wagon brakes, water motors, whips, wire goods, wood pulp, wood-working machinery, wheels and woolen blankets.

The most important industries of the city are those devoted to the manufacture of cigars, boots and shoes, chairs, carriages and sleighs, leather, overalls and clothing, scales, grass seeds, combs and buttons, outing garments and machinery, engines and boilers. The Lestershire Boot and Shoe Company recently moved to Lestershire, two and one-quarter miles west of the center of the city, is one of the largest industries of its kind in the country. The Whitney-Noyes Seed Company is the largest enterprise of its kind in the world. Binghamton is the second cigar producing city in the United States, and the great cigar factories of Barlow, Rogers & Simpson, Reynolds, Rogers & Co., George A. Kent & Co., Hull, Grummond & Co., C. B. Smith, Jr., & Co., John Gumberg & Co., Lyman Clock, Son & Co., have an output varying from ten to twenty millions each, annually, the first named having one year reached the enormous quantity of over 22,000,000. The engines and boilers of Shapley & Wells are shipped to all parts of the civilized world, while the scales made by Jones of Binghamton are used in every country on the globe. The overalls, pants and shirts made by the Bennett Manufacturing Company, Reed B. Freeman, the Freeman Overall Company and Smith, Kinney & Co. bear the highest reputation in the market and are in demand in all parts of the Union. The chairs manufactured by Wilkinson & Eastwood, the Binghamton Chair Company and Stickley Brothers have the lead in the great markets of the country. The Osgood & Thompson combination hay scales are a wonderful improvement in farm scales and are in great demand. The cutters and sleighs of the Sturtevant-Larrabee Company are widely recognized as the best in the market, and the sleds and express wagons made by the Wilkinson Manufacturing Company go away in car-load lots to lighten the hearts of millions of children in all parts of America. The Binghamton Manufacturing Company control a high-class trade for their superior outing garments, which reaches from the Atlantic to the Pacific. The great tannery of J. B. Weed & Co. is the largest in America, and that of Wilkinson, Sons & Co. makes a new process leather that is in demand throughout the country. Alonzo Roberson's new wood-working plant is the largest and most advantageously situated of any in the State, and both he and Bartlett & Co. are shipping sash, doors and blinds and other lumber products in enormous quantities to the trade. Of the other industries named each is represented by from one to half a dozen or more concerns and all are in a prosperous condition with uniformly increasing trade and output.

Commercial.

The wholesale trade of Binghamton has long been one of its most important features and it has kept pace with the general growth and prosperity of the city. All goods are procured direct from manufacturers, both at home and abroad, and not only do our merchants compete successfully with neighboring cities, but they have held the territory against the encroachments of all. In a general way it may be said of the wholesale and jobbing trade of the city that it occupies all the territory to which it is rightfully entitled, and, in addition to this, it has very considerably extended into the territory of other cities, notably Syracuse and Elmira. The trade now is in the most satisfactory condition, and while it has had a steady growth for many years, the increase in the past five years has been particularly gratifying. In groceries the great wholesale houses of S. Mills Ely & Co., Bean & Co., McKinney, Everts & Co., and H. W. Chubbuck & Co. transact a business that is not exceeded by any similar houses in the State, outside, possibly, of the metropolis. The boot and shoe trade is well represented by Stone & Germond and Goff & Macomber, and Babcock & Stowell and Geo. M. Harris are extensive jobbers of hardware as well as retailers. Lloyd & Gardiner are the only strictly wholesale confectioners in the city. The Whitney-Noyes Seed Co. and Conklin & Mersereau each do a very heavy jobbing trade in grass seeds, the John Ray Clarke Co. in hats, Casper & Crittenden in crockery, North & Shaw in provisions, and

White & Co. and John J. Moses in wines and liquors, and others in various lines are each transacting large and annually increasing operations. The Empire Grain and Elevator Co. handle grain in large quantities and the Berwind-White Coal Mining Co. through their branch office in this city transact a very extensive business in bituminous coals. Arguing from the success of the jobbing enterprises already located here, an equally profitable field is open for the establishment of wholesale dry goods, notions and millinery houses as well as for other specialties.

In the retail department of commerce no other city in the State is better supplied with facilities for obtaining goods of all kinds at reasonable prices, and the opportunities for engaging in any kind of retail enterprise here are of the most favorable nature.

PHELPS BANK BUILDING.

Susquehanna Valley Bank.

The Susquehanna Valley Bank is one of the oldest and best known banks in the Southern Tier. It was organized in 1855, with a capital of $100,000, to which has since been added a surplus fund of $40,000. The bank is located in the massive stone structure known as the Phelps Bank Building, an illustration of which is shown above, and the banking rooms are spacious and convenient, affording ample accommodations for the public and possessing every modern convenience for facilitating the business in hand. A general banking business is transacted, including the receiving of deposits, the discounting of approved commercial paper, the making of collections and issuance of exchange. From its inception this bank has enjoyed the confidence of the public, and under its present wise and conservative management it has done and is doing a large and safe business, all its operations being marked by prudence, caution and honorable business methods, and it is generally recognized as one of those solid and carefully conducted institutions which reflect credit alike upon its officers and the community in which its influence is felt. Prompt, courteous and efficient in all their dealings with the public, its officers are naturally popular and fully uphold the credit and dignity of the bank. The officers are Messrs. J. W. Manier, President; J. B. Weed, Vice-president, and Arthur Griffin, Cashier. The Board of Directors is as follows: James B. Weed, George A. Kent, S. J. Hirschmann, Charles M. Stone, Norman A. Phelps, Arthur Griffin, Hon. William B. Edwards, Gilman L. Sessions, Asa R. Tweedy, William G. Phelps, Alonzo C. Matthews, James M. Stone and James W. Manier. Mr. Manier has been connected with the bank as cashier and president since 1865, and Mr. Griffin, the cashier, has also spent the best years of his life in the service of the bank.

First National Bank.

The First National Bank, which is one of the oldest and most reliable institutions of the kind in the country, was organized December 19, 1863, and for twenty-eight years has been a prominent factor in the industrial development of Binghamton, and its career has been one of the most creditable character, alike conducive to the financial welfare of its stockholders, depositors and customers. Its capital stock is $200,000, backed up by a surplus fund of upwards of $100,000, and while its management has always been characterized by a proper conservatism, yet it has been progressive in all matters that gave promise of growth and permanence to the industrial advancement of Binghamton. The executive officers of the bank are Messrs. F. T. Newell, President; Harper Dusenbury, Vice-president; and John Manier, Cashier, who may well be numbered among the foremost financiers of Binghamton. A general banking business in all its usual forms is transacted, including the receipt of deposits, granting loans and discounts, and making collections at all available points. It is a bank of business in every sense of the word and indulges in no shaky speculation or uncertain investments. Its record is one of which its managers have every reason to feel proud, and it has done much to enhance the welfare and advancement of this city by its judicious fostering of all reliable industrial endeavors.

Binghamton Savings Bank.

The Binghamton Savings Bank was chartered April 18, 1867, and its business is confined exclusively to receiving and caring for savings deposits and funds deposited in trust, and the deposits now amount to

$1,330,000. Sums as small as one dollar are received on deposit, and semi-annual dividends at the rate of four per cent per annum are paid upon all deposits which have remained in the bank for a period not less than three months next preceding the quarter day. To mechanics, laboring men, women and children, as well as to all persons, the facilities afforded by this bank for securing a bank account by means of smaller or larger savings cannot be overestimated. The high character and sound financial standing of the officers and trustees of the bank are sufficient guarantees that no loss can possibly reach depositors, and as all investments of the resources of the bank are rigidly prescribed by law to be made only in securities which cannot depreciate in value, a further insurance is secured. The officers of the bank are Messrs. Harper Dusenbury, President; W. H. Wilkinson and W. B. Edwards, Vice-presidents; Harris G. Rodgers, Treasurer; Charles M. Stone, Secretary and Charles W. Gennet, Teller. The Binghamton Savings Bank has always been conducted upon a sound and conservative policy which has always proved advantageous and satisfactory to depositors, and the institution is one in which this community has every reason to take just pride.

The other banks are the City National, the National Broome County, the Merchants and the Chenango Valley Savings Bank.

Transportation.

Railroads are the great arteries through which the commerce of the country seeks the markets of the world. A number of roads leading to or from any central point gives to that point a superiority over all others in transportation facilities and an equalization of rates which naturally draws and concentrates manufacturing, commercial and other interests. Binghamton is nearly equi-distant from the cities of New York, Philadelphia and Buffalo. The distance to New York is 207 miles; Philadelphia, 220 miles; Boston, 340 miles; Buffalo, 208 miles; Albany, 142 miles; Syracuse, 80 miles; Oswego, 116 miles; Utica, 100 miles; Rochester, 180 miles; Scranton, 60 miles.

The various lines centering here are, the New York, Lake Erie & Western, a trunk line from the metropolis to the great West; the Delaware, Lackawanna & Western, a second line from New York to Buffalo, and which also operates lines from Binghamton to Utica, and from Binghamton through Syracuse to Oswego; and the Delaware & Hudson railroad, the most important carrier of summer travel in the country, and in connection with the Erie, in Binghamton, the Troy & Boston and Fitchburg in Troy, and the Boston, Hoosac Tunnel & Western at Mechanicville, the D. & H. gives a through line from the West to Boston.

The number of passenger trains arriving at Binghamton every twenty-four hours, and departing therefrom, on the different railroads, aggregates 109.

Real Estate.

The demand for real estate during the past year has, in Binghamton at least, been a sure indication of the faith placed in its future by the many thousands who have made investments. Real estate has not in a single noticeable instance been offered for less than was paid for it. It has invariably been disposed of at a figure warranted by the growth and prosperity of the city. Although the price of property has advanced, there are few who believe that it is at present undervalued. There has been no "boom" to excite wild-cat speculation on the part of the investor, but the demand and increase in value has emanated from legitimate sources, founded on the belief that the city offers great inducements, both as a manufacturing and trade center and as a beautifully situated residential city. Many new and handsome business blocks and attractive apartment houses and flats, built in the prevailing architectural styles of the day, have been erected within a few years, and more are now in progress.

The Moeller Estate.

One of the most desirable pieces of property in Binghamton, now on the market, is the well-known Moeller estate, which contains ninety acres within the city limits, and which is beautifully situated on high ground in the eastern section of the city, and within ten minutes' drive of the Court House. This property was formerly the summer home of the late Captain B. J. Moeller, U. S. N., and was selected by the citizens' committee of Binghamton as the site for the State Masonic Home, had this institution been located here. It is on the direct line of the Robinson street electric railway and is but one block distant from the Court Street & East End street railway. The property includes a handsome residence located in a beautiful grove, and there are a number of small groves of oak, hickory and maple trees, scattered about the property. No more eligible piece of property could be desired than this, and it would prove a bonanza indeed for some syndicate to purchase, plat out and sell in building lots, while the individual purchasers would secure the most desirable home sites in Binghamton. It has now for the first time been placed upon the public market, and if not sold in whole, will be cut up into acreage plots and be disposed of the coming season. Mr. Alex. E. Andrews of 56 Court street has control of the sale of this valuable property, two photographic views of which accompany this article.

The Coal Supply.

Among the conditions which have for many years united in promoting the growth of the city is the cheapness of fuel for domestic use, and the supply of our manufacturing industries. No towns in the State, not excepting those nearest the coal deposits, have been able to obtain their fuel at rates as low as have been charged to our consumers. The difference during the last twenty years has ranged from ten to thirty per cent, as a comparison of sales in the various towns will show. As the cost of living and the cost of production are largely contingent on the price of fuel, the fact here stated is one that must be taken into

RESIDENCE ON THE MOELLER ESTATE.

account in estimating the advantages of any town as a place of residence, or as a location for manufacturing purposes. The extensive business conducted by the large coal dealers in Binghamton, when reduced to figures, presents the most astonishing proportions. The direct railroad communications with the coal fields of Pennsylvania, and the competition existing here between the rival corporations which are extensive miners and shippers of this valuable product, have resulted in fixing the delivery price of coal in Binghamton at lower figures than are enjoyed by any other important manufacturing center in the State.

Street Railroads.

Few cities of its size are better accommodated with street railroads than Binghamton. Eight different lines and branches gridiron the various parts of the city and afford quick and cheap transportation to its citizens. Electricity is the motive power applied on several of the lines, and the system is being rapidly extended.

Financial.

Binghamton's banking business is perhaps the strongest support of the manufacturing and mercantile interests of the city, and working in alliance with these interests in all their legitimate phases, each appreciably influences and partakes of the tone and methods of the others. Hence, the banks of the city, like her business enterprises, are noted for their sound, energetic, yet conservative management, command the entire confidence of business men and capitalists and hold a high rank among the financial institutions of the State. There are three national banks, two State banks, one trust company, two savings banks, one safe deposit company and two private banking houses.

Churches.

The churches of Binghamton are widely distributed over the city, and are confined to no section. The ecclesiastical edifices are mostly of substantial and enduring proportions and the condition of their financial affairs attests the most skillful and conservative direction. The number of church societies holding regular services either in their own edifices or other suitable places is twenty-six, of which nine are Methodist, four Presbyterian, three Episcopal, two each Baptist, Congregational, Catholic and Lutheran, and one each Christian and Universalist.

Amusements.

Binghamton being so readily accessible to the metropolis enjoys the luxury of first-class theatrical entertainments. Many of the very best of metropolitan actors and companies visit this city and are always sure of a generous support. A magnificent new opera house is now being erected, which will be ready for occupancy about August 1, 1892.

THE CITY OF BINGHAMTON.

EMPIRE GRAIN ELEVATOR.

Ross Park.

The public park known as Ross Park was donated to the city in August, 1875, by Erastus Ross. It contains an area of 90 acres, largely covered with trees, and is a pleasant and healthful resort for picnic parties and people of the city generally. It is connected with the city by electric cars, and is under the jurisdiction of the city government. Spirituous liquors, ale and strong beer are prohibited from being sold in the park and a police force is kept on guard to preserve order.

Societies.

Binghamton has numerous organizations for fraternal, beneficial and helpful purposes, all of which are in a flourishing condition and are accomplishing the objects of their existence.

The Press.

Four daily newspapers are published in Binghamton, one morning and three evening. Each daily has a weekly. There are two weeklies besides those published from the offices of the dailies, also one temperance publication.

The Court House.

The Broome County Court House stands on a beautiful knoll and esplanade fronting Court street, opposite Chenango. Near by is a pagoda, from which delightful open-air concerts are given during the summer evenings. The building is massive and substantial, and being sufficiently elevated above the surrounding streets, it invites attention. A magnificent soldiers' and sailors' monument attests the fact that the city is not unmindful of her fallen heroes ; it stands in the public square fronting the Court House and is an ornament to the city.

Binghamton Industrial Exposition.

Through the enterprise of a few of the citizens an annual Industrial Exposition was organized last fall and the first exhibition, lasting five days, was held and met with a remarkable success. The grounds are situated on the bank of the Chenango river and contain a race track and numerous buildings, and are within five minutes' walk of the centre of the city. The important success of the first exhibition has so encouraged the management that next year it is proposed to hold a ten-days' exhibition, which it is confidently predicted will exceed any similar exhibition in the State both in numbers of exhibitors and attendance.

Ackerman Building.

The latest, as well as one of the most elegant, office buildings erected in Binghamton is the Ackerman building, which has just been completed and is ready for occupancy. The building, which is owned and was erected by Mr. Cornelius H. Ackerman, occupies the plot of ground bounded by State, and Henry and Commercial avenue, thus giving it a frontage on three streets, affording an abundance of light, and in fact, every room in the building has the advantage of plenty of windows. The building is six stories high and is constructed of red sandstone for the first story, the remaining stories being brick. It is provided with steam heat and electric lights and an Otis fast elevator. Wide halls and stairways have also been provided, as well as ladies' and gentlemen's toilet rooms on each floor, and every modern conven-

ACKERMAN BUILDING.

ience demanded by modern business methods has been incorporated in the construction. As an architectural ornament to the central business portion of the city, the building is an important feature and has few rivals for beauty of appearance, solidity and graceful design. The interior has been especially laid out for office purposes, singly and en suite, and already a number of well-known and enterprising business men have secured offices in the building, while other equally desirable rooms are still at the disposal of tenants. The ground floor is a specially commodious and attractive room, and will prove a fitting home for one or two banks, for which it has been specially designed. The second, third and fourth floors contain ten offices on each floor and each room has two or more large windows fronting on one of the three streets. The fifth floor has been laid out for a gentlemen's club room, with handsome parlor and reading room, billiard room and grill room and a central corridor into which all rooms open. The sixth floor has been arranged for a lodge room, the main hall being supplemented by two large ante-rooms. A janitor will be in constant attendance on the building, and it will be maintained in a manner that will be pleasing to the tenants and creditable to its projector. Mr. Ackerman is deserving of commendation for his enterprise in adding to the business conveniences of the city by the erection of so superb a structure, which while being a valuable acquisition to the architectural beauty of the city is destined to prove a judicious investment of capital. We present herewith an illustration of the Ackerman building.

Prospects for the Future.

The location of Binghamton is one which renders it impossible for any combination of circumstances to arrest its growth, either as a place of business or residence. Lying as it does at about equal distances from New York, Philadelphia, Rochester, Buffalo, Albany and Troy, and occupying the centre of which these cities are on the circumference, it is sure to become an important feeder for these overcrowded localities. The past of Binghamton having furnished a record of continuous and sustained growth it is a fair presumption that the future will present results of proportionate advance or even accelerated expansion. This is an age of speed, and the industries of the close of the Nineteenth Century are surrounding themselves with forces and agencies as amazing in their results as those of steam and electricity. Already the developments of electrical science have given us a revolution in methods of obtaining motive power which bids fair to supplant all others. In the utilization of all the resources which nature has furnished or science unveiled, there is every reason to believe that Binghamton will be fully abreast with the most progressive cities. It has no lack of men with business sagacity equal to the improvement of every opportunity and it is safe to predict that the historian of the industries of the future will be able to point back to those of to-day as the auspicious beginnings of a greater and brighter destiny.

The present of Binghamton is magnificent and full of promise. It is the handsomest, richest, busiest, most public spirited and most progressive city and community of equal extent and numbers between the two great oceans. Its natural advantages were never better supplemented by its acquired resources for the development of its progress than they are to-day, and the opportunities to obtain homes, occupation, happiness and prosperity lie waiting open for all. Binghamton is the home of intellectual vigor and refinement, wealth, manufactures and commerce, with a past full of interest, a present full of earnestness and a future full of brightness. Binghamton presents a thousand attractions to the student, the patriot, the statesman, the wage earner and greatest of all to that most practical of all philanthropists, the enterprising capitalist seeking safe investments in real estate or the establishment of productive industries. The time is not far distant when

GEORGE A. KENT'S BLOCK, STATE STREET.

Binghamton's 38,000 enterprising inhabitants will have become doubled and when of the United States it shall be, what it now is of the great Empire State, its most attractive city.

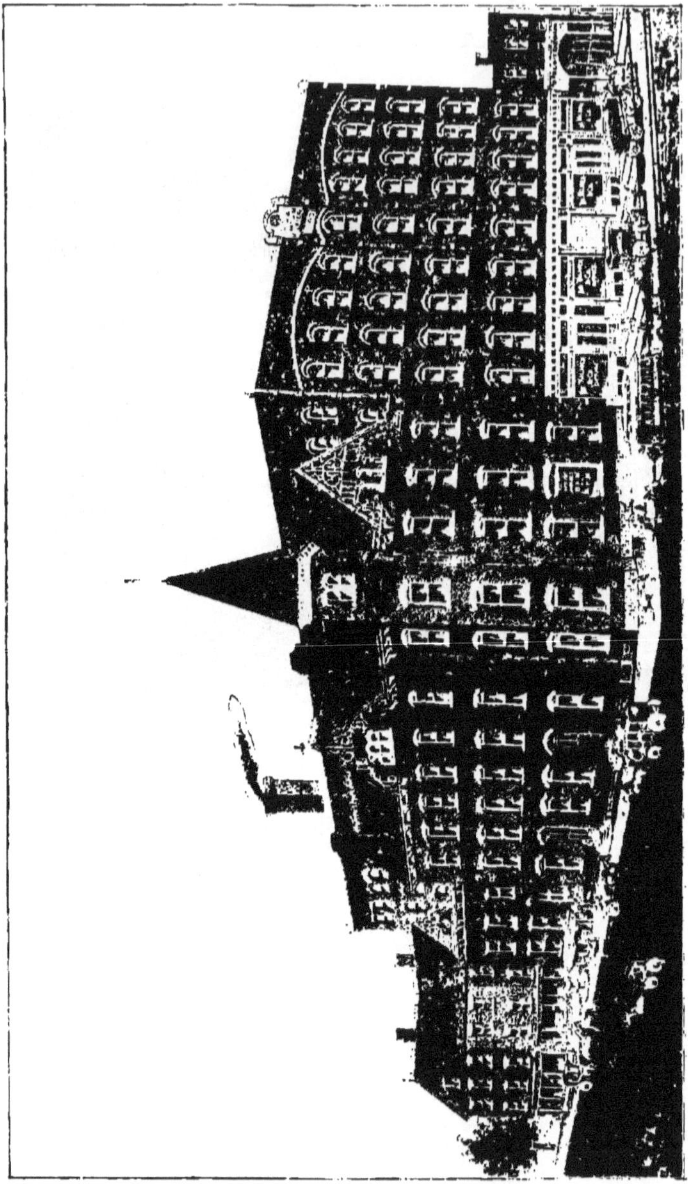

THE CITY OF BINGHAMTON.

DR. KILMER & CO.'S LABORATORY. (See Opposite Page.)

The City of Binghamton.

Its Leading Industries and Principal Mercantile Establishments, with Sketches of their Foundation, History and Progress, and Notes on the Character and Extent of their Operations.

DR. KILMER & CO.,
Manufacturers of Proprietary Medicines.

Binghamton has every reason to be proud of being the home and headquarters of the enterprising firm of Dr. Kilmer & Co., manufacturing chemists, where the compounding of Swamp Root and other herbal remedies is carried on. The prominent success that has attended the sale of these remedies is almost unparalleled in the history of the proprietary medicine business. Scarcely ten years have gone by since the remedies were first offered to the general public and their first introduction covered but a few minor counties of the State, yet to-day they are sold in enormous and annually increasing quantities in all parts of the United States, throughout South America and the West Indies, branch houses having been already established at Rio De Janeiro, Brazil and Kingston, Jamaica, and another is in contemplation in Canada. An enterprise of so important a character as this to have grown up in so short a time must have possessed great inherent merits from its inception, and these merits are to be found, first in the unfailing medicinal properties of the remedies themselves ; second, in its able and energetic management. Dr. Kilmer, the discoverer, has for many years been a practicing physician in this city ; he is a regular accredited graduate of two high class colleges. His great success in private practice, which he still continues with annually increasing call upon his services, led him to desire a larger field for his various specifics than was possible by simply prescribing them to his patients. Therefore in 1881 he associated with him as an equal partner, his brother, Mr. J. M. Kilmer, who for 18 years previous had been engaged in the wholesale dry goods business in New York city. From a modest beginning has grown up the present enormous business, which under the able management of Mr. J. M. Kilmer, leaves Dr. Kilmer and his assistant physicians free to continue the practice of the profession, and his patients, both in person and by letter, are now numbered by thousands and come from every part of the United States. In fact, to obtain a personal consultation with the Doctor, it has become necessary to make an appointment in advance. The present facilities of the firm for compounding their remedies are large and important. The plant covers about one-quarter of a city square, and consists of a four-story dispensary, adjoining which is the laboratory, a five-story brick building, and the firm has in contemplation the erection of another large building, which will then give them the largest manufacturing plant of its kind in the United States. On the ground floor occupying Nos. 374 and 376 Chenango and 2, 4 and 6 Virgil streets are located the main business, advertising and private offices of the concern. They are very elaborately, but substantially fitted up in antique oak furnishings, manufactured from special designs. Connecting with private entrance from Virgil street are the private offices, consulting rooms and waiting parlors used by Dr. Kilmer in his practice. They are complete and handsomely equipped with all the latest scientific apparatus and instruments known to the profession. The firm do all their own printing in a special department located at Nos. 370 and 372 Chenango street, running the entire length of the building. The equipment of this office is most complete and comprises a 50-horse power engine, a number of high speed cylinder presses, turning out a large number of books per hour, smaller job presses, etc., etc. They print daily an enormous amount of paper, one press alone having a per diem capacity of 176,000 sheets printed on both sides in two colors. Some idea of the amount of paper used can be gleaned from the fact that from twelve to fourteen million large sixteen-page pamphlets or books are issued every year. Here are printed the labels, wrappers, pamphlets, etc., found accompanying each and every package of medicine. The "Invalid's Guide to Health," their leading publication, unlike all other pamphlets issued by manufacturers of medicines that have come under the notice of the writer, contains no funny stories, receipts or jokes, but is edited and compiled in all seriousness for the use and benefit of the temporary sick, or the chronic sufferer. The laboratory proper occupies the entire fifth floor, and is replete with all equipments and scientific apparatus for quickly and accurately compounding the preparations. In the bottling department, which is immediately under, the writer's particular attention was called to the bottling machine, the firm's own invention, which fills twenty-six hundred bottles per hour. The concern have lately added a Novelty Department, where are manufactured by a secret process all the large board signs, banners, transparencies and other novelties printed on wood. In fine, in their plant Dr. Kilmer & Co. make all their wares, with the exception of the corks and bottles, used in the production of their remedies, and throughout the entire building the point that impressed the writer most forcibly was its wonderful completeness in every detail, and to undertake to describe the special features in each department would necessitate compiling a volume. It is a noticeable fact that Dr. Kilmer & Co.'s Remedies have acquired their wide popularity almost wholly by means of their growing reputation and merit. The drug sale fully expresses the fact that the Kilmer goods are the most popular with the people and that Swamp Root has the largest sale of any similar preparation on the market. The once popular summer resort known as Hiawatha Island was purchased by the firm three years ago, and after entirely renovating the buildings and adding new ones, they converted it into a private summer home. The property consists of an island of 137 acres, situated in the Susquehanna River, comprising a magnificent park, shady drives and walks and a large stock farm. It is but 18 miles from Binghamton and is accessible by the Erie and D., L. & W. R. R., and by ferry from the station. Altogether it is a very charming spot, affording beautiful views of both mountain and water scenery. The firm of Dr. Kilmer & Co. consists of B. A. Kilmer, M. D., and J. M. Kilmer, who are each one-half owners of the plant, business and real estate held and occupied by the firm.

O. W. SEARS,
Wholesale and Retail Dealer in Coal, 19 Clinton St.

It is to the cheapness and quality of coal that the manufacturing interests of a community are largely indebted for their advance and prosperity, and no concern in this section has accomplished more, as regards its facilities for furnishing a high grade of coal, than has that of Mr. O. W. Sears, who instituted his enterprise here about ten years ago, and has since developed a large and growing trade with manufacturers and for domestic purposes. The facilities of the house embrace an extensive yard and series of coal pockets, having a capacity for the storage of 1,000 tons of coal. The yards adjoin the Erie R. R. and cars are run into the coal pockets, where they are unloaded without handling. About fifteen thousand tons are handled annually, and only the best grades of anthracite and bituminous coals are dealt in, which are furnished to the trade and consumers at lowest market prices. Seven assistants are employed in the conduct of the business and all orders either by mail or telephone are promptly filled. Mr. Sears is also a member of the firm of Bartlett & Sears, strictly wholesale coal dealers of Buffalo, N. Y. His relations with producers and first hands are of a most intimate nature, and every advantage accruing to the most progressive houses in the trade are placed at the disposal of patrons.

C. B. SMITH, JR. & CO.,
Manufacturers of Fine Cigars, 301 to 305 Water St.

The cigar manufacturing industry of Binghamton has long been its most important productive feature and Binghamton cigars rank high among the very best made in the country. Among the leading establishments which are contributing largely to this importance and whose efforts are constantly directed towards fully maintaining the reputation and character of their output is the house of Messrs. C. B. Smith, Jr., & Co., which was instituted about twelve years ago, and has since acquired a reputation that fully entitles it to a prominent position among the cigar factories of the Empire State. The premises occupied for the business are comprised in a new four-story and basement brick building, which is equipped with improved machinery operated by steam power and furnishes employment to 150 skilled workmen. The products of the house embrace a large variety of cigars, from medium to the highest grades, a specialty being made of fine Havana cigars. All their goods are sold under their own registered brands, of which they have about forty, all of which have gathered high favor with the trade. Among the leading brands we note: "Del Monte," "Flor de Palmeta," "King William," "Los Gatos" and "Santa Garcia," which are in wide demand by the trade and consumers wherever introduced. The trade of the house extends throughout the United States and is with jobbers only, the annual output reaching 4,000,000. The individual members of the firm, Messrs. C. B. Smith, Jr., and Charles H. Hall, are both experienced manufacturers and expert judges of leaf tobacco, and possessing, as they do, unsurpassed facilities for economical production, they are making a line of fine and medium cigars which is in every respect well worthy the attention of the trade. They are honorable competitors for legitimate business, and enterprising and progressive manufacturers.

A. CORBIN, SON & CO.,
Wholesale and Retail Druggists, 38 Court St.

This house, which is the only one in the city doing a considerable wholesale trade in drugs, was instituted in 1881 by Messrs. A. Corbin & Son, the present firm having been organized in 1886. The business premises are embraced in a three-story and basement building, which is supplied with every convenience for the advantageous display of the stock and the prompt fulfilment of orders. The first floor is devoted to the retail salesrooms and office in front, and the wholesale operations in the rear, a prescription department being also provided for, and the remaining floors and basement are used for storing the surplus stock, which embraces large and complete lines of pure drugs and chemicals, dyes, paints and oils, whole and ground spices, perfumes, proprietary medicines, fancy goods, etc. The stock also includes herbs, roots, barks, etc., and druggists' glassware and sundries, and in fact everything required by the trade and public in the way of drugs, medicines and pharmaceutical preparations. All goods are procured direct from the most eminent manufacturers and importers, and in each department the stock will be found ample, varied and of the highest quality. Fine wines and liquors for medicinal use are carried, and indeed everything for the complete equipment of a first-class drug establishment. The trade of the house extends throughout Southern New York and Northern Pennsylvania along the lines of railroad centering at Binghamton, this territory being frequently covered by a travelling salesman. The members of the firm are Messrs. A. Corbin, F. G. Corbin and Samuel Higgins, gentlemen thoroughly familiar with all departments of their business, and who have always conducted it on a liberal and enterprising basis.

J. B. TALBOT & CO.,
Hides, Pelts and Skins, 173 Water St.

The original inception of this business took place in 1864, when it was founded by Livermore & Co., the present firm having been organized in 1881. The premises occupied for the transaction of the business are commodious and afford ample storage facilities, and are the headquarters for the transaction of a large and growing trade in the purchase and shipment of hides, pelts, skins, furs, wool, tallow, etc. These staples are purchased in any quantity from dealers, collectors, or producers, and after being graded are shipped to the trade in the large cities of the East chiefly. The firm solicits consignments of anything in their line for which the highest market cash prices will be paid upon receipt. The members of the firm are Messrs. J. B. and Page W. Talbot, and Lester W. Potter, all gentlemen of enterprising and energetic methods and closely identified with the growth of this city. Their house occupies an eminent and esteemed position in the trade, and its age, solidity and honorable record render it one of the most advantageous with which to form relations that are sure to be pleasant and profitable.

WILKINSON, SON & CO.
Manufacturers of Leather, Foot of Carroll St.

The enterprise of Messrs. Wilkinson, Son & Co. was originally instituted many years ago by Lewis Abbott. In 1870 the business came into the possession of Messrs. Wilkinson Bros., and in 1884 they were succeeded by the present firm. The plant is located on the bank of Susquehanna river, from which power is obtained, an auxiliary engine of 40-horse power being occasionally used. The tanning and currying shops embrace a series of suitable buildings, which are fully equipped with all the latest improved machinery known to the trade, and large yards are also utilized for storing bark. Fifty-five skilled workmen and others are given employment in the several departments of the business and about three hundred hides are handled each week, all being of home production. The firm manufactures chiefly upper leather which is known to the trade under the names of Imitation Goat, Grain, Imitation Kangaroo from Calfskins and Cowhides, and London Seal, Boot Grain, also flexible insole, both grain and splits. The products are taken by the boot and shoe manufacturing trade throughout the country, generally, and their goods have a high reputation in the market for superior quality. Their imitation Kangaroo under their trademark of "American Kangaroo," has a wide popularity with the manufacturers and it possesses all the qualities of the genuine both as regards fine finish and durability, while it is furnished at a much less price. While the firm uses large quantities of bark in the processes of tanning, in the manufacture of their London Seal leather they use no bark at all, but reach the end by a new and improved process, which results in a perfect leather that is in great and growing demand with the trade. The members of the firm are Messrs. W. H. Wilkinson, Arthur R. Wilkinson and Charles Thorne, all well known and prominent citizens of Binghamton. Mr. W. H. Wilkinson is also president of the Wilkinson Manufacturing Co., of this city, Vice President of the Binghamton Savings Bank, a member of the Board of Trade, and otherwise prominent in the best interests of the city.

OSTROM, BARNES & CO.,
Cigar Manufacturers, 179 Water St.

This house was established in 1886 and has since built up a trade extending throughout New York and Pennsylvania requiring the services of two travelling salesmen, sales being made to both jobbers and retailers, the average output of the factory being 2,000,000 cigars annually. The premises of the firm are comprised in a four-story brick building 25x75 feet in dimensions, of which the three upper floors are utilized for manufacturing purposes. Fifty skilled cigar-makers are given employment and the products are strictly hand-made cigars, no machinery being employed, as is the case with many other manufacturies. The goods of the firm are all put upon the market under their own brands, among the chief of which are: "Walt Whitman," "Post E," "Trophy," "Lavender," and "Something Good." These are all standard goods, made from carefully selected and thoroughly seasoned stock, by skilled workmen, and are confidently recommended to smokers as being unsurpassed for fine flavor, delicate aroma and even combustion. The active management of the business devolves upon Messrs. E. D. Ostrom and J. T. Barnes, who are both experienced judges of leaf tobacco and expert manufacturers, and all the operations of their factory are conducted under their personal supervision.

REYNOLDS, ROGERS & CO.
Manufacturers of Cigars, 19 to 25 N. Depot Street.

One of the first among the great enterprises devoted to this branch of productive activity stands the representative establishment of Messrs. Reynolds, Rogers & Co. This house was founded in 1884, and is to-day a monument to the enterprise, energy and progressive ideas of its projectors. The factory of the firm is comprised in a large four-story and basement brick building, having a floorage area of 35,000 square feet. It is equipped with a 60-horse power boiler and a 35-horse power engine and all the latest improved special machinery known to the trade, employment being given to from four to five hundred operatives. The factory is well lighted, heated by steam, and supplied with all modern facilities for the orderly and systematic conduct of the business, and the annual output of cigars ranges from fifteen to twenty millions, an idea of which enormous quantity may be obtained, when it is said that if these cigars were all placed in a line end to end they would cover a distance equal to that from New York to Chicago. The products of the house embrace all kinds of fine and medium grade domestic cigars, none of the cheapest grades being produced. They are supplied extensively to the jobbing trade and are sold throughout the United States from the Atlantic to the Pacific. All the goods are made and packed under the firm's own copyrighted brands of which they have a large number, among the most popular of which we note: "Pride of Egypt," "Sheriffs' Sale," "Josh Billings," "Blue Point," "Bengal," "Moxie," "Wild Waves," "Malto," "Seals of the North," "Seals of the South," "Seals of the East" and "Seals of the West," the latter four being the self-same goods packed under the change in name for the four principal sections of the country named. The individual members of the firm are Messrs. F. B. Reynolds, G. T. Rogers, and F. E. Lay, each of whom takes an active interest in the management of the business, and each is an expert in his special department. No other house is better equipped in every respect to offer marked inducements to the trade, and it is no small tribute to the abilities and business talents of the management to say that they have not only maintained, but constantly increased, the operations of their industry, until now this house stands among the first of the cigar trade of Binghamton.

BINGHAMTON GLASS WORKS,
Manufacturers of Green Glassware, McLean Street and Railroad.

The manufacture of glass ware is one of the oldest of industries and one of the few in which the methods of modern manufacturers are practically the same as those of its earlier followers. Binghamton is the seat of an important manufactory of glass ware which is known as the Binghamton Glass Works and of which Mr. William Burrows is the sole proprietor. These works were erected about fourteen years ago, and are located in the western section of the city, adjoining the two main trunk lines of railroad, with which they are connected by side tracks. thus affording every facility for the receipt of raw materials and the shipment of the finished products without rehandling. The plant covers about two acres upon which are erected two furnaces, each having a capacity of five tons daily. Besides these are other minor buildings, warehouses, etc., and the whole is equipped with all the latest improved tools and appliances known to the trade, including a 40-horse power steam engine. The products are what are known to the trade as green glassware and consist of vials, bottles and flasks of all sizes and shapes, chiefly manufactured to order for use by manufacturers and bottlers of proprietary articles, medicines, condiments, beverages, etc. and includes also bottles for all commercial purposes. The number of bottles produced so varies according to the sizes made that the total produced daily is not attainable. Sufficient to say that when both furnaces are in operation about ten tons of glassware are produced daily and as the production is almost wholly the result of hand-labor a force of no less than 200 men and boys are given employment. As these are largely highly skilled workmen, it is evident that the operation of these works is an important feature of the industrial thrift of this city. The products of the house are taken by the trade throughout the United States generally east of the Mississippi and their high character is well understood and appreciated by the trade. Mr. Burrows is a native of England where he learned the business and is a practical glassware manufacturer. He also conducts another similar enterprise at Stroudsburg, Penn., where he makes his headquarters. With unrivalled conveniences for shipping, an established excellence of product and a liberal and fair dealing business policy it is but just to say that as conducing to the advancement of the material prosperity of this city by the employment of many skilled workmen, the Binghamton Glass Works is performing a beneficent work while in the pursuit of legitimate profits and may be regarded as a representative concern fully worthy the pronounced success it has attained.

C. L. SAUNDERS & SON,

Dealers in Armour's Chicago Dressed Beef, Prospect Ave and R. R.

This firm are handlers of the products of the world-renowned packing house of Armour & Co. of Chicago. This great firm slaughter immense quantities of cattle daily in Chicago, and ship the dressed beef in refrigerator cars to all points in the East, where it arrives fresh and sweet as the day it was killed, with no perceptible loss in weight, and it can therefore be sold to the consumers at much less prices than was possible under the old system of transporting live cattle long distances and slaughtering them while in a feverish condition from the effects of such transportation. The facilities of the firm consist of a two-story refrigerator building which adjoins the railroad system of the city and admits of the unloading of the cars direct into the building. The capacity of the refrigerator is about thirty-five carcasses and other products dealt in, which embrace dressed mutton and lambs, pork, sausage, smoked meats, hams, lard, etc. The firm handle about two car-loads of dressed beef weekly, and supply a trade that besides embracing the city also extends throughout a large section of Central and Southern New York and Northern Pennsylvania, and which is annually increasing in volume. The members of the firm are Messrs. C. L. Saunders and W. L. Saunders, both experienced men in the business and progressive and enterprising merchants.

S. MILLS ELY & Co.,
Wholesale Grocers, N. Depot St. and Prospect Ave.

In connection with the wholesale grocery trade of Binghamton, a few brief facts with relation to the history and business of the house of Messrs. S. Mills Ely & Co., the oldest wholesale grocery establishment in the city, are replete with interest. Founded in 1843 by Messrs. McKinney & Co., as dealers in flour and provisions, and succeeded in 1871 by Mr. S. Mills Ely, who had been a member of the firm since 1863, this house has been continuously conducted for nearly half a century, with annually increasing trade, influence and reputation. In 1872 the present extensive salesrooms and warehouse of the firm were erected and in 1875 Mr. Edward F. Leighton became associated with Mr. Ely under the present firm title. The headquarters of the firm are embraced in a substantial four-story brick structure 70x120 feet in dimensions, located as above indicated, besides which they utilize a large two-story brick warehouse on State street, which combines a cold storage warehouse, a mincemeat factory and a stable, and they also have a two-story warehouse on Prospect avenue, where heavy groceries are stored, the whole affording ample accommodations for a large and varied stock, which has no equal in extent between New York and Buffalo, and embraces staple and fancy groceries, teas, coffees, spices, grocers' sundries, flour, provisions, smoked and salt meats and fish, butter, eggs, wooden ware, etc. Twenty assistants, including several commercial travellers, find occupation with the firm. Both members of the firm are energetic, prompt and intelligent representatives of the best element of our business community. Mr. Ely has been a resident of Binghamton for thirty-five years, and Mr. Leighton may be said to have grown up in the house, and is thoroughly acquainted with all the details of the business.

THE CHENANGO VALLEY FLOUR MILLS,
George Q. Moon & Co., Proprietors.

The Chenango Valley Flour Mills were established in 1865 by Mr. George Q. Moon, who conducted them until 1880, when Mr. Robert J. Bates became associated with him under the above named firm title. The mill and elevator of the firm, which is the most prominent building to meet the eye of a stranger on alighting from the cars at passenger stations, is located adjoining the railroad system of the city, and switches from the Erie, D., L. & W. and D. & H. C. railways enter the premises, thus affording the most advanced receiving and shipping facilities. The elevator has a storage capacity of 100,000 bushels of grain, and the mill is equipped with the full roller system, embodying all the latest improvements of the day, and has a capacity for producing 300 barrels of flour and three car-loads of meal daily. About fifty workmen are given employment and an engine of 200-horse power furnishes the motive force to the mechanical equipment of the mill and elevator. The gentlemen at the head of this enterprise are influential members of the community, who are closely identified with the city's progress and development.

ISAAC LAUDER & SON,
Marble and Granite Works, 61 Eldredge St.

A prominent and old established house engaged in the production of marble and granite monuments is that of Messrs. Isaac Lauder & Son, which was originally founded in 1879 by Mr. Isaac Lauder, who commenced business at Oneonta, removing here some years later, and in 1890 the present firm was organized by the admission of Mr. James Lauder to an interest in the business. In connection with the work in hand, premises are occupied comprising a shop, yards, etc, where an average of six skilled workmen are steadily employed. The firm manufacture everything in the way of monumental and cemetery work both in marble and granite. Their productions are distinguished for their good taste and artistic design, and thus a large and widely extended patronage has been achieved, spreading throughout the city and surrounding territory. The facilities of the firm are such that all orders may be promptly filled, and estimates and drawings are cheerfully submitted. The firm also carry a considerable stock of finished headstones and monuments from which selections can be made. Operating under the most favorable conditions, we may also state that the prices are dictated by a spirit of moderation which has done much to gain patronage. Many handsome specimens of the firm's handiwork may be seen in the cemeteries of Binghamton and vicinity, and references to patrons will be made to those desiring. Mr. Isaac Lauder is a practical marble and granite workman and is possessed of a high order of artistic skill and good taste, and his son may be said to have been brought up in the business. Their enterprise is doing its full share in the industrial development of Binghamton and is certainly one of its leading and representative establishments.

THE CLARENCE E. BEACH ELECTRICAL SUPPLY CO.,
136 State Street.

The enterprise forming the caption of this article is the outgrowth of the electrical department of the firm of Vickers, Brooker & Co., which was instituted in 1890 and came under its present management and title in October last past. The management is in the capable and energetic hands of Messrs. Clarence E. & George S. Beach, who are in every way equipped by experience and study of the science and practice of electricity to skillfully conduct all its operations and make the enterprise one of the important industrial resources of Binghamton. The firm carry in stock a full and complete line of electrical goods and supplies, and novelties in electrical goods are constantly being added as fast as introduced. They are also prepared to undertake the faithful performance of all kinds of electrical work for private residences, manufactories and public buildings. They make a specialty of electric bell wiring, electric light wiring and fitting of buildings, hotels and apartment houses with electric bell annunciators, letter boxes, speaking tubes, etc., and in fact are ready with all facilities to promptly execute all kinds of electrical work. Already a large and growing trade has been built up by the firm which extends generally throughout this section of the State and Northern Pennsylvania and gives ample evidence of steady increase. The enterprise being in the hands of pushing and energetic men of broad-gauge ideas and fully abreast of the times in all that leads to success and influence, its future prominence and usefulness may be confidently predicted.

J. B. WEED & CO.,
Manufacturers of Upper Leather.

This enterprise, which is one of the largest of its kind in the country as well as one of the oldest, was originally founded in 1838 by the late Marshall H. Weed, who was a pioneer in his line and who created a national reputation for the superiority of his leather. The present firm, consisting of Messrs. J. B. & F. M. Weed, sons of the founder, succeeded to the business in 1860. The firm's plant in this city, including yards for storing bark, covers about five acres, upon which are erected several extensive buildings. The tannery is a two and one-half story brick building, 80x250 feet in dimensions, the currying shop is a five-story brick building, 40x250 feet, and besides these main structures are others used for storage, boiler and engine-houses, etc. The mechanical equipment embraces two steam engines of 250-horse power combined, five steam boilers, and all the latest improved machinery known to the trade. About 200 workmen find employment in the tannery, and about 100,000 hides are annually made into leather. The product consists of boot and pebble grain, split leather, buff glove and oil leather and imitation goat, the latter being a prominent specialty of the firm. All their products bear the highest reputation in the trade for superior quality. In connection with their manufacturing operations in this city the firm own extensive tracts of forest land in Potter County, Pennsylvania, from which they obtain their supply of bark for tanning purposes, and of which they use upwards of 8,000 cords annually. Upon this land they have saw-mills and a large number of laborers are employed in getting out lumber and bark and preparing it for shipment. The trade of the house extends throughout the United States, wherever boot and shoe manufacturing is carried on, and their products are also exported to foreign countries. The members of the firm are among the most active and progressive manufacturers of the Empire State and few, if any, have done more to promote the industrial thrift of Binghamton.

JOSEPH P. NOYES & CO.,
Manufacturers of Combs and Buttons, 13 Ferry Street.

The enterprise of Messrs. Joseph P. Noyes & Co. is the direct successor of one of the oldest manufacturing houses in America, and one of the very few in this country which have been continuously conducted by members of the same family for so long a period. It was originally instituted in Essex county, Mass., in 1759, by the ancestors of the present proprietors, who were the pioneers of the comb making industry in this country. After a series of changes in the composition of the proprietorship, the business was removed to this city in 1865 by Messrs. E. M. Noyes & Bro., the present firm title having been adopted in 1879, the present proprietors being Mr. Joseph P. Noyes, and his son, Joseph K. Noyes. The manufacturing plant is comprised in a series of suitable buildings, the main factory being a modern five-story brick structure, which are equipped with all necessary machinery, much of which is of the firm's own invention and was especially designed for their uses, power being obtained from a valuable and ample water privilege, and employment being furnished to from 50 to 75 operatives. A feature of the plant is a well equipped machine shop, which is maintained by the firm for the production and repair of their own mechanism. The products of the house are of two entirely different classes—combs and buttons. The former consist of nickle plated, patent metallic-back raw horn combs, of which the firm were the original inventors, and which are made in a variety of shapes, sizes, styles and manners of finishing.

The latter product is a specialty, and consists solely of patent hand-snap buttons. These buttons are made in two parts, and are designed to replace missing buttons on garments without the use of a needle and thread. They are applied instantly and the two parts snap together with firmness and strength by the force of the hand, and by the use of them the traveller, the farmer, the laborer, the mechanic, the growing boy, and men of every profession can instantly replace missing buttons with these and with the assurance that the hand-snap buttons will prove far more serviceable than any that could be put on with thread. Both lines of goods are widely sold throughout the United States and are in the hands of the jobbing trade in all the cities of the country, besides which considerable quantities are exported. The enterprise has been an important factor in building up the industrial resources of Binghamton, and has added to the diversified character of the manufactures of this city, which is so much better for a locality than a preponderance of one kind of production. Mr. Joseph P. Noyes is one of the substantial and public-spirited citizens of Binghamton, closely identified with its advance and prosperity and active in all measures promising good to this community. He is also largely interested in other business enterprises of this city, is a large real estate holder, and is prominent in matters relating to the amelioration of the needy; at present he is the President of both the Susquehanna Valley House for Children and the Board of Associated Charities. One hundred and thirty-two years is a long period, longer even than the history of our nation, and this well-known establishment, with such a record, has substantial claims to the high reputation and eminent position it has so long enjoyed in the commerce and industry of this country.

WILLIAM F. YOUNG,

Manufacturer of Butter Tubs, Firkins and Cooperage, 7, 9 and 11 Washington Street.

The cooper shop of Mr. William F. Young was originally instituted in 1850 by its present proprietor, who is one of the pioneers of the manufacturing advancement of the city and is probably the only manufacturer in the city to-day who has continuously, without change, conducted one and the same enterprise in one place for so many years. His enterprise embraces the manufacture of butter tubs and firkins for butter packers in this vicinity chiefly, for which he has all the necessary facilities, including a commodious shop, outbuildings for storage, etc., the equipment including a 12-horse power steam engine. He also deals in cooperage stock of all kinds and coopers' tools, supplying the same to the trade in Southern New York and Northern Pennsylvania in quantities to suit. He carries a full and complete stock of staves, hoop poles and heading, procured direct from the original sources of supply, which he offers at the lowest market prices. Mr. Young is a practical cooper and at one time was engaged in the business of making sugar casks on the island of Cuba. After his establishment in this city, for many years he was a large shipper of cooperage stock to Cuba, which was obtained from the forests near this city and forwarded to New York by canal for shipment. The exhaustion of the timber in this neighborhood resulted in a stoppage of this department of the industry, the staves required for the manufacture of butter tubs now being procured from Kentucky, Tennessee and other Southern States. Mr. Young is one of the most esteemed and respected citizens of Binghamton, is a large holder of real estate here and has done much toward the building up of the city. For ten years he was city assessor, which office he conducted to the entire satisfaction of the community and honor to himself, voluntarily declining re-election.

JONES OF BINGHAMTON,
Manufacturer of the United States Standard Scales, Office and Works, Binghamton, N. Y.

American genius and enterprise challenge comparison with the world. The character of our products has made for them a market in every land the sun shines on, and most of the valuable contributions to mechanics have had their origin, or else have been developed to perfection in the United States. In no line of production is this fact more prominent than in the construction of scales and weighing machines. Strength, durability and perfect accuracy have made American scales famous throughout the world, and eminently, those manufactured by Jones of Binghamton far excel in all desirable qualities those of any other nation on the globe. This great enterprise, the pride of Binghamton, and one which has done more to advertise this city at home and abroad than any other located here, was founded in 1865 by the Hon. Edward F. Jones and in 1888 was incorporated under its present title, which had become a household word in every town, village and hamlet from ocean to ocean as well as in many foreign lands. The enterprise was begun upon a very modest scale when compared with its present extensive proportions, but its growth and expansion was assured from its start, and each year has added to its importance until to-day in its special line it has few if any equals and no superiors, either as to extent of territory covered by its trade or reputation for quality of products. That the operation of an extensive industry of this character should require a large plant is self-evident. The works cover an area of about four acres, upon which are erected numerous substantial brick buildings, each designed for some specific department of the business and each possessing every facility that ample capital could provide or experience and progressive enterprise could suggest, and the whole replete with an enormous equipment of general machinery, besides many special appliances and delicate devices necessary for the prosecution of a business requiring such accuracy of detail. During the past summer important additions and improvements have been made to the works in the way of several new buildings. A new brass and iron foundry 50x150 feet in dimensions has been erected, as well as a new forge-shop 40x60 feet, and a new two-story machine shop 30x50, which with the main four-story machine shop and other former buildings place the company's facilities on a par with the largest concerns of the kind in the world. The motive power is supplied from a 100-horse power steam engine. In the manufacture of their scales the company use about ten tons of iron daily and their yearly consumption of lumber aggregates upwards of half a million feet. Since the completion of the company's improvements to their plant, the force of workmen has been augmented and two hundred and fifty now find employment in the several departments of the works, and thus the influence of their location here is of incalculable benefit to Binghamton, as by the disbursement of a large sum weekly in wages the material prosperity of the city is greatly enhanced.

Jones of Binghamton manufactures every description of scale known from the minute letter scale weighing a fraction of an ounce to the powerful track and platform scales capable of accurately weighing one hundred and fifty tons and upwards. In all of these, perfect accuracy is the distinguishing feature. The Jones of Binghamton scales are in use in every part of the world where commerce exists and they have become the standards of the world of weights. They are in use in many of the principal elevators, stock yards, mills, warehouses and upon leading railroads in this country and abroad, and are being universally adopted in the departments of the government. Every scale is guaranteed to be a correct weighing machine, made only of the best materials by the most skilled workmen and is warranted for five years. They also warrant their scales to suit, and in order that the customer may judge for himself as to that, the scales are sold to any responsible person in any part of the United States, on trial, and the price includes cost of freight to any railroad station or steamboat landing in the United States or Canada. From this feature originated the expression, "Jones, he pays the freight," which has become one of those happy advertising phrases so familiar to every inhabitant of America, that has never been equalled either in popularity or pointedness. While all the scales manufactured by this company are of the latest and most improved patterns and are absolutely correct in principle and operation, their track scales of all sizes and capacities are made upon a principle entirely different and in advance of all others, and under patents owned solely by themselves. The theory and principle which obtain in all scales of this company's make and their original improvements and adaptations make them first in strength, simplicity, economy of construction, accuracy and durability, and these features when added to the recognized low prices make them indeed the choice of all thinking people. This great industry now successfully entered upon its second quarter of a century's usefulness has been a powerful factor in attracting attention to Binghamton as an advantageous location for the establishment of industrial or commercial operations. Concerning its founder and present head, little could be said in a volume of this character that would add to the esteem in which he is so widely held by the public and trade at large. If, perchance, however, there might be some corner of the country into which his name and fame as a scalemaker or as a public man has not yet penetrated, it may be said that the Hon. Edward F. Jones, now and since 1886 Lieutenant-Governor of New York State, is a native of Utica, N. Y. He was Colonel of the valorous 6th Massachusetts Regiment, whose desperate march through the streets of Baltimore is one of the historic events of the great rebellion. The regiment was the first to reach Washington and to it has been accorded the credit of saving the capitol. Having gained distinguished honors in the service of the Union he came to Binghamton at the close of the war and founded the great scale-works which bear his name. His voice has always been raised for such measures as would benefit the people and he was one of the earliest members of the New York State Grange. Concluding this brief sketch of the facilities and products of this organization, we may be permitted to say that its present extent and high reputation has been built up and maintained by a constant aim to make only the most reliable goods and the most strict integrity in every transaction, and its history and success should be considered as significant incentives to those who would know the benefits to be derived from patience in well-doing, untiring industry and uncompromising honesty in all dealings.

LYNCH & CHRISTIE,
Grates, Mantels and Tiles, 86 State Street.

Nothing adds so greatly to the interior decoration of a room as a handsome mantel with fireplace and grate, while the usefulness of this adjunct both as a matter of comfort in the early fall and spring and as adding to the cheerfulness of an apartment, hotel reading room or public room is well attested by all. Messrs. Lynch & Christie of this city are prepared to furnish everything in this line of the highest artistic character and in the greatest variety of styles and designs. The firm occupy commodious premises at the above indicated address, which are handsomely and attractively arranged so that patrons may make selections understandingly. The main floor is divided into a number of apartments, in which the mantels are set up and surrounded with carpets, rugs and furniture in such a manner as to give the appearance of a finished room, enabling the customer to see the design as it would appear in a finished residence. Besides the large and varied stock carried, any special design is promptly furnished, and in fact every advantage and accommodation is offered by the firm that can be obtained in the great metropolitan trade centres. This enterprise was instituted in 1885 and has since built up a large and growing trade that extends throughout the city and vicinity. Aside from the above mentioned enterprise in which as a firm they carry on the business, each of the members is largely engaged in a separate industry on his own account. Mr. J. R. Lynch has been engaged since 1880 in the execution of tin and iron roofing of all kinds and galvanized iron cornice work, in which he has met with great success, and Mr. Walter Christie has since 1876 been engaged in handling all kinds of roofing slate at wholesale and retail and in the erection of slate roofs, as well as the production of marbleized slate mantels, enjoying a trade that extends throughout Southern New York and Northern Pennsylvania and giving employment to from twelve to fifteen skilled workmen. In each of these several branches of trade these gentlemen have long been leaders, and the success and prominence attending their efforts have added no little to the reputation of this city as a source of supply for first-class goods.

BINGHAMTON GLOVE AND MITTEN M'F'G. CO.
91 State Street.

The marked diversity of the industries of this city is particularly illustrated in the establishment of the Binghamton Glove and Mitten Manufacturing Co., which was organized in 1888 by Mr. Frederick J. Bryant, its present sole proprietor, and has since acquired a reputation and a trade that extends throughout New York, Pennsylvania, Ohio and Michigan, and is annually increasing in volume. The premises occupied for the business are commodious and fully equipped with all the latest and most improved machinery and tools for the economical production of light and heavy gloves and mittens, employment being given to about twenty-five skilled operatives. The company's specialties comprise a general line of fine grades of gloves and mittens in calfskin, hogskin, buckskin and other materials. The goods are made for men's and boys' wear and they are specially designed for first-class trade. The facilities of the house are altogether of the best character, assuring perfection of product, at the same time that the prices will be found fair and reasonable and based on liberality. No goods made anywhere give any better satisfaction to the public and dealers will find them the most advantageous to handle. Mr. Bryant is a practical and experienced manufacturer and an enterprising business man. All goods manufactured receive rigid inspection at his hands before shipment and as a result, only those that can be classed as perfect in all respects are allowed to go out of the establishment. The enterprise is a valuable addition to the industrial resources of the city, and its growth and prosperity are alike creditable to Binghamton and to its projector. We commend the house to the trade, wherever located, with the assurance that relations entered into with it will prove pleasant, permanent and profitable.

H. T. ALDEN,
Cigar Manufacturer, 247 Water Street.

The cigar manufacturing enterprise of Mr. H. T. Alden has done much to promote the industry in this city, and while its annual output is not so great in quantity as that of some others, this lacking in quantity is more than made up in the fine quality of the cigars produced. Mr. Alden manufactures cigars for fine retail trade only, and his products are all hand-made, the finest qualities of Havana and domestic tobacco being used. The business was established about nine years ago, since which time a trade has been built up that extends throughout Pennsylvania and New York and an annual production of about 800,000 cigars is turned out. The manufacturing facilities embrace two floors and the basement of the building at the above indicated address, where an average force of seventeen skilled workmen is employed. Among the chief brands of the house are "H. A.," "La Flor de Sota," "Key West" and "Order of Railroad Conductors." These are strictly first-class domestic cigars, made from carefully selected leaf, by skilled workmen, and are guaranteed to be of invariable uniformity. Some five-cent goods are also produced, which are also the best of their grade and are kept fully up to the standard. Among these the "Jockey Queen" and "Camp Fire" are each in popular demand and are commended as being full value for the money. Mr. Alden is widely known in the trade as a genial gentleman and enterprising manufacturer, and his success is alike creditable and gratifying to both his customers and himself.

C. S. DARLING,
Wholesale Dealer in Chicago Dressed Beef, 25 North Depot Street.

The method of slaughtering cattle, sheep and hogs in the West and shipping the dressed meats to the East where it arrives as sweet and fresh as the day it was killed, has proved to be a most satisfactory one, and is carried out to perfection by the house of Mr. C. S. Darling in this city, who is a wholesale dealer in Chicago dressed beef, mutton, lambs and packing house products. The premises occupied are embraced in the first floor and basement of the large building, located as above indicated, which is so situated with reference to the railroad tracks that refrigerator cars used for transporting the beef are unloaded direct into the building. Constructed in the building is a large refrigerator, or cooler, which is capable of storing 60 carcasses, and this room is kept at an even temperature of about 38 degrees. Mr. Darling handles N. Morris & Co.'s Chicago beef exclusively, and he also deals in frest mutton, lambs, pork, etc. The trade of the house extends throughout Southern New York and Northern Pennsylvania. Mr. Darling instituted his enterprise in January, 1889, and has since built up a large and growing trade, induced here by the superior quality of the products handled. He is a pushing and progressive business man and an esteemed citizen and his house is one of the important factors of the trade resources of this growing commercial city.

J. E. SEARLES,

Wholesale and Retail Tobacconist and Confectioner, 154 Washington Street and 122 Court Street.

A leading and representative factor of the jobbing trade of Binghamton is the house of Mr. J. E. Searles, who commenced business here in 1880, and has since built up a large clientage among the retail dealers in the city and surrounding country, which is annually growing in importance. Mr. Searles conducts two stores, the main headquarters of the business being located at 122 Court street and a branch store at 154 Washington street. At the latter a wholesale and retail trade in tobacco, cigars, cigarettes and smokers' articles is carried on, while at the main store the stock embraces, besides full lines of tobacco, cigars and smokers' articles, a particularly complete stock of confectionery suitable for general trade, walking canes in large variety, jewelry and cutlery. All goods are procured direct from manufacturers in large quantities and are offered at prices that command attention and are quite as low as may be obtained elsewhere from more distant localities, while prompt and immediate delivery and in quantities to suit are advantages not obtainable when purchases are made in other cities. A specialty of the house is the finest brands of case goods in original packages direct from manufacturers. Mr. Searles is a progressive business man and enterprising in all his methods. He is thoroughly acquainted with the demands of his trade and he affords the most advanced accommodations for procuring anything in his line.

THE M. I. S. T. COMPANY.

Factory and Headquarters, Washington, D. C. Binghamton Office, 168 Water Street.

The fame of the great remedy made by the above company is widespread, and apart from the making of money by legitimate enterprise the benefit thus conferred upon suffering humanity is almost incalculable. In this city the company's office is under the efficient management of Mr. D. W. Hill, and his territory embraces the whole of Broome county. M. I. S. T. signifies Murray's Infallible System Tonic. It is a well-known fact that upon the purity of the blood depends the health of the human being. The Scriptures declare that "the blood is the life," and well is that fact demonstrated by modern science. M. I. S. T. is a tonic which regulates the blood, purifies it and frees it from poison and stimulates the circulation. It acts directly upon the liver and kidneys, secures a perfect evacuation of the system through the natural channels, thus expelling all poisons. It is particularly beneficial in cases of catarrh, liver complaints, kidney diseases, constipation, female weakness, scrofula, heart disease, skin diseases, piles, rheumatism, fever and ague, dyspepsia and other maladies. It is compounded from natural vegetable products, according to an approved and well-tried formula, and it will absolutely perform all that is claimed for it. Thousands of testimonials have been received from all parts of the country, and at the office in this city may be seen letters from well-known residents, right here, who will be glad to testify to the benefits they have derived from its use. This specific is sovereign in its effects, and our readers will be repaid a hundred-fold if they will but investigate the merits of M. I. S. T. To those who are afflicted with disease of any kind, the only way to assure recovery is to purify and enrich the blood. M. I. S. T. will do this; it will cure the sick, give them new life and thus make their surroundings once more rosy-hued and happy.

G. H. & E. A. FORD,
Wholesale and Retail Dealers in Coal, 210 Chenango Street.

One of the most important factors of the coal trade in Binghamton is the enterprise of Messrs. G. H. & E. A. Ford, which was established in 1871 by Mr. R. A. Ford, father of the present proprietors, who succeeded to the business in 1891. The firm are the most extensive retail dealers in coal in Binghamton, and they fill orders by the car-load at wholesale, shipments being made direct from the mines to destination without breaking bulk, while their facilities for supplying the retail trade by the ton, embrace the possession of a large yard located on the line of the railroad system of the city, admitting of cars being unloaded direct into the storage sheds without rehandling. The natural as well as the acquired resources of the firm are unsurpassed by those of any of their cotemporaries and these advantages are promptly shared with their customers. Their location is a most central one and telephone connection insures the most prompt delivery of orders. The firm gives employment to twenty-five hands, including teamsters for delivery. They handle chiefly the D. & H. C. Co.'s anthracite coal, than which there is no better for all purposes, and also Kentucky, Ohio and Pennsylvania bituminous coals. About 25,000 tons of anthracite coal are handled annually, and their business is constantly increasing in volume. In all their operations the firm will be found prompt, liberal and enterprising, always solicitous for the benefit of their patrons and always prepared to offer advantages in keeping with such a reputation.

BEMAN & BAYLESS,
Manufacturers of Keg and Barrel Heads, Tub Covers and Packing Boxes, 5, 7, 9 and 11 Frederick Street.

The extensive manufacturing business conducted by Messrs. Beman & Bayless in this city is one which has been called into existence by other large manufacturing houses of this and other localities. Although to the casual reader the caption of this article may not have great signification, a little investigation will prove that a great deal underlies it and that an industry of an important and growing character has been built up with these articles for chief products. This enterprise was founded in 1868 and has since grown to such proportions that it requires several million feet of lumber annually to supply the material for the product of this factory. The plant is embraced in a series of suitable buildings covering about half a city block and adjoining lumber yards embracing six acres. The mill is fully equipped with late improved special machinery and large modern dry kilns and is operated by 100-horse power steam plant. Employment is given to from 50 to 75 workmen. The firm also have a saw-mill at Great Bend, Pa., where about 30 men are employed getting out stock with which to supply the works in this city. The firm make a specialty of heads for soda, nail and horseshoe kegs and cement and cracker barrels. They also turn out butter tub covers and packing boxes. All these products are turned out in large quantities by machinery at lowest possible cost and are widely distributed to the trade chiefly in the Eastern markets, shipments being made in carload lots. In packing boxes the product is largely taken by local manufacturers, thousands of boxes being annually made for Dr. Kilmer & Co.'s medicines, Frank E. Harris' extracts and the cigar industry. The individual members of the firm are Messrs. E. A. Beman and John Bayless, both well-known and influential residents of Binghamton who enjoy the esteem and consideration of this community whose industrial advancement is greatly benefited by the enterprise they so ably conduct.

BINGHAMTON BRANCH, U. S. BAKING CO.,
Wholesale Cracker and Cake Manufacturers. Factories: 154 and 156 State Street and 3, 5 and 7 Commercial Avenue.

The Binghamton Branch of the United States Baking Company was formed by the combination on August 1, 1891, of the enterprises formerly conducted by Messrs. Ira J. Meagley & Co. and C. C. Jackson, respectively. This company now operates upwards of thirty cracker manufactories in the various principal cities of the country and, while by this means ruinous competition has been to a considerable extent cut off, the prices of the products have not been advanced, but on the contrary in many cases lowered, this being made possible by the introduction of the very latest improved methods and the consequent reduction of the cost of production. The business of the company in this city is conducted under the management of Mr. Ira J. Meagley. Two plants are operated, each being fully equipped with all the latest improved machinery and appliances operated by steam power and furnishing employment in the several departments to about forty skilled assistants. Here crackers, cakes and biscuits are made from the best obtainable materials, after the most scientific process and with chemical exactitude, resulting in a uniform good product, which is in large and growing demand throughout Southern and Central New York and Northern Pennsylvania to the exclusion of all others. The variety of goods produced by the company seems almost interminable and includes oyster, butter and milk crackers, water crackers, soda crackers, ginger snaps, lemon cakes, iced cakes, menagerie crackers, tea cakes, etc., and a multitude of other equally popular and salable crackers and cakes for family use, hotels and restaurants. The goods are put up attractively in barrels, boxes and cartoons, and the trade and consumers exhibit by the increasing demand for the products their due appreciation of their high character.

BURHANS & BARNES,
General Insurance and Real Estate Agents, Hagaman Block.

There is no more inviting field for real estate operations than the city of Binghamton presents at the present time. The scale upon which public improvements are being conducted, with the vast outlying territory constantly being laid out, augmented by a rapidly increasing population, all combine to give real estate investments a stability, with assurance of rapidly enhancing values which would be hard to duplicate. Messrs. Burhans & Barnes occupy a prominent position among the leading and reliable real estate agents of this city, and they possess unsurpassed facilities for buying, selling, exchanging and renting real estate. They have a large list of business and residence properties on their books as well as vacant lots and tracts in all parts of the city. They have one tract of 100 lots in the east end of the city, which is one of the most important and attractive suburban sections of Binghamton and is destined to become one of its most thickly settled. A number of large manufacturing establishments have already been erected in this vicinity and others are to follow, and lots purchased now in this section

THE CITY OF BINGHAMTON. 51

are sure to increase in value to many times their cost, and that, too within a very short period. The firm transact a general real estate business, collect rent, take full charge of estates and for non-residents pay taxes, effect loans on bond and mortgage, and buy and sell real estate, and their reliability and responsibility are proverbial. The firm also transacts a general insurance business and are among the leading underwriters of this vicinity and represent the following staunch companies: The St. Paul Fire and Marine of St. Paul; the Caledonian of Scotland; the Manchester of England; the New Hampshire and the People's of Manchester, New Hampshire; the Reading Fire of Reading, Pa.; the Mechanics' and Traders' of New Orleans; the American Central of St. Louis; the State Investment of California; the Northwestern of Milwaukee; the Hartford Steam Boiler Insurance Co. of Hartford, Conn.; the American Surety Co. of New York, and the Preferred Mutual Accident Insurance Co. of New York. The combined assets of these companies represent many millions of dollars, and with such a list of prominent insurance organizations, the firm is prepared to accept the largest risks, guaranteeing absolute indemnity in case of loss. The firm also represent in this section the American Loan and Trust Co. of Ashland, Neb., and the Equitable Mortgage Co. of Kansas, and investors and capitalists will find opportunities through these companies for profitable and safe investments in improved Western farms and city property with rates of interest far greater than is obtainable in the East. The members of the firm are Messrs. P. K. Burhans and Fred E. Barnes. The former has been prominently connected with the real estate and insurance interests of Binghamton for the past twenty years, having founded the business in 1872, and few men in the city are better qualified for its successful management. Mr. Barnes has been associated in the firm since 1888, and is a particularly energetic and active underwriter, to which branch of the business he gives his special attention. The firm is well-balanced, prompt in adjusting losses, and an authority on real estate values, and with superior facilities in both departments of the business, command the confidence and respect of a large clientage.

O. R. MASON, Agt.,
Plumber, Steam and Gas Fitter and Dealer in Gas Fixtures, No. 1 Wall Street.

O. R. Mason is one of the oldest plumbers in the trade here having originally established himself here in 1863. His facilities embrace commodious show-rooms and shop, located as above indicated, where a full and complete stock of plumbers' materials and supplies is carried as well as gas fixtures in large variety and steam and gas fittings. Mr. Mason makes a specialty of sanitary plumbing and ventilating according to the most scientific modern investigations, and all work performed by him is guaranteed to be as perfect as it is possible to procure anywhere. A large and growing business has been established and many of the finest public buildings and private residences of this city and vicinity contain examples of his skill in this line of trade. Among them we note the Griffin & Burroughs block, the Water Works building, E. P. Smith's residence on Main Street and E. D. Vosbury's residence on Main Street. From four to six skilled workmen are steadily employed one being recognized as the most skilfull and capable plumber in the city and excelled in either theory or practice by none other in the country. We commend this enterprise to such of our readers as are contemplating the erection of new buildings or the improvement of old with the assurance that relations formed with it will prove eminently satisfactory.

M'KINNEY, EVERTS & CO.,
Wholesale Dealers in Teas, Coffees and Spices, Etc., 186 and 188 State St.

This enterprise was originally instituted in 1865 by Messrs. McKinney & Everts, the present firm having been formed in 1891, and for over a quarter of a century it has enjoyed an annually increasing business, enlarging the scope of its operations and extending the territory of its trade. The premises occupied as salesrooms, warehouse and manufacturing departments are embraced in a three-story and basement brick building 45x90 feet in dimensions, which is furnished throughout with every modern facility for the prompt fulfilment of orders and the economical handling of goods. In the manufacturing department the latest improved machinery and appliances are in use, including coffee roasters, spice mills, etc., power being furnished by a 20-horse power steam engine. The firm grind their own spices and put them up under their own trade marks, such being guaranteed strictly pure. They also roast and grind their own coffees, which bear an especially high repute in the market, and they also manufacture a superior grade of baking powder, besides a full line of extracts, etc. Besides goods of their own production their stock embraces teas, coffees, spices, canned goods, fancy groceries, grocers' sundries, etc., their chief specialties, however, being teas, coffees and spices. A recent innovation of the firm is the direct importation of teas. The large trade built up by them in teas induced the firm, with commendable energy, to provide their customers with the most advanced facilities for procuring them, and early in October of the present year the first invoice of "May pickings" of Japan teas was received in Binghamton direct from Yokohoma by Messrs. McKinney, Everts & Co. This example of enterprise created quite a stir in the tea trade of the city and has resulted in great advantage not only to the firm accomplishing it, but to all the customers of the house. The individual members of the firm are Messrs. Edward P. McKinney, C. A. Everts and Edward McKinney, the latter being a son of the senior member of the firm. They are assisted in the management of the business by a force of ten employes, including five commercial travellers, and the trade of the house extends throughout Southern and Central New York and Northern Pennsylvania.

WIEDMAN SHOE CO.,
Manufacturers of Ladies', Misses' and Children's Solid Shoes, 70 and 72 State Street.

This business was founded in 1884 by Messrs. W. L. Wiedman and G. H. Buck, its present proprietors, to whose experience and ability in introducing new and desirable methods and processes in the manufacture of superior shoes, is largely due the pronounced success the house has attained in the trade. The company's plant is embraced in a four-story brick building of which they occupy three floors and which are equipped with all the latest improved machinery known to the world for the production of superior goods at a minimum cost, power being obtained from an electric motor and employment being given to about twenty-five skilled workmen. The products of the house consist of a general line of ladies', misses' and children's fine and standard sewed shoes in kid, morocco, calf, grain and other leathers. All the products are strictly first-class goods made from the best and carefully selected materials and by skilled workmen, and for elegance of style and finish, beauty of appearance and durability are not excelled by those of any other house in the country. A recent novelty of the firm is a misses' and childs' shoe made from a new process tanned leather without the use of bark. This leather is peculiarly soft in texture and yet is possessed of great strength, it being next to impossible to tear and it will withstand any amount of pounding without cracking, a test that no leather of any other tannage will endure. The firm call this leather London Seal and they guarantee shoes made from it to out-wear those made from any other leather in existence, yet their prices for these are no higher than for other standard goods. The trade of the house extends throughout New York, Pennsylvania and New Jersey, and in the manufacture of an extra good quality of shoes it is doing much to attract the attention of the public to Binghamton as a source of supply for first-class manufactured products.

WILKINSON & EASTWOOD,
Manufacturers of Fancy Rockers, Binghamton, N. Y.

This house was instituted in 1879 for the purpose of manufacturing boys' express wagons and sleds, but in 1886 the character of the product was changed to the manufacture of fine upholstered and cane-seat fancy rockers. So rapid has been the growth of the demand for the firm's productions, superinduced by their artistic character, beauty of design, fine finish and low cost, that within the space of the last two years the firm have been obliged to more than double their capacity and further enlargements are still in contemplation. The manufacturing plant covers nine city lots, upon which are erected large four-story brick and wooden buildings, large yards being also used for storing lumber. The mechanical equipment embraces all the latest improved modern machinery, operated by steam power, and employment is furnished to one hundred skilled workmen. The products embrace fine upholstered chairs and fancy rockers in silk plush and silk tapestry, and these are made in many new and attractive designs, in various kinds of wood, highly polished, carved and ornamented. New and original designs are constantly being introduced and the firm have earned a high reputation for being fully abreast and in advance of the times with artistic novelties in their line. The products are all attractive, well made, artistically designed and finished, are salable and therefore just what the trade wants. While the trade of the house has so far been chiefly confined to the Eastern and Middle States, it is constantly increasing and extending to more distant sections of the country. By reason of the proximity of Binghamton to all the great distributing centers of the East, the unsurpassed shipping facilities afforded here, and the complete plant of the firm as well as their progressive and pushing methods, they are enabled to offer the trade inducements in prompt filling of orders and low prices that bid fair to long insure a steady continuance of past success. The members of the firm are Messrs. C. A. Wilkinson and W. H. Eastwood, both active and enterprising business men, in the prime of their usefulness, who take a pride in their business as well as in the city. The policy upon which the business is conducted is a fair and liberal one and the goods manufactured can be classed among the best which any market affords.

FOLMSBEE & IVES,
Manufacturers of Fine Cigars, 37 and 39 Hawley Street.

The aim of the proprietors of this house has always been to make a class of goods that should fully merit the good opinion of smokers, and to scrupulously maintain their brands, and the result has been the establishment of a permanent and growing trade which gives every indication of rapid and steady increase in the future. The facilities of the firm embrace a commodious factory, where a force of skilled workmen is employed, all operations being conducted under the immediate personal supervision of the proprietors, both of whom are practical and expert cigarmakers. The products of the factory are exclusively hand-made cigars. The chief brands of the firm are the "Puritan" and "Folmsbee & Ives No. 1," which are beyond question the very best ten-cent cigar made in Binghamton and equal to any made elsewhere. Each cigar is the product of the labor of one person in its entirety, and for uniformity in material and workmanship is unsurpassed. They are made from the finest Havana leaf tobacco, and are warranted to be exactly as represented. The firm being practical manufacturers are also expert judges of tobacco and only the best is used for these brands. To accommodate their trade they also manufacture a cheaper grade of cigars, which under the brand of "F. & I.," are equally in demand at the price, are long-filler and hand-made, and sold at five cents. As an evidence of the quality of the goods made by the firm, it may be remarked that their product is almost entirely taken in the local market, which, in the view of the fact that Binghamton has the choice of the products of all the factories located here, is a tribute to the superior quality of those made by this firm. The members of the firm are C. E. Folmsbee and G. O. Ives.

THE BINGHAMTON WIRE GOODS CO.,
Manufacturers of Wire Work and Wire Goods, 198 and 200 State St.

This enterprise was originally founded in 1881 by the late F. A. Hoag. In 1886 the firm of Hoag & Titchener was formed and they in turn were succeeded by the Binghamton Wire Goods Co. in 1890, of

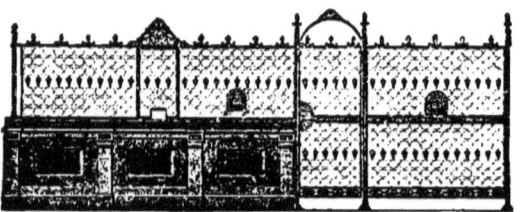

which F. A. Hoag, since deceased, E. H. Titchener and E. Harris were the co-partners. The company occupy about 12,000 square feet of floorage and the works are equipped with special machinery, operated by steam power, and furnish employment to about a dozen skilled workmen. The business is divided into two separate departments, one for the manufacture of wire nails, staples, double-pointed tacks, etc., and the other for the manufacture of plain and ornamental wire work of all descriptions. For the former class of goods the company has agencies in all the principal cities of this country and their wire nails, staples and double-pointed tacks are shipped to all parts of the country and exported to Canada and other foreign lands. The architectural revolutions of late years have wrought many important changes not only in forms but in materials employed, not the least important being the substitution of metals where wood was formerly used. In the second department of the company's business

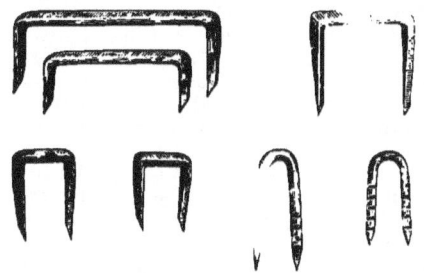

one part of this change is supplied in the manufacture of all kinds of plain and ornamantal wire work for office, counter and bank railings, window guards, elevator enclosures, piazza panels, brass and iron grilles for windows, etc. These goods are made in a great variety of styles and designs from bright, coppered, galvanized, tinned and flat wire, plain and brass wire, from architects' drawings or otherwise as may be desired.
Other goods handled by the firm are wire fencing, poultry netting, flower stands, spark guards, etc. Having unsurpassed facilities for promptness and good work, the firm make estimates for all kinds of wire work and wire goods and guarantee satisfaction and lowest prices. In this department of their business the Binghamton Wire Goods Company have a large local trade and also cover a large part of Southern New York and Northern Pennsylvania. The management of the business is in the hands of gentlemen of experience and pushing energy, who are closely identified with the growth and prosperity of Binghamton.

WILLIAM H. OGDEN & CO.,
Manufacturers of Fine Cigars, 78 and 80 State St.

Binghamton owes much to the enterprise and ability of the houses engaged in the cigar manufacturing industry, and a leading and well-known representative of the trade is the house of Messrs. Wm. H. Ogden & Co., which was established August 14, 1889, and has since grown from modest beginnings to be one of the leading and shining lights of the trade. The firm occupy two floors of the building, located as above indicated, for manufacturing purposes, where employment is given to thirty-five skilled workmen, no machinery being employed, the products being chiefly strictly hand-made cigars, and the better grades. All their goods are made and packed under their own brands and are distributed to the retail trade in New York and Pennsylvania, where they have attained a popularity that is as widespread and permanent as it is gratifying. The principal specialty of the firm is their "Escribanos" brand, which has probably met with as great favor as that of any other cigar ever before put upon the market, necessitating almost the entire attention of the firm to keep up with their orders. It is widely known for its fine natural aroma, its uniform quality and reliability, and for genuine merit it is fully entitled to be classed as the finest made in this market. It is a straight ten-cent cigar and is for sale by leading dealers throughout the circuit of their trade. Their leading five-cent cigar is the "Bow Knot," which is equally popular at the price. The annual output of the factory is about 2,000,000 cigars and the demand is steadily increasing. The members of the firm are Messrs. William H. Ogden, J. S. Ogden and William Ogden, Jr., all of whom take an active interest in the management of the business, and the result of their progressive methods is a superior grade of cigars, which the trade has been prompt to appreciate. The firm enjoys a high reputation for integrity and liberality and they are to be congratulated upon the success they have achieved, which their enterprise so fully merits.

L. DOOLITTLE,
Binghamton City Mills, 8 South Street.

The grinding of cereals for food is one of oldest and most prominent industries of all ages and is represented in Binghamton by a number of houses whose united operations are very large. Prominent among them is the Binghamton City Mills, of which Mr. L. Doolittle is the proprietor. This mill was first started about a quarter of a century ago, the present mill having been erected about six years ago. It is a three-story building 40x86 feet in dimensions and is provided with four run of stone operated by water power and has a capacity for grinding about 650 bushels of grain daily. Only custom flouring is done, but considerable feed is ground and shipped to the trade throughout this and the adjoining counties, and Western flour, grain, and feed are also handled at both wholesale and retail. Mr. Doolittle is one of the pioneers of Binghamton's industrial progress and has been a resident of the city for nearly half a century. He was at one time engaged in the lumber business and for a number of years also conducted a retail grocery store. Another of his enterprises was the carding of wool, which he carried on until the change in business methods resulted in this branch of production being transferred to other localities. Though actively engaged in business for so many years, he is still an energetic and progressive manufacturer and his present industry is one of the features of the commercial supremacy of this growing metropolis.

W. W. HEMINGWAY,
Plumber, Steam and Gas Fitter and Dealer in Hardware, Stoves and Ranges, 175 and 177 Washington Street,

The most extensive establishment in Binghamton, devoted to the branch of commercial industry, implied in the caption of this article is that of Mr. W. W. Hemingway, which was originally founded in 1867 by Mason, Root & Co., who were succeeded in 1880 by J. W. Doubleday & Co., of which latter firm Mr. Hemingway was a member, and in 1889 he assumed sole control of the business. The headquarters of the business are embraced in a large double store and basement 43x120 feet in dimensions, which is handsomely fitted up and attractively arranged and contains a large and varied stock of goods embracing parlor heating stoves, furnaces, ranges, tinware and kitchen furnishing goods, gas fixtures, gas and steam fittings, plumbers' materials and supplies and indeed everything in these various lines required by the demands of the public. The house has the agency in this city for the Pease Economy Furnace, which is undoubtedly the very best furnace ever contrived for heating and ventilating dwellings, schools, churches, stores or other buildings, and is in use by many in this city and vicinity. Mr. Hemingway has executed the plumbing, steam and gas fitting in very many private residences and public buildings in Binghamton, and his trade in stoves and ranges is widely recognized as being a most important one. A large variety of different styles and makes of stoves is shown here and courteous assistants are pleased to explain their merits to all inquirers. As a representative progressive house this one is a marked feature of the trade resources of Binghamton and is justly entitled to the prominence it has achieved in the exercise of its liberal business policy.

CHARLES E. LEE,

Wholesale and Retail Dealer in Lumber, Building Materials, Cut-Stone, etc., 200 Chenango St. and 100 to 150 Eldredge St.

The oldest and most prominent house engaged in handling all the varied products implied in the caption of this article, in Binghamton, is that of Mr. Charles E. Lee, which was established in 1870, and has been conducted under his sole proprietorship since 1883. With headquarters as above indicated, where two extensive yards, one for lime and sewer pipe and the other for lumber and stone cutting, are occupied, the house is in possession of every modern facility that tends to decrease the cost of handling or promote the prompt fulfillment of orders. The yards are connected with the railroad system of the city by side tracks, which permits of the receipt and shipment of stock without rehandling, and large warehouses and sheds protect the materials from the weather. The stock handled embraces lumber of all kinds, hardwoods, shingles, lath, lime, cement, plaster, sewer-pipe, fire-brick, fire clay, chimney tops and cut-stone, the latter forming a very important branch of the business, requiring the services of a large number of skilled stone-cutters during the building season. All the goods handled by Mr. Lee are unrivalled for high quality and general excellence, and are received direct from the most noted manufacturers of the country in large quantities, and are offered to the trade at lowest prices. A full and complete assortment of regular sizes of fire-brick slabs is carried in stock and special sizes are made to order, while in general builders' materials the stock is ample to promptly meet the largest orders. From forty to seventy-five workmen are employed, the number varying with the exigencies of the season, and besides an extensive and growing local business a large wholesale trade is transacted that extends throughout a large part of Southern New York and Northern Pennsylvania. In every respect the facilities of the house are such as to have gained for it a wide reputation and placed it in the foremost rank of the successful establishments of the Parlor City.

BINGHAMTON WOOLEN CO.,

Manufacturers of Blankets, Binghamton, N. Y.

A recent and important addition to the diversified character of the industrial resources of Binghamton is the Binghamton Woolen Co., which commenced operations here in July last. The manufacturing plant of the company is embraced in a three-story and basement building 40x110 feet in dimensions, which is equipped with all the latest improved machinery known to the trade, and of a very superior character, power being obtained from a 35-horse power steam engine, and employment being given to about fifty operatives at present, which number it is contemplated will be gradually increased. The products are made in a variety of fine and medium grades and in all the usual sizes in white and grey, and are trimmed and finished in the best manner. Only the best qualities of raw materials are used in their production, and already a large and growing demand has been built up for the goods which extends throughout the United States generally. The executive officers of the company are Messrs. C. A. Lull, President, and R. W. Meeker, Secretary and Treasurer, both gentlemen of comprehensive business experience and enterprising methods equal to the requirements of the successful management of so important an enterprise.

PERSELS & MACK,
Manufacturers of Saddlery and Harness and Jobbers of Saddlery Hardware, 40 Chenango St.

No single firm in the city enjoys a higher reputation than Messrs. Persels & Mack. This house was originally instituted in 1872 by Messrs. Smith and Persels. In 1874 the firm style changed to Smith, Persels & Co. In 1876 it became Persels, Nicoll & Mack, and in 1890 the present firm of Persels & Mack, composed of Messrs. Henry Persels and Daniel H. Mack, succeeded to the business. The present extensive premises occupied by the firm were erected and taken possession of in 1886. The building has three floors each 24x115 feet in dimensions, the ground floor being used for office and salesroom and the upper floors for manufacturing purposes. The firm are wholesale dealers in saddlery hardware, and they carry an extensive stock of everything pertaining to the trade, of both foreign and domestic manufacture, from the cheapest buckle to the most expensive harness trimmings, and including also parts of harness gig saddles, winkers, bridles, housings, fronts, halters, reins, etc. In the manufacturing department a large force of skilled workmen is employed, and fine hand-made single and double, light and heavy harness is manufactured. The productive capacity of the factory is about 2,000 sets of harness annually. Two travelling salesmen are employed and their trade extends throughout New England and the Middle States. The members of the firm are both gentlemen of high standing in this community, of sound business judgment, who by energy and enterprise have built up from small beginnings this important addition to the manufacturing and jobbing interests of Binghamton.

STONE & SANDERS.
Dealers in Paints, Oils, Glass, etc., 7 Court St.

The above named house is the oldest and most prominent representative of the paint and oil trade of Binghamton, and its transactions form an important feature of the wholesale and retail accommodations of the city. The business was instituted in 1879, and has steadily expanded with the growth and development of the city, increasing its facilities and the scope of its operations as the requirements of its trade and this market made necessary. The premises occupied for the business are embraced in three floors, each 22x80, which afford ample accommodations for the storage of a large and complete stock and the prompt fulfillment of orders. The assortment carried is not only complete, but is also of admirable selection and quality, is purchased direct from the most noted manufacturers, and is offered to the trade, large consumers and the public upon the most advantageous terms. It includes all kinds of ground and mixed paints, colors and white lead, oils, varnishes, glass and painters' materials, brushes, glue, japans, and in fact every conceivable article incident to the trade. A specialty is made of Liquid Fillers and Stains, Water Proof Floor Finish, Magic Primer and Furniture polishes made by the Star Furnishing Co., of Dayton, O., for which the firm are general agents. They also carry a full line of sash weights in all sizes from three to thirty pounds. A full and complete line of artists' materials and colors is also a feature of the stock. The facilities of the house are complete in all particulars, and their trade extends throughout a radius of fifty miles from this city. The members of the firm are Messrs. W. J. Stone and H. H. Sanders, both thoroughly conversant with all the details of the business to which they devote their close attention. Those concerned will find their best interests well served in dealing with this firm, which has inducements to offer fully equal, at least, to those of metropolitan trade centers.

BINGHAMTON PRODUCE CO.,
Produce Commission Merchants, 187 Water Street.

Among the later additions to the produce branch of trade is the solid and progressive house of the Binghamton Produce Co., combining energy and experience with a complete knowledge of the wants of the trade and enjoying the confidence of a wide circle of shippers and patrons extending throughout a large part of Southern New York and Northern Pennsylvania. This enterprise was founded in 1889 by Messrs. W. D. and W. F. Cady and R. S. Cotton. Their premises comprise a store and basement and one upper floor of the new building located as above indicated, which afford ample accommodations for the stock and admirable facilites for handling it. An elevator connects the floors, and a cold-storage room insures the proper care of perishable products. The business of the house, which is of a strictly wholesale character, embraces the handling of fresh gathered eggs, butter, cheese and country produce as specialties, and no house in Binghamton is in a better position to supply the demands of the retail trade in these food supplies. They also handle hay, straw, feed and flour to a limited extent, and are always prepared to sell goods on commission, consignments being solicited for which the highest market prices and quick returns may be confidently assured. The firm are in daily receipt of the products of firstclass dairies, which they offer the trade upon favorable terms. The house is probably the largest handler of butter and eggs in this market, and as one of the most important of the trade facilities of Binghamton, having for its sole object the furnishing of food supplies of high quality to the public at lowest prices, the Binghamton Produce Co. is fully entitled to the success and prosperity it has achieved in its chosen field of enterprise.

EUREKA ADVERTISING AGENCY,
Ackerman Block.

The Eureka Advertising Agency, was organized in 1889, and has since built up a large and growing patronage and a high reputation among newspaper publishers. The agency does a general advertising business, placing advertisements in any and all newspapers throughout the United States, at the lowest possible rates. The agency having no axe of their own to grind with the publishers, are enabled to quote net cash prices, and the record of the past business done assures publishers of prompt cash payments, which encourages them to afford the agency advantages not easily duplicated elsewhere. The agency offers advertisers all the facilities that modern methods have made advantageous, and their advice and experience are promptly put at the disposal of patrons. The agency also has the exclusive control of all street car advertising in Binghamton and other cities. This medium of advertising is recognized by the leading advertisers of the country as one of the most profitable that can be obtained. Mr. G. S. Ackley is the manager of the business, to whose progressive ideas and energetic methods its prominent success is due. The enterprise is a valuable acquisition to the business resources of Binghamton, and fully merits the prominence it has attained.

EMPIRE GRAIN AND ELEVATOR CO.
Office 192 Chenango St., Elevator and Warehouse, Robinson St.

One of the most important enterprises of the kind in the State and the only one of considerable proportions in this section is the Empire Grain and Elevator Co., of this city, which was organized in June, 1891, and has a paid up capital stock of $75,000. This prominent concern may be said to have been instituted by reason of the labors of Mr. L. M. Wilson, its present secretary, treasurer and general manager, and the success of the company since its organization is an evidence of the good judgment shown in locating it here. The company's business embraces the buying and shipping of grain, hay and mill-feeds, buckwheat grain and also the manufacture of clipped oats. The company are heavy buyers of grain in the Western markets, which they supply to millers and local dealers in car lots, either direct from the original sources of supply without transhipment, or from warehouse here, as may be desired. They are also large buyers of buckwheat grain and baled hay in this market, the former being disposed of in Illinois, Wisconsin and other Western states, as well as the middle and New England states. The chief trade of the company, however, is in supplying millers and dealers in New England and the middle states with grain, hay and mill-feeds, for which department of the business they enjoy the most advanced and modern facilities. The company's elevator and warehouse is located in the north-eastern section of the city and is literally surrounded by railroad tracks. The building is equipped with a 100-horse power steam engine, elevating and cleaning machinery, oat clippers, power shovels, steam car pullers, separators, etc., and in fact every mechanical contrivance and convenience that would in any way serve to save labor or secure promptness in filling orders. About 1000 feet of tracks insures receipt and shipment of stock with a minimum of handling, and a sixty-ton track scale insures correct weights. The capacity of the elevator is 50,000 bushels of grain and the warehouse furnishes

storage for 5,600 tons of hay, and mill-feeds, and this stock, supplemented by large shipments daily in transit, insures the prompt fulfillment of all orders. By reason of its central location, and being upon the main highway from the west to the east, Binghamton offers the greatest advantages to the trade as a source of supply for the above named staples, and the Empire Grain and Elevator Co. has developed these advantages in the interest of their customers, and made it possible for the trade to use this market at a saving over that of any other in the East. This company lays down grain and other products throughout the circuit of its trade, with greater promptness and frequently at less prices than it is possible to obtain it from more distant markets. A special feature of the business of the company is the manufacture of clipped oats, which are in demand by the trade and consumers. Mr. L. M. Wilson is assisted in the management of the business by Mr. T. H. Wilson, Associate Manager, and no enterprise in the city gives greater promise of continued growth and prosperity than does the Empire Grain and Elevator Co. Correspondence from the trade is solicited and prompt replies and quotations may be assured. This city is to be congratulated upon being the headquarters of so prominent and valuable an institution as this, which by its advanced facilities and accommodations is a credit alike to its management and this community.

LLOYD & GARDINER,

Manufacturers and Wholesale Dealers in Confectionery, 215 State Street.

The enterprise of Messrs. Lloyd & Gardiner is the chief representative of the confectionery branch of the wholesale trade of this city and is the only exclusively wholesale confectionery house in the city, such others as do any jobbing, being also retailers. This house was founded in 1885 by Lloyd & Shrimpton, the present firm, composed of John E. Lloyd and C. L. Gardiner, having succeeded to the business January 1, 1890. The premises occupied are comprised in a four-story and basement brick building, the ground floor being utilized for salesrooms and office purposes and the upper floors for manufacturing and surplus stock. The equipment of the establishment embraces all necessary appliances, no power machinery being used, the products being all hand-made confectionery. The firm manufactures a full and complete line of fine and medium confectionery, including some penny goods, making a specialty of fine moulded cream goods, which are unsurpassed for quality, handsome appearance and attractiveness. Another specialty is fruit tablets, packed in glass jars, which for fine flavor and high quality are in the highest repute with first-class retail trade, druggists and confectioners generally. The firm pack their own goods under their trade-mark of "Wild Rose," which has become a well-recognized guarantee of superior quality. Only the best ingredients, pure sugar, flavorings, etc. are used and all the products are guaranteed to be exactly as represented. Besides the goods of their own production, the firm carry a complete line of candies, confectionery, chocolate goods, penny goods, novelties, chewing gum, etc., which are procured direct from the largest and most noted manufacturers of the country and are offered to the trade at manufacturers' prices. They also handle a full line of foreign and domestic nuts. The trade of the house extends throughout this State and Pennsylvania within a hundred miles of Binghamton, and four travelling salesmen represent the house on the road. Notwithstanding the keen competition of New York and other markets, the "Wild Rose" brand of confectionery produced by this house is to be found in the hands of the principal retailers of this section, and the particular excellence and attractiveness of these goods are annually increasing the demand for them. The members of the firm are both experienced and practical manufacturers and they devote their close personal attention to all the details of the business in the interest of excellence of product. The extent, variety and character of the entire stock of this house merit the attention of critical and prudent buyers and the trade will find upon forming relations with Messrs. Lloyd & Gardner many advantages impossible to procure elsewhere in this market.

H. L. BUSH & CO.,

Cigar Manufacturers, 249 Water Street.

The cigar manufactory of Messrs. H. L. Bush & Co., established in 1889, has since come to be an important factor of the industry in this city. The firm occupy commodious premises in the building located as above indicated, where they give steady employment to twenty cigar makers and annually turn out about 850,000 fine and medium grade cigars. Their goods which are chiefly designed for fine retail trade are also in demand by leading jobbers and are distributed to the trade throughout New York and Pennsylvania principally. Their leading brands are "Governors," "Refined" and "La Rosa" in five cent cigars, and "Local," "Honor" and "The Hand Made" in ten cent cigars. These are particularly popular with consumers and the trade, and are fully maintained to the high standard originally set for them. No power machinery is used and all the goods produced are strictly hand-made cigars and as such are confidently recommended to the trade and consumers as possessing every attribute for perfect satisfaction. The members of the firm are Messrs. H. L. and A. J. Bush, both progressive manufacturers, who devote their close personal attention to all the operations of the business, in the interest of a superior product. The success and continued growth of the business have been matters of favorable comment both in the trade and this community and every promise of future expansion is given.

W. D. STEVENS,

Mason Contractor and Builder, 36 Susquehanna Street.

Mr. W. D. Stevens began operations in 1869 and during the interval since elapsed has erected a large number of the principal churches, business blocks, manufacturing establishments and private residences of Binghamton as well as a large part of the central business structures in Oneonta. For a number of years he confined his attention to mason work only, but of late years has undertaken the entire work of building, including brick, stone and frame buildings. His present facilities embrace a wood working shop, which is a two-story brick building 80x175 feet in dimensions, which is equipped with all necessary improved machinery and tools, operated by a 50-horse power steam engine and capable of turning out everything in the way of builders' finish, after the most approved methods and at a minimum cost. Planing, carving and turning are also accomplished here for the trade at reasonable prices. The energies of the house are devoted to the erection of all kinds of public and private buildings and also include all kinds of jobbing and the production of stair and cabinet work. Among the principal buildings erected by Mr. Stevens, either in whole or in part, are the High School, Weed's tannery, Hamlin block, Ackerman block, Pope & Johnson block, Dunk block, Cady block, Tabernacle church, Congregational church, Hammond block, Westcott block, Rich block, Lester block, Stone & Jenks' block and many others. These are but a few of the prominent exemplifications of his skill and ability as a builder.

C. A. CORBIN,

Wholesale Dealer and Shipper of Eggs, 152 Main St.

The facilities afforded by Binghamton for the transaction of an enterprise such as that forming the caption of this article, by reason of the numerous and far-reaching lines of railway centering here and the contiguity of the city to unsurpassed producing localities are particularly favorable, and have resulted in the acquisition by Mr. C. A. Corbin of a very extensive business, which, while also being an unique one is annually increasing in the volume of its transactions. Mr. Corbin founded his enterprise in 1872 at Otego, N. Y., and removed its headquarters to this city in 1889, and he also operates branch packing houses at Otego, Unadilla, Bloomville, Trout Creek, Afton, Morris, Canton and Hartwick. The facilities of the house embrace storage warehouses at the several receiving points, and in this city alone there is a storage capacity for half a million dozen eggs. The operations of the business embrace the collection and the purchase of eggs from the producers in this state and Pennsylvania and their shipment to New York city, a specialty being made of strictly fancy fresh eggs. Eggs are also packed in lime and stored to meet the demand at seasons when the supply of fresh eggs is limited. During the season the daily outlay for eggs reaches the sum of $1,000, and the aggregate results in an annual turnover of very large proportions. The greatest care is taken in the selection of stock, and the connections of the house with producers are such that the sources of supply are practically unlimited. The trade of the house is entirely with New York city and daily shipments are made to this market. Mr. Corbin is an enterprising and progressive business man, and since his location here has closely allied himself with the commercial development of Binghamton.

C. A. SMITH,
Cigar Manufacturer, North Depot Street.

As a leading representative of the cigar manufacturing trade we quote with pleasure the enterprise of Mr. C. A. Smith, which was originally established in 1886 at Oneonta, and was removed to this city in 1888. The factory and salesrooms are located in the five-story building, opposite the "Erie" passenger station, where every improved mechanical facility is at hand for the economical production of fine seed and Havana cigars, power being obtained from a 20-horse power steam engine and a 40-horse power boiler, and employment is given to sixty skilled workmen. All the operations of the factory are conducted under the personal supervision of the proprietor, who is an experienced manufacturer and an expert judge of leaf tobacco, and has been actively engaged in the business for the past fifteen years. The result is a line of medium and fine cigars that have no superiors in the market and are in active demand both by the trade and consumers. The goods are produced chiefly under registered brands of the house, among which we note "Havana Bouquet," "Santa Clara," "El Cometa," "Crown Jewel," "Elkoe," "Big Gun," "899," "Red Skin," "Happy Coon," "Gold Anchor," "Big 23," "Cherry Ripe," "Liberty" and "Yum Yum," each of which has a high reputation and great popularity in wide-spread localities throughout the United States generally as far West as the Pacific coast, sales being made almost exclusively to jobbers, three travelling salesmen representing the house on the road. The principal and leading brand of the house, however, is the "C. A. S. Bouquet," a strictly fine hand-made Havana filled cigar, which is confidently recommended as the best ten cent cigar on the market. It is widely known for its fine natural aroma, reliability and uniformity and for genuine merit is fully entitled to be classed as the finest made in this market. The annual out-put of the house is about 2,000,000 cigars, and the volume of production is annually increasing, necessitating frequent increase of facilities. The establishment is in every way entitled to the confidence of the trade and ever since its advent here it has been a leading representative of the cigar manufacturing industry of Binghamton.

GAYLORD'S STORAGE WAREHOUSE.
178 State Street, Branch Office, 78 Court St.

The above named enterprise is an important adjunct to the commercial resources and conveniences of Binghamton. The warehouse is a four-story and basement brick building, 25x125 feet in dimensions, which is provided with an elevator connecting all the floors, and in every respect affords the public with all necessary facilities for the storage and safe keeping of merchandise, furniture, pianos, pictures, carriages, gold and silver plate and goods of all descriptions at reasonable rates. A special feature of the enterprise is that the management insures all goods for its patrons free. A large covered van for moving furniture is also one of the facilities of the house, and this van may also be secured for removing furniture to any desired place. This warehouse was first thrown open to the public in 1888 and has since proved the wisdom of its inception by the large patronage it has received from the community. The management of the business is in the hands of Messrs. A. D. Gaylord and H. J. Gaylord. The former has been actively engaged in the packing of leaf tobacco in this city for the past quarter of a century and the latter is now and long has been the leading real estate dealer of this city and is also president of the Security Mutual Life Association of Binghamton.

HEATH & HARRIS,
Machinists, 227 and 229 Water St.

This business was instituted in 1882 by Knapp & Heath, the present firm succeeding to the business in 1890. The firm occupy a two-story brick building which is fully equipped with all necessary machinery operated by a 15-horse power steam engine, employment being given to a number of skilled mechanics. The products of the house embrace improved foot-power lathes, which have a high reputation in the trade and are in demand throughout the United States. Other products are milling machines, improved iron shapers and vises. Besides the manufacture of the above, the firm do a regular jobbing and repairing business, for which they are prepared with all necessary facilities. Anything in the line of special machinery or tools is constructed to order and inquiries are invited on this class of machine work. Both members of this firm, Robert Heath and J. Fred Harris, are thoroughly practical machinists who take an active part in all the operations of their business.

HULL, GRUMMOND & CO.,
Manufacturers of Cigars, 220 Water St.

The manufacture of cigars is the leading industrial interest of Binghamton, and among the most creditable establishments devoted to their production is that of Messrs. Hull, Grummond & Co., which has developed a large and annually increasing trade that extends throughout the United States generally. This house is also one of the oldest of the larger establishments manufacturing cigars, having been originally founded in 1874 by Mr. John Hull, Jr., the present firm having succeeded to the business in 1886. The factory of the firm is a large four-story and basement brick building, which is fully equipped with all necessary improved machinery, including stripping, bunching and scrap machines, operated by a 25-horse power steam engine and supplied with elevator and all other modern facilities for the economical production of the goods and the prompt fulfillment of orders. The products embrace a large variety of medium and fine domestic cigars ranging in price by the case from $20 to $60 per thousand, the output of the factory ranging from ten to fifteen millions annually, employment being given to from four hundred to five hundred male and female operatives. No very low grade cigars are made, and sales are made to the jobbing trade exclusively. The individual members of the firm are Messrs. John Hull, Jr., Charles A. Hull and Fred W. Grummond, all progressive and enterprising business men, closely identified with the industrial advance of Binghamton.

KNAPP & SON,,
Machinists, 196 State St.

Among the manifold manufacturing industries which distinguish Binghamton as a prominent trade center, there is no more useful branch of production carried on here than that which engages the attention of Messrs. Knapp & Son. This enterprise was originally begun by Mr. William Knapp in 1869, the present firm having been formed in 1885, after several changes in the proprietorship of the business. The premises occupied for the business are embraced in three floors of the building located as above indicated, and are equipped with a full complement of machinists' tools and machinery operated by steam power, employment being given to an average force of seven skilled artisans. The firm are builders of all kinds of special and general machinery, steam engines, etc., and also do a large jobbing and repairing business for local manufacturers. They undertake the manufacture of any mechanical device in brass and iron, besides the manufacture of special machinery and tools, shaftings, hangers, pulleys, etc. They turn out on contract large numbers of lubricators, damper regulators, water regulators and other specialties for the Hoffman Lubricating Oil Co. of this city. The members of the firm are both practical and expert machinists and engineers, and possess a thorough knowledge of the varied details of the business over which they preside.

W. F. RAHILLY & CO.,
Wholesale Dealers in Wines, Liquors, Etc., 138 Washington Street.

The enterprise of Messrs. W. F. Rahilly & Co. among its contemporaries occupies an eminent position in the liquor trade here. It was originally established in 1870 by John W. McTighe, the present firm assuming control in 1890. The premises occupied comprise a well appointed and convenient store at the above address where may be found a large stock of foreign and domestic wines and liquors of the choicest selected quality. While a general line is handled, specialties are made of the following celebrated brands of whiskey, viz: Hermitage, Beaver Run, Finch's Golden Wedding, Old Crow, Mt. Vernon and Duffy's Pure Malt. These are all goods of tried and national reputation, pure in quality, delicious in flavor, wholesome and reliable. In addition to the above a very fine stock of American and imported gins, rums, brandies, whiskies, champagnes, clarets, ports, sherries, Bass ale, etc., are carried which have been specially selected for the trade of this house. Altogether the facilities of the concern are fully equal in every respect to those of dealers in any city in the country. The trade of the house extends throughout a wide range of territory embracing mainly Southern New York and Northern Pennsylvania. The individual members of the firm are Messrs. W. F. Rahilly and F. E. McTighe, both of whom are thoroughly experienced in the business to which they give their close personal attention.

JOHN RAY CLARKE CO.,
Wholesale Dealers in Hats, Caps, Straw Goods, Robes and Blankets, Cor. Henry St. and Commercial Ave.

This house was originally established by the late John Ray Clarke, the present company having been organized in 1891, since the demise of the founder. The warehouse of the company is embraced in a handsome new five-story building, erected in 1890, which covers an area of 80x90 feet. The building is furnished with all modern improvements, including an elevator and is one of the most complete commercial edifices in the city, and is also notable for its substantial and graceful architecture. The stock carried is large and well selected and embraces hats and caps of all kinds, shapes and styles of the ruling fashion, as well as straw goods in season, and a complete line of sleigh-robes, plush and wool lap-robes of their own manufacture, and horse blankets, no other concern in the state, outside of New York, showing so complete and varied a stock. All goods are procured direct from manufacturers both at home and abroad in large quantities, and are offered at prices which command the most favorable attention. Eight assistants in the warehouse and ten travelling salesmen are employed in the several departments of the business, and the trade of the house extends throughout New York, Pennsylvania, Ohio and Michigan.

JULIUS P. MORGAN,
Manufacturer of Cigars, 1 and 3 Carroll St.

The extensive cigar manufacturing establishment, now and since March, 1891, under the proprietorship of Mr. Julius P. Morgan, was originally established in April, 1888, by Messrs. Schubmehl, Cox & Co. The factory is comprised in a three-story brick building, which is fully equipped with all late improved machinery, operated by a 20-horse power steam engine, and furnishes employment to one hundred and twenty-five skilled operatives. The products of the factory embrace a variety of brands of fine and medium grade domestic cigars, which are produced after the most improved methods from the best qualities of leaf tobacco, and while in no particular can they be classed as cheap in the sense of inferiority, they are offered to the trade at lowest possible prices considering the quality. Among the chief brands, of which there are many, we note: "Our Veterans," "Scarlet Letter" and "Oaken Buckets" in five-cent cigars, and "Brook Trout" and "La Gladiosa" in ten-cent cigars, which have had a phenomenal sale and are justly popular with the trade and smokers wherever introduced. The trade of the house extends generally throughout the United States and is with jobbers exclusively, a number of travelling salesmen being constantly on the road. Mr. Morgan, the proprietor of this enterprise, though a recent accession to the industry, is a gentleman of large and varied business experience and attainments, and is prominently connected with other important enterprises in this city. He has surrounded himself in his present enterprise with able and progressive lieutenants, and has not only succeeded in maintaining the large and growing trade of the house, but has also extended the scope of its operations and augmented the demand for its products.

THE L. BOLLES HOE AND TOOL CO.,

Sole Manufacturers of Bolles' Cast Steel Field and Garden Hoes, Office and Works 124, 126 and 128 Walnut Street.

The enterprise of The L. Bolles Hoe and Tool Co. is one of the oldest of Binghamton's industrial enterprises, having been originally established in 1840, and its products having been in the market for over half a century are everywhere recognized as the highest standard for quality and superiority. The company's plant is located in the western part of the city and adjoins the railroad system, thus affording the most complete facilities for the economical receipt of raw materials and the shipment of the finished product. The works consist of a series of brick buildings, which are fully equipped with all necessary machinery and tools, operated by a 150-horse power engine and employment is given to forty skilled workmen. The products consist of Bolles' celebrated cast steel field and garden hoes, mortar or street hoes, handled planters' hoes, handled cotton hoes, socket cotton hoes, weeding hoes, riveted hoes, etc. These are made in various numbers and sizes from the best materials by experienced and skilled workmen and after the most approved patterns, original with this company. These hoes have no equals in the market for high quality and finish and the trade-mark of the company is a guarantee of perfection. From the inception of the business, the distinguishing feature of this company's operations has been the superiority of their goods. Thus the favor of the trade and consumers has been attained and a large and prosperous business created which extends throughout the United States, besides which their goods are also exported to foreign countries. The officers of the company are Messrs. J. T. Whitmore, President; E. N. Abbott, Secretary, and J. W. Manier, Treasurer, who give the management of the business their energetic attention. Mr. Manier is also President of the Susquehanna Valley Bank. The enterprise is an important factor in the make-up of the city's industries, and with a record of a half century for the production of the best goods of the kind in the market is fully entitled to the confidence of the trade it has so long enjoyed.

BENNETT BROTHERS,
Manufacturers of Cigar Boxes, South Street.

This house was originally instituted in 1884 by A. R. Wilkinson & Co., the present firm having succeeded to the business in 1889. Their facilities embrace a well-equipped factory operated by water power and supplied with all the late improved machinery known to the trade, including sawing and planing machines, nailing machines, etc. The firm manufacture all kinds of cigar boxes from the best materials and in the highest style of workmanship and, having all modern facilities, they are turned out at the minimum cost. From ten to fifteen employes are required in the business and the trade of the house, while being largely with local manufacturers, also extends to all the neighboring towns and is annually increasing in volume. The members of the firm, Messrs. J. M. and W. E. Bennett, are both practical men at the business and give all the details of manufacture their close personal supervision in the interest of superior products.

H. J. GAYLORD,
Real Estate, 78 Court St.

The old-established and representative real estate agency of Mr. H. J. Gaylord, which is the most prominent enterprise of the kind in the city, has done much to advance the corporate growth and business interests of Binghamton, inviting men of capital here and at the same time offering inducements to residents to own homes or purchase lots for manufacturing, mercantile or residence purposes. This agency is second to none of its kind in the State, either in facilities for doing business, experienced management or reputation for reliability and fair dealing, and has for many years been actively engaged in developing Binghamton's industrial and commercial growth, and the benefits conferred upon the city through the energy and enterprise of its founder and proprietor, Mr. H. J. Gaylord, have been many and valuable. Mr. Gaylord conducts a general real estate business, buying, selling and exchanging real property of all kinds both on his own account and on commission for others. He also negotiates mortgage loans, furnishes buyers of lots with money to erect houses, when desired, upon terms that are most liberal, and furnishes opportunities to industrious working men and others to own their own homes, which no prudent man can afford to neglect. He takes full charge of estates and property for non-residents, collects rentals, pays taxes and transacts all business relating to real estate at a moderate compensation, and his experience and standing in the business community are such as to justify the most implicit confidence of clients. Mr. Gaylord has been instrumental in laying out and disposing of a number of valuable sub-divisions and additions to the building sites in the most desirable sections of the city, many of which have been sold and built upon, and others equally desirable still remaining. Mr. Gaylord is a broadgauge man, of comprehensive views, thoroughly identified with Binghamton in the best sense, and extremely liberal toward all who would invest in the soil and thus become permanently attached to the city. His suite of offices is centrally located, and headquarters for real estate investors in Binghamton. A hearty welcome is extended here to all strangers and investigators of the advantages of Binghamton, and all inquiries will be answered and information furnished to visitors. Correspondence from capitalists, investors, and those seeking a profitable and advantageous location for a home or industry is invited, and to such is offered the full benefit of the sagacity, knowledge and business experience of the management.

BAYLESS PAPER CO.,
Manufacturers of Book, News and Manilla Paper, Binghamton, N. Y.

The Bayless Paper Co. was instituted in 1882 and has since developed a large and annually increasing trade extending throughout New England, the Middle and Central Western States. The company's plant, located in the north-eastern section of the city is most extensive in character and complete in equipment. The buildings are several in number and are adjoined on all sides by the tracks of the railroad system of the city, affording the most complete facilities for the receipt of raw materials and the shipment of finished products, cars being loaded and unloaded direct at the doors. Large yards for storing wood from which wood-pulp is made, are also utilized, and the machinery and appliances in operation are of the most modern character, representing all the improvements that have been made, during recent years, in the art of paper making. Two steam engines with a combined force of 400-horse power serve to operate the mechanical equipment and employment is furnished to about thirty workmen. The company make about 3½ to 4 tons of wood pulp daily and turn out from five to seven tons of paper per day, the quantity varying with the kind of paper made. Book, news and manilla paper are produced which may be said to represent the very acme of perfection in their various grades. The proprietors of the enterprise are Messrs. Geo. C. and F. J. Bayless.

BINGHAMTON BLACKBOARD CO.,
Manufacturers of Blackboards, 9 Ferry Street.

This enterprise, of which Mr. L. A. Ash is the founder and proprietor, though instituted so recently as March 1891, has already built up a large trade that extends throughout a large part of the Eastern, Southern and Western States and is gradually extending its territory. The manufacturing facilities of the company embrace a two-story factory, which is fully equipped with all necessary machinery, operated by water power. The products embrace a variety of sizes and styles of Portable Blackboards, which may be used for many different purposes. They make excellent bulletins for newspapers, railroads, ticket offices, merchants and for business purposes generally, while for the home they prove an inexhaustible source of amusement for children, and at the same time afford instruction as well, in drawing, writing and figures. The styles made are neat and attractive in design, durable and well finished, and the material used for the surface of the blackboard is the most perfect article of the kind in the market, making a smooth and durable blackboard that will not crack or become otherwise useless. The company's blackboards are for sale by the stationery and school supply trade, and dealers in fancy goods, etc., and by reason of the excellent shipping facilities, and prices at which lumber is obtained at Binghamton they are placed on the market at prices that command attention. Mr. Ash, the proprietor of the enterprise is a practical man at the business, to which he gives his close personal attention.

CRANDAL, STONE & CO.,

Manufacturers of Carriage Hardware and Trimmings, Office and Works 336 Court Street.

The enterprise of Messrs. Crandal, Stone & Co., was originally founded in 1871 by Messrs. John Doane & Co., and it came into the possession of the present firm in 1881, since which time the business has been largely increased and the scope and field of its operations materially extended. The firm's plant is located in the eastern section of the city, and adjoins the railroad system, thereby affording all facilities. The works of the firm, which were erected in 1887, are of the most complete and modern character and are fully equipped with all the latest improved special machinery and tools known to the trade. The main building is a large four-story brick structure, besides which there are minor buildings, and a 50-horse power engine provides the motive force for the machinery, employment being given to about one hundred workmen. The firm are extensive manufacturers of carriage hardware and trimmings of various descriptions, making a specialty of a medium grade of goods, which however, are the best of their class. Many of the firm's products are of their own invention, protected by patents and are the best of the kind in the market. The firm publish a large and handsomely illustrated catalogue and price list, which goes exhaustively into the subject of their products and which will be forwarded to the trade upon application. In connection with their business, the firm maintain a fully equipped electro-plating plant, where all their own goods are silver-plated by themselves, and in fact, their works are among the most self-contained of any of the kind in the country. The trade of the house extends throughout the United States and Canada, and their goods are also exported to all parts of the civilized world. The members of the firm are Messrs. G. L. Crandal, C. M. and W. H. Stone and C. E. Titchener, all prominent and well-known residents of the city, who are adding much to the high reputation Binghamton enjoys as a manufacturing city.

S. E. OFFENHEISER,

Wholesale Fruit and Commission Merchant, 132 State Street and 25 Commercial Avenue.

Largely engaged in this department of commerce is the well-known house of Mr. S. E. Offenheiser, which he established here in 1885, he having previously carried on a similar business in New York city for twelve years. The premises occupied are comprised in two floors and a basement which afford ample storage room for the stock which embraces all kinds of foreign and domestic fruits in their seasons, and includes oranges and lemons, peaches, bananas, grapes, berries of all kinds, melons, dried fruits and nuts, and southern early vegetables and produce. The facilities of the house embrace intimate relations with shippers and producers throughout the country and the principal importers at the seaports, and the choicest products of the market are constantly being received. The trade of the house extends throughout a large section of Southern New York and Northern Pennsylvania, along the several lines of railoads centering at Binghamton and is annually increasing in volume. Seven assistants and one travelling salesman are employed by the house and the prompt fulfillment of all orders may be assured. The reputation of this house for reliability, quick sales and prompt returns to shippers is a wide-spread and honorable one, and consignments of anything in this line is solicited for which liberal advances will be made.

F. B. RICHARDS & CO.,

Cigar Manufacturers, 11 and 13 North Depot Street.

The firm whose name forms the caption of this article, while not being such large producers as some others located here, has become a well-known and highly esteemed one in this branch of manufacture, by reason of the high character of its out-put. It was founded in 1887, since which time a trade has been established that extends throughout New York and Pennsylvania and is annually increasing in volume. The premises occupied are comprised in a part of the extensive five-story and basement brick building, where at present about seventy-five skilled hand workmen are employed, which number, however, will shortly be largely increased. No machinery is used in making cigars, the products being all strictly hand-made and designed for first-class retail trade. The average out-put of the factory is about 3,000,000 cigars annually and of these fully two-thirds are made to be retailed at ten cents each. Four travelling salesmen are employed by the firm and sales are made almost exclusively direct to the retail trade. Among the chief brands of the firm are the "F. B. R.," "Bouquet," "Cuba Mail," "Special Drive," "Princesa," "Drummer's Dream" and "Brotherhoods," all of which are in marked favor with discriminating dealers and consumers. In fact the aim of this firm has always been to make a first-class cigar, worthy the good opinion of smokers and to scrupulously maintain their brands. The members of the firm are both widely and well-known to the trade as gentlemen of pushing and progressive methods and honorable in all their dealings.

C. D. MIDDLEBROOK & Co.,

Wholesale and Retail Dealers in Lumber and Shingles, Cor. State and Lewis Sts.

This enterprise is the largest establishment of the kind in the city, and has long been an important factor in supplying lumber to builders and manufacturers in this section, as well as controlling a large wholesale trade that extends throughout a considerable part of Southern New York, Pennsylvania, and New Jersey. The business was first instituted in 1869 by W. W. Rope & Co., of which firm Mr. C. D. Middlebrook was a member, though at that time he was a resident of Oswego, N. Y., where he conducted a similar enterprise. In 1885, the present firm succeeded to the business, since which time the scope and operations of the house have been largely augmented. The premises of the firm cover an area of 60 x 250 feet, upon which is erected a brick storage warehouse, 57 x 200 feet in dimensions, partly two, and partly three stories high, the whole affording the best possible facilities for the receipt and shipment of lumber and the prompt fulfillment of orders. Open driveways permit teams to enter the buildings and load and unload while all the principal stock being housed insures its perfect condition. The stock carried embraces all kinds of builders' lumber, shingles, doors, windows, blinds, mouldings, etc., all of which are procured direct from the original sources of supply in large quantities and upon the most favorable terms. The firm carry the largest stock of lumber and lumber products in this vicinity, and they are enabled to offer to the trade and consumers inducements in quality and prices difficult to procure elsewhere. The members of the firm, Messrs. C. D. Middlebrook and R. R. Griswold, are both gentlemen of long experience in the lumber trade, and both are closely identified with the growth of this city.

BINGHAMTON WIRE WORKS,

David Campbell, Manufacturer of Plain and Ornamental Wire Work, 140 State Street.

The Binghamton Wire Works has long been a leading representative of this industry in this section. It was established in 1881 and occupies commodious premises at the above indicated address. The plant is equipped with all necessary tools and appliances and furnishes employment to a number of skilled workmen. The works have long held a high reputation for the superiority of their out-put, and the trade of the house extends throughout a large section of Southern and Central New York and Northern Pennsylvania. The products of the Binghamton Wire Works include chairs, bank and office railings of every description, flower stands, settees, florists' designs, coal and sand screens, wire cloth, wire window and door screens, trellis frames for gardens, spark arresters, wire fencing, poultry netting, etc., and all kinds of special wire work to order; the facilities of the house for the manufacture of anything in its line being unsurpassed in the Southern tier. Mr. David Campbell, the proprietor of this useful enterprise, is a practical man at the business to which he gives his close personal attention, and he is widely known in the trade as a liberal and progressive business man.

BARTLETT & CO.,

Manufacturers of Sash, Doors and Blinds, Etc., Office 43 Collier St.

A leading and most important concern devoted to this branch of production is the widely-known house of Messrs. Bartlett & Co., which is the direct successor and outgrowth of the enterprise originally founded in 1845 by Isaac L. Bartlett, father of the senior member of the present firm. About 1861 the business was known under the title of Blanchard, Bartlett & Co.; in 1875 Bartlett Bros. succeeded to the business and in 1886 the present firm was organized and is composed of Arthur S. Bartlett, Emily B. Bartlett, L. B. Smith and E. B. Clark. The manufacturing plant covers the greater part of a block and has a frontage on three streets, the lot being 180x285 feet in dimensions. The main building is a three-story and basement brick structure, besides which there are several minor buildings, dry houses, engine house, storage buildings, office, etc. The works are fully equipped with all the latest improved machinery known to the trade, are operated by two steam engines having a combined power of 250-horse power and employment is furnished to about 125 workmen. The firm also have a yard for storing lumber located elsewhere which covers about four acres, and where they carry a large stock of all kinds of lumber both to supply their factory and the local trade. The business of the firm embraces the manufacture of sash, doors, blinds and builders' trimmings, and large quantities of these products are turned out and shipped in all directions, notably to Philadelphia and New England as well as to near-by towns and villages. The firm procure all their lumber and raw materials in large quantities direct from the original sources of supply and having unexcelled facilities for manufacturing are enabled to offer the trade inducements both in quality and price that insure them a constantly increasing demand for their products. Great care is exercised that all wood used in their products should be thoroughly seasoned and to accomplish this a large stock of lumber is kept so as to be maturing, besides which recourse is also had to dry-kilns which greatly expedites matters. The trade of this house forms a large element in the makeup of Binghamton's industrial activity, and the management is energetic, enterprising and thoroughly alive to the wants of the trade both at home and abroad, uniting the highest qualities of the skilled manufacturer and the pushing merchant.

THE STURTEVANT LARRABEE CO.,
Manufacturers of Carriages & Sleighs, Charles St.

The Sturtevant Larrabee Co. was incorporated in August of the present year and succeeded to the business founded in 1883 by Messrs. Kingman, Sturtevant & Larrabee. Their manufacturing plant is located in the western section of the city and adjoins the tracks of the two trunk line railroads traversing this section of the State, thus affording the company the most advanced facilities for the economical receipt of raw materials and the shipment of the finished products. The plant covers upwards of an acre, upon which are erected two spacious four-story factories with several minor structures for storage and other purposes, the whole having a floorage area of 75,000 square feet and employment being given to about 150 skilled workmen. The products of the house include fine light carriages, pleasure and road wagons, surreys, etc., and the capacity of the establishment is about 10,000 vehicles annually. The company's sleighs and cutters have long enjoyed the highest favor with the trade and public throughout the United States and Canada and the result has been an annually increasing demand for their products. The company manufactures their vehicles complete from the raw materials and with their superior facilities they are enabled to cheapen the cost and at the same time maintain the highest quality. Their carriages are especially noteworthy for lightness combined with strength, beauty of design, good workmanship and fine finish. The company issue handsomely illustrated, descriptive catalogues of their vehicles which will be forwarded upon application. From these we note road wagons, Concord wagons, Brewster surreys, Tuxedo double spindle wagons, runabout wagons, phaetons, buggies, market wagons, grocery delivery wagons, etc., finished in many styles and all guaranteed first-class in material and workmanship and warranted, with fair usage, for one year. Those who have used the sleighs and cutters made by this house will feel no hesitancy in accepting their carriages, since the same care in manufacturing, which enabled them to build up the largest sleigh trade in the country from a small beginning, is exercised in producing carriages that satisfy all the reasonable demands of the trade and public. The management of the business is in the hands of Messrs. O. Britton, pres., H. Chester Larrabee, vice-pres., F. T. Newell, treas., and J. W. Sturtevant, secy., gentlemen of experience and enterprise and closely identified with the growth and prosperity of Binghamton's industrial supremacy.

STAR ELECTRIC CO.,
Electrical Engineers and Contractors, Cor. State and Henry Streets.

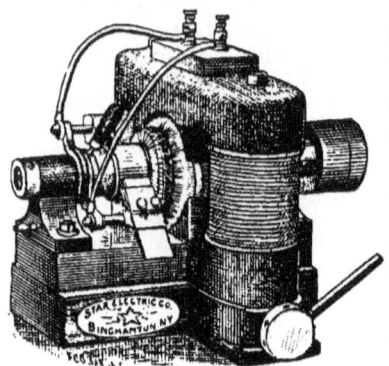

The Star Electric Co. was organized October 1, 1891, and succeeded to the business originally instituted in 1887 by the Otis Electrical Supply Co. The company is under the able management of Messrs. M. M. Jacobs and F. G. Winter, who are both enterprising and progressive business men and thoroughly proficient in all matters relating to the application of the electrical current for architectural and other purposes. They are prepared with all facilities to undertake the construction and supply of all electrical contrivances for the facilitation of business operations or for the comfort, convenience and security of private residences, including electric call bells and door bells for houses, hotels and offices, gas lighting apparatus, burglar alarms, hotel annunciators, electric watchman's clocks, electric lighting plants, dynamos, etc. and all other forms of electrical apparatus and appliances. The company carries a full and complete stock of all kinds of modern electrical appliances, as well as are agents for many special lines of goods. The company is also interested in the manufacture of the Star automatic and slow speed dynamos which were designed by Mr. M. M. Jacobs of the firm, and are widely recognized as first-class dynamos and are sold at a less price than others of less capabilities. They furnish the trade with supplies at wholesale and have a large and growing trade that extends throughout Southern New York and Pennsylvania, as well as to more distant sections of the country. Ten assistants are employed by the company in fulfilling contracts for electrical construction, and among other buildings fitted out by them in this city the following named are exemplifications of their skill and good workmanship: the Strong block, Ackerman block, Lestershire Boot and Shoe Co.'s factory at Lestershire, Bayless Paper Mill, Ross building, the Republican building, Hotel Bennett, Arlington Hotel, Hotel Crandall, Jones of Binghamton and many other public buildings and private residences.

M. McMAHON,
Manufacturer of Carriages and Business Wagons, 85 to 91 Eldredge St.

This business was founded in 1838 and has since annually increased in volume of trade as well as in augmentation of plant. The premises occupied embrace a series of suitable buildings, utilized for the several departments of manufacture and for office and warerooms, a full stock of finished carriages being always on hand from which selections may be made. The equipment of the factory embraces a 12-horse power steam engine and the usual wood-working machinery, employ being furnished to about twenty-five skilled workmen. The products of the house consist of light pleasure and business carriages, buggies, phaetons, surreys, run-about wagons, road wagons, etc., and business wagons of various styles and designs, in the manufacture of which the house has no superior, a fact that is fully attested by the large and annually increasing number in use by the residents of this city and vicinity who prefer them to any other make, the sales of the house being made direct to the consumer. The house turns out about 125 carriages and wagons of all sorts annually, all of which are sold within a circuit of 50 to 60 miles of Binghamton. It is a self-evident fact that a house turning out a moderate number of vehicles such as this, and with each vehicle constructed under the personal supervision of the proprietor, would be able to supply the consumer with a better carriage for the money than could be produced by very much larger factories. In connection with the production of new work the house does a very extensive business in repairing all kinds of carriages and wagons, which is done promptly at reasonable prices.

D. J. MALANE,
Sanitary Plumber and Gas Fitter, 88 State St.

The enterprise of Mr. D. J. Malane is one of the leading establishments of the kind in the southern tier. The premises occupied consist of a commodious and attractively fitted up store and basement, where is shown a very full and complete stock of improved plumbing materials and apparatus, and artistic gas fixtures, fancy gas globes, sanitary specialties, etc., exhibiting, perhaps, the largest and finest selection of these goods to be found in the city. A specialty is made of sanitary plumbing and ventilating which work is performed in its highest perfection, only the best materials being used and only the most skilled workmen being employed. About fifteen hands are employed during the season, and all contracts entered into are executed under the close and practical supervision of Mr. Malane, who possesses the broadest ideas and widest experience in everything relating to the trade. Among the many buildings fitted up with sanitary appliances by this house, we cite, as examples of first-class work, the Hotel Bennett, the Arlington Hotel, the Strong Block, the new Ackerman Block, the U. S. Government building and Court House, besides which very many of the private residences in the city have been fitted from this house. In all his relations Mr. Malane will be found energetic, enterprising and liberal, and the success and prominence which has attended his business are but the just reward of well directed efforts.

BEAN & CO.,
Wholesale Grocers, 162 and 164 Water Street.

A leading representative of the wholesale trade here is the house of Messrs. Bean & Co., which was originally founded in 1871 by J. Bean & Co., the present firm composed of I. W. and Arthur J. Bean succeeding to the business in 1881. The premises occupied by the firm consist of a four story and basement building which is equipped with elevators and coffee roasters operated by steam power, and the whole is stored with a most complete stock of staple and fancy groceries, attractively and systematically arranged, and every facility is offered the trade for the speedy and satisfactory selection of purchases and the prompt fulfillment of orders. The stock comprises a full assortment of groceries, teas, coffees, spices, tobaccos, sugar, molasses, dry and salt fish, canned goods, etc., all of which are offered at prices which cannot fail to give satisfaction to retail dealers within the circuit of their trade which extends throughout Southern New York and Northern Pennsylvania. An advantage of no small consequence that insures to purchasers dealing in this market is found in the saving of freights over goods shipped from more distant localities, as well as in prompt receipt of orders. Four traveling salesmen are employed by the firm and an annually increasing business is transacted.

WINTON & HARROUN,

Manufacturers of Car Trimmings, and Electrical Brass Goods and Brass Founders, 39 and 41 Whitney St.

One of the most prominent manufacturing enterprises of Binghamton, both as regards the special excellence of the products, its complete facilities, and the extent of territory covered by its trade, is that of the above named house, which was founded in 1888, and since Nov., 1889, has been conducted under the sole proprietorship of Mr. T. A. Harroun, the original firm title, however, being retained. The manufacturing facilities embrace a large three-story brick factory with an extension in the rear, the whole covering about 40x150 feet. The mechanical equipment, which embraces all necessary improved machinery and tools, is operated by a 15-horse power steam engine, and employment is furnished, in the several departments, to about twenty skilled workmen. The products of the house consist of a general line of car trimmings, which are largely in demand by car manufacturers throughout New York, Pennsylvania and Canada chiefly, and also a line of electrical brass goods, dynamos, electric motors, generators, etc., of all sizes and for all purposes. A complete electro-plating plant is one of the features of the establishment, and a general jobbing brass casting and electro-plating business is also done, much work of this character being accomplished for other manufacturers who have not similar facilities of their own. A specialty is made of refinishing coach and car trimmings, and in this branch of the business a high reputation has been acquired for good work and moderate charges.

W. C. BRONSON & CO.,

Cigar Manufacturers, 7 and 9 North Depot Street.

Among the large industrial establishments of Binghamton is the extensive cigar factory of Messrs. W. C. Bronson & Co., which, though instituted as recently as July 1, 1891, bears all the marks and possesses all the substantial qualities and advantages of the oldest and best known houses in the city, and is pushing with rapid strides towards a prominent position among the leaders of the cigar industry of Binghamton. Though as a firm, Messrs. W. C. Bronson & Co., have been engaged in the business but a few months, the members of the firm, Messrs. W. C. Bronson and C. B. Cooke are fully equipped by experience and capabilities to carry to a successful finish the industry which they have inaugurated. Their factory is comprised in a commodious five story and basement brick building 30 x 80 feet in dimensions, which is equipped with all the latest improved machinery known to the trade, operated by steam power. At the present writing the firm give employment to fifty workmen, which number is being daily increased, and by January 1, 1892, they confidently expect to have one hundred and fifty or more at work, when they will be able to turn out about 30,000 cigars daily. The products of the house are mainly confined to a good quality of medium grade cigars, no very cheap ones being produced. They are all manufactured from well cured tobacco of good quality and by the most advanced process resulting in a class of goods that gives good satisfaction to smokers and insures permanent trade with the houses handling them. The trade of the house is exclusively with jobbers and extends from Portland, Me., to Portland, Oregon, three traveling salesmen being employed by the firm. The cigars are packed under special brands to suit customers when desired, and also under their own copyrighted brands, of which they have a large number. Many of these brands have long enjoyed the highest reputation and popularity in the market, having been the property of a house now out of business, and the present owners fully maintain the high character of those brands. Among the leading ones we note "Our Actors," "Our Actresses," "Salmon," "Art Boquet," which enjoy a popularity and sale in the west that have never been exceeded by those of any other firm in Binghamton, and are staple with almost every dealer in that section. The policy upon which the business of the firm is conducted is one of liberality, enterprise and fair dealing, and its success and prosperity in the future has already been fully demonstrated, and gives every promise of steady and permanent growth.

E. ADAMS & SONS,
Brass and Iron Founders, 227 and 229 Water St.

This house commenced operations here in the spring of 1890 and has since built up a trade that extends throughout a large section of Southern New York and Northern Pennsylvania. The facilities embrace a commodious foundry having a capacity for turning out about three tons of iron castings and 800 pounds of brass castings daily, employment being given to about a dozen skilled workmen. In the brass foundry department, everything in the way of brass, bronze and composition castings is made for all mechanical purposes and from one quarter ounce up to 1,000 pounds or over in weight. In the iron department the range of products is equally varied. A large variety of patterns is on hand, enabling the firm to readily supply all staple goods, and castings are promptly made to order to suit the special requirements of patrons. All the details of the work are executed under the personal supervision of the members of the firm, all of whom are experienced practical brass and iron founders. All orders are promptly filled and only first-class castings are made. The members of the firm are Messrs. E. Adams, V. P. Adams and C. P. Adams, who are closely identified with the industrial development of Binghamton.

JOHN NOWLAN,
Parlor City Boiler Works, 75 and 77 Robinson Street.

The manufacture of boilers and plate iron work is well represented by the Parlor City Boiler Works, of which Mr. John Nowlan is the proprietor and Mr. Thomas Dunlea is superintendent. This enterprise was established about ten years ago and from small beginnings has built up a large and annually increasing trade that extends throughout Southern New York and Northern Pennsylvania as well as being largely local. The growth of the business necessitated enlarged facilities, which have been provided by the erection of two large frame buildings in the eastern section of the city adjoining the railroad system. One of the buildings is utilized for plate iron work, the other as an iron foundry. The products of the works consist of steam boilers of every description, stills, retorts, tanks, chemical pans and every description of plate iron and sheet iron work as well as iron castings of all kinds. A specialty is made of Dunlea's steam and hot water automatic steel heating boilers, which are the best and most economical boilers in the market for heating purposes and are in large demand by the building trade and consumers throughout a wide section of the country. Both Mr. Nowlan and Mr. Dunlea are practical and skilled plate iron workers and give their close personal supervision to all the operations of the enterprise. They devote particular attention to repairing which is promptly and efficiently performed at reasonable prices. Estimates for anything in the line will be promptly furnished and ultimate satisfaction assured in the performance of all contracts.

VANDEBOGART'S PAPER BOX FACTORY.
123 South Street.

The vicinity of Binghamton is a large consumer of paper boxes and in this important industry Vandebogart's Paper Box Factory must be accredited a foremost place, which, as a house, was the pioneer in this industry in this city and is the only representative of it for public accommodation. It was founded in 1882 by Spaulding & Vandebogart and assumed its present title in 1890. The premises utilized are embraced in a two-story factory, which is fully equipped with all the latest improved machinery known to the trade, operated by an eight-horse power engine and furnishes employment to an average of sixteen operatives. The products of the factory comprise all kinds of plain and fancy paper boxes, honey boxes, fancy candy boxes, wedding cake boxes, etc., which are principally made to order. Any desired shape or style is made and the reputation attained for first-class workmanship and tasteful designs by this house is unexcelled. During eight months in the year the factory ships 2,000 boxes per day to New York to be used in putting up Ely's Cream Balm and large quantities are also manufactured for Dr. Kilmer's medicines of this city. The trade of the house extends throughout the city and vicinity and also over a considerable portion of New York and Pennsylvania, the bulk of the products being taken by local manufacturers.

J. W. LACEY,
Cigar Box Manufacturer, 4 and 6 State St.

This enterprise was originally founded in 1880 by Lacey & Wilkinson, the present proprietor succeeding to the sole control in 1886, since which time the business has been largely increased. The premises occupied embrace two floors of the three-story building located as above indicated, which are equipped with all the latest improved machinery known to the trade, operated by steam power, and furnish employment to from twenty to thirty operatives, according to the exigencies of the season. The average capacity of the factory is about 2,500 boxes per day, and the facilities are such that all orders are promptly filled and the products are of the very highest character. A specialty is made of fine embossed work, in which variety of boxes the house has no superior for the production of fine work. This style of boxes is now being largely used, and they prove to be attractive and help to sell the contents. The trade of the house, while being largely with local manufacturers, also extends throughout Southern New York and Northern Pennsylvania, and orders are also received from more distant sections. The stock of labels, trimmings, etc., carried is always varied enough to meet the requirements of a large trade, while the liberal and fair dealing business policy of the house is such as to attract a large and growing patronage.

H. W. CHUBBUCK & CO.,
Binghamton Spice Mills, 4 & 5 Wall Street.

This house, the pioneer in its line of trade, must be recognized as having promoted in more than an ordinary degree, the commercial interests of this city, since, during all these years, it has continued on a progressive and successful career, until the trade-mark of its specialties has become a familiar household word throughout a large portion of southern New York and northern Pennsylvania. The premises occupied are embraced in ten floors of the buildings located as above indicated, where every modern mechanical appliance for the production of pure spices, mustard, baking powder and other specialties, has been provided and is operated by a 15-horse power steam engine. The firm carry a large and complete stock of teas, coffees, spices, fancy groceries, canned goods and grocers' sundries, which are all procured from first hands in large quantities and are offered to the trade at lowest market prices. The firm roast and grind their own coffees fresh every day and warrant them true to quality represented. Their spices are put up under their own brands and in attractive and salable packages, and they make a specialty of a large and varied stock of teas. While they do not make any false claims to be direct importers of teas, they do claim to compete with any other jobbing house located here or elsewhere. The house is represented within the circuit of its trade by three experienced traveling salesmen and an annually increasing business is transacted. Since the demise of the late senior member of the firm the active management of the business has devolved upon Messrs. D. W. & J. L. Chubbuck, both of whom are prominently identified with the commercial growth and prosperity of Binghamton, and are progressive and pushing business men. The house was originally founded in 1865 by S. D. Beach & Co., the present firm succeeding to the business in 1872.

THE SECURITY MUTUAL LIFE ASSOCIATION, OF BINGHAMTON, N. Y.,

Home Offices, Phelps Bank Building.

The propriety and necessity of life insurance is no longer questioned by prudent men, the chief thought being given to an investigation of how safe and reliable life insurance can be procured at the least cost. For some years the great objection to "old line" companies has been that insurance, as furnished by them, is too expensive, the premium charges being out of all just proportion to the amount necessary to pay losses and economical expenses. An insurance contract combining safety with economy has long been much desired by the insuring public. The Security Mutual Life Association was incorporated November 6, 1886, to efficiently meet this want. It is a purely mutual company, and its object is to furnish life insurance as reliable and safe as law, science and capital can make it, and at as low rates as is consistent with absolute safety. The system of insurance adopted by the company was devised by Mr. Chas. M. Turner, a gentleman of large experience and thorough knowledge of life insurance matters, who occupies the position of secretary and general manager of this association. This system avoids the excessive premiums of the "old line" companies and at the same time is not dependent upon uncertain contributions, as are the purely after-death assessment societies. The plan or system occupies the middle ground between these two extremes of life insurance, and is the out-come of long study, patient investigation and scientific analysis of all the life insurance methods of the past. Every member who enters this association makes advance premium payments which provide the association with the means to establish three separate funds: first, the Mortuary Fund, which is created for and can be used only for the payment of death claims, all the accumulations to this fund from lapses and interest beyond such requirements and one hundred thousand dollars as an Emergency Fund being returned to the policy-holders in reduction of premiums; second, the Reserve Fund, which, with all its accumulations from lapses and interest, is equitably apportioned to persistent members each five years with the privilege of using it to still farther reduce the premiums, to purchase paid-up insurance, or to make the policy self-sustaining with all surplus accumulations added; third, the Expense Fund, which is the only fund from which the expenses of management can be paid. The three funds are, under the by-laws, kept separate and apart, and can only be drawn upon for the specific purposes for which they were created. The premiums always payable in advance are rated at age of entry according to the American experience table of mortality. To these amounts are added an equitable sum which provides for the Emergency and the Reserve Funds. The premium payments are less than those demanded by "old line" companies, and are still further reduced by an equitable proportion of all the profits which may accrue to the company by reason of lapses, interest, accumulations and careful selection of risks. That the plan of the company has all the elements of sound, safe and reliable insurance in its composition is evidenced by the fact that it already has the largest surplus, in proportion to out-standing insurance, of any co-operative company in the world, and exceeds the most of the "old line" companies. Its system has the endorsement of the best insurance authorities of America, and that it has struck a popular chord is evidenced by the last statement of its financial condition, at the end of its fifth year of co-operate existence, which shows an unparalleled growth. By this statement dated January 1st, 1892, the association shows a surplus of over $150,000.00, with insurance in force of $6,000,000.00. The company issues Equation and Annuity policies, at rates, "which to persistent members" are much cheaper than those of after-death assessment societies can possibly be, while all the uncertainties of those organizations are eliminated, the premium payments being in advance, the expense of management being limited and inflexible and all surplus accumulations periodically returned to persistent members. The system contains every element of permanence and security claimed for the strongest "old line" companies. This association has not and never has had a death claim due and unpaid: its policies are incontestable, non-forfeitable and free from technicalities and burdensome restrictions. Its methods should be investigated by all who are contemplating additional life insurance. The officers of the Company are: Messrs. H. J. Gaylord, pres., J. M. Stone, vice-pres., J. W. Manier, treas., and Chas. M. Turner, sec'y and gen'l manager, under whose able management The Security Mutual Life Association has attained a position of which they may well feel proud and its future gives every promise of usefulness, honor and prosperity. The Association is recognized as one of the strongest in the country, while none presents to the policy-holder a greater amount of benefit.

CHAS. C. WELLS & CO.,
Manufacturers of Fine Cigars, 34 Whitney Street.

The cigar manufacturing enterprise of Messrs. Chas. C. Wells & Co. was founded in June, 1886, by the head of the present firm which was organized in August, 1891. From its inception the success of this house has been a prominent one, each year witnessing an extension of its trade and an increase of its facilities and the scope of its operations until at present its products are to be found in the hands of the trade in all the towns, cities and villages within a radius of 200 miles of Binghamton. The facilities of the house embrace a commodious factory affording employment to from twenty-five to thirty skilled cigar makers, the products being fine domestic and Havana hand-made cigars of which the firm produce about one million two hundred thousand annually. Their cigars are put up chiefly under their own special brands, among the best-known of which are: "Social Club,"

"Electric City," "Duke of Anjou," "My Own," "Opera," "Caprice" and "La Rosas" in ten cent goods, and "Prize Winners," "New Ad," "Special Permit," "Key West," "Toboggan," "Little Dandies," "Mc-Ginty," "Telephone," "Hustler," "Blazer" and "Little Beauty" in five cent goods. The trade will find a line of these cigars added to their stock will result in greatly increased patronage. The members of the firm are Messrs. C. C. Wells, L. H. Scott and S. J. Clark, all experienced and practical cigar manufacturers, who in the conduct of their enterprise in this city are adding greatly to the name and fame of Binghamton as a source of supply for fine domestic and Havana cigars.

CONKLIN & MERSEREAU,
Re-Cleaned Grass Seed by their New Patent Process, Office 128 State St. Warehouses 21, 22, 24 and 26 Commercial Avenue.

Until comparatively recently one of the most discouraging features of the seeding for grass was the impossibility of obtaining pure seeds. All the stock offered for sale on the market contained a large per cent. of weed seeds and other impurities, which not only failed to produce grass when sown but re-produced weeds in countless quantities, in many cases entirely destroying the value of the crop to the farmer. Many realizing the reward awaiting any one who would invent a cleaner that would remove the bull's-eye daisy, black plantain and other objectionable seeds, experimented at the expense of much time and money, but on account of the difficulty of making the separation, failed to accomplish the desired result. Not discouraged by the failure of others and spurred on by the demand of the trade, Conklin & Mersereau after much labor succeeded in inventing and perfecting a cleaner which from its simplicity and superiority of workmanship left nothing further to be desired, and so completely accomplishing the desired result that they immediately challenged the world to produce a class of seed equal in purity to those re-cleaned by their New Patent Process, and also offered a reward for finding a single plantain or bull's-eye daisy in timothy re-cleaned by their patent cleaner. And although this offer has been made thousands of times in writing, verbally and printed, and many experts have visited Binghamton with their magnifying glasses in their pockets, to secure the same, the reward has never been won, although it was first offered over eight years ago and the firm has cleaned and sold many thousands of bushels since that time. Many dealers who formerly bought their seeds in the West now buy them in Binghamton, as no where on earth can there be found as pure a class of seeds. To this fact alone Binghamton is known abroad as well as in the United States, as the headquarters of pure grass seeds, and the increase in this business in the last few years has surprised even those that are well acquainted with its details. Their premises are embraced in a large five-story warehouse extending from State street to Commercial avenue, and a four-story warehouse on the opposite side of Commercial avenue. These warehouses are equipped with special patented machinery, mentioned above, which are run by steam and are fully protected by the patent laws of the United States, and can be used by them only. They are also large dealers in other kinds of grass and field seeds, including field and ensilage seed corn and seed peas, which are grown for them in different sections of the United States and Canada, thereby insuring the most improved variety and germinating qualities true to name at prices that defy competition. The members of the firm are E. W. Conklin, T. T. Mersereau and H. E. Conklin, all pushing and enterprising business men and closely identified with the growth of the industrial development of Binghamton. Their enterprise is a prominent one of its kind and it has done much to attract the attention of the outside world to Binghamton.

BINGHAMTON MANUFACTURING COMPANY.
Manufacturers of Outing Garments.

No concern in Binghamton has made greater or more substantial progress in its special line of production than has the Binghamton Manufacturing Co., whose efforts, from its inception, have been ably directed to the perfection of the manufacture of outing garments for ladies, gentlemen and children, and so practical has been the result of their endeavors that to-day their productions are in active demand by the most discriminating class of trade in all the large cities of the country from the Atlantic to the Pacific coast. The company's record is one of honorable progress and steady expansion of facilities and, first, last and all the time, of improvement in quality, style and finish of all garments. The enterprise was instituted in 1885 by Messrs. A. H. La Monte, T. P. Learned and C. L. Peak and the present extensive premises utilized were occupied in 1888. They are comprised in a four-story brick structure which is completely equipped with every modern facility for the orderly and systematic conduct of the business. An elevator connects all the floors and electric bells, speaking tubes, steam power and heat, electric lights and gas are provided. The office, sample room and stock room are on the first floor, the cutting room is on the second floor, the packing and finishing rooms are on the third floor and the top floor, which is lighted by sky-lights as well as windows on three sides, is used for the work room, the shipping being done in the basement. One hundred and fifty operatives, male and female, are given employment, and as all the work is done on the premises under the supervision of the members of the firm, a uniformity of makeup is secured, which is not possible under the contract system, so common with manufacturers in other large cities. The Binghamton Manufacturing Company employs only help of good character and standing and while they command and receive higher wages, the goods that they turn out fully justify the policy by their superior excellence of makeup and finish. The products of the house consist of original designs in outing garments for men, women and children, made from the finest and most fashionable materials, and cut, designed, made up and finished in the best possible manner, fully equal, in all respects, to any produced by the most respectable custom tailors or dressmakers. They include negligee shirts for men, youths and boys, outing and tennis suits for ladies and children, ladies and misses' waists and blouses, tennis blazers and sashes for ladies and gentlemen, tennis caps for ladies and misses, outing and tennis suits for gentlemen, house and office coats, boys' waists and blouses, sailor blouse kilt suits for boys and girls, and bathing suits for ladies and gentlemen. These are made in many styles and sizes and of many and varied materials; in one particular, however, all the garments are alike—the high quality. The firm issues an elaborately illustrated, artistically printed and exhaustively edited pamphlet which will be forwarded the trade upon application. The company neglects no single part of their garments, slights no part of the manufacture, employs no poor materials, dispenses with no operations and omits nothing that can in any possible manner add to the style, fit, finish or quality of their products, and while they do not wish or claim to compete in prices with cheaply made, inferior garments, they cannot be undersold by any concern on the same plane of quality and that is the very best in the market. While all their products bear the stamp of perfection, particular merit has been attained in the Binghamton shirts, as their negligee shirts for men, youths and boys have become so widely known. These shirts fit like custom made and, unlike the majority in the market, the collars have a respectable and permanent roll. They are formed so as to fit the neck and shoulders; the collars, collar bands, yokes and sleeves are adapted to the wearer's figure and in all their features combine to make attractive, serviceable articles of apparel. The company's trade relations extend to all parts of the United States, two traveling salesmen representing the house on the road and the fine city trade everywhere find the Binghamton outing garments the best and most salable of their kind. In every respect the management of the Binghamton Manufacturing Company is adequate to the maintenance and augmentation of their present large and increasing trade; they have established a reputation in the past of such a character as to make personal comments unnecessary and bringing to their enterprise an unusual degree of discernment, liberality, industry and integrity are fully entitled to the general estimation in which they are held and the pronounced success their establishment has attained.

JOHN M. RUSSELL,

Manufacturer of Cigars and Jobber of Tobacco, etc., 60 Court Street.

Prominent in the cigar and tobacco trade of Binghamton is the enterprise of Mr. John M. Russell, which, established in 1883, has since come to be the headquarters for a large and growing jobbing trade in tobacco, cigarettes and smokers' articles as well as fine cigars. The premises occupied are embraced in a commodious store and basement, with manufacturing department in the rear where a force of skilled cigar makers are steadily employed in the production of fine hand-made domestic and Havana cigars. All the products are strictly hand-made, and the chief brands are the "Medallion," "J. R.," and "A 1," in ten cent goods, and "Pilot," "The Best," "Specials," and "Our Five," in five cent goods. In the jobbing department a full and complete stock of all the leading brands of smoking and chewing tobacco and cigarettes is carried which are offered to the trade at manufacturers' prices, and goods are also sold at retail. The trade of the house is chiefly confined to Binghamton and vicinity, and is annually increasing in volume.

DEXTER D. BROWN,

Dealer in Furniture, 170 Washington St., and 121 State St.

Mr. Dexter D. Brown instituted his business in 1881, and has since conducted it with annually increasing success and influence. This house is now widely recognized as one of the leading concerns of the kind in the State, devoted to the sale of fine furniture. The premises occupied are embraced in a four-story and basement building, 22 x 157 feet in dimensions, extending through from Washington to State street, and affording a floorage area of over 17,000 square feet. The stock of furniture here displayed is as complete as energy and enterprise can make it and is as elegant as good taste and skill can execute. It embraces furniture for all purposes in fine and medium grades from the most inexpensive chairs and tables to the most highly finished and elaborately upholstered and carved parlor and drawing room suites, and includes parlor, library, chamber and dining room furniture, fancy chairs and rockers, folding beds, cabinets, desks, side-boards, mirrors, etc., in large variety of styles and in all the fashionable woods. Though all articles are substantially and well made from good materials and finely finished, the prices charged are most reasonable, the large trade of the house enabling them to procure the stock in large quantities direct from producers and upon the most advantageous terms and any article of furniture either for the humblest cottage or the most costly mansion may be procured here. The enterprise is in every respect a most reliable one and always stands ready to accord the greatest inducements and advantages to customers.

OSGOOD & THOMPSON,

Scale Manufacturers, Office 217 Water St.

If there is one thing of more importance than all others in the affairs of commerce, it is just measurement in the transfer of commodities; therefore an establishment devoted to the manufacture of scales, that most vital instrument in the prosecution of trade, must receive significant mention in these pages. The Standard Scales of Messrs. Osgood & Thompson have for many years been well known in all parts of America and in many foreign countries. Especially is this true in recent years of the Osgood Combination Wagon Scale, which is the only radical and valuable improvement in wagon scales since they were first perfected. This scale, patented by Mr. Osgood in 1876, is the result of over thirty years' practical experience and patient investigation. From the first it has forcibly appealed to the scale-using public, as it reduced the cost of manufacture materially and, therefore, the price to the purchaser, so that an equally reliable standard scale could be bought at a price impossible to be furnished by any other manufacturer making the old style of scales. That it has been appreciated has been evidenced by the growth of the enterprise, which has since come to be one of the most important concerns in this line in the country. The manufacture of "Osgood" scales was begun by Mr. H. B. Osgood and others at Thompsonville, Conn., in 1846. After several changes and two disastrous fires the business was removed to Binghamton in 1865. Mr. H. B. Osgood, the senior member of the firm, is the oldest and one of the most thoroughly posted and practical scale men in the country to-day. He devotes his entire attention to the manufacturing department, which he personally superintends. The junior member, Mr. L. K. Thompson, who is a pushing and progressive business man in the prime of his usefulness gives his time to the finances and sales and has entire charge of the business outside the factory. Since the establishment of the present firm the business has steadily grown and it has been twice necessary to enlarge the factory to supply the demand. To-day it is one of the most important manufacturing enterprises in the city. The products of the works embrace a complete line of the larger class of scales, but a specialty is made of the Combination Wagon Scale. These machines are all set up at the factory and carefully tested before being packed for shipment and every scale is fully warranted for five years. They are the only cheap scale on the market that is accurate and durable and their simplicity makes them specially desirable, as they can be set up by an ordinary carpenter and do not easily get out of order. A large illustrated catalogue is published annually by Messrs. Osgood & Thompson, and will be furnished interested parties free of charge. The firm's products are sold in all parts of the United States and Canada, and are also largely exported to South and Central America, Mexico, the West Indies and Great Britain. The steady progress of the business and the triumph of the "Osgood" Wagon Scale is very gratifying to the proprietors and they take special pride in the thousands of satisfied customers who are using and recommending their scales.

EDWARD R. MASON,
Graduate Optician, 114 Court Street.

With the advance of civilization and the consequent studiousness of the masses generally and the severe tax made upon their eyes, it is not to be wondered at that those organs should suffer from the strain. It is no unusual thing to see young boys and girls wearing glasses now-a-days and particular attention should therefore be given to caring for the eyesight. Only the best glasses should be used and these should always be obtained from and be properly adjusted by some competent optician and never be purchased from a dealer in miscellaneous goods, who having procured his stock in the open market where he could buy the cheapest has thought only for profit in the sale of his goods. Fortunately for this community it numbers among its commercial resources an establishment devoted to the supply of optical goods, which is presided over by one of the most expert and accomplished opticians in the State. This is that of Mr. Edward R. Mason, who is a graduate optician and has made a study of the profession as well as of the practical manufacturing part of the business for a period of nearly twenty years. The enterprise he now conducts was founded by his father, Mr. J. H. Mason, in 1878 and was later conducted under the style of J. H. Mason & Son, Mr. E. R. Mason assuming sole control in 1890. At his handsomely appointed place of business he carries a large and complete stock of optical goods, eye glasses, spectacles, miscroscopes, etc., as well as watches and clocks. Special attention is here given to the scientific fitting of spectacles and eye glasses and oculists' prescriptions are also filled. Fine watch and clock repairing are also features of the facilities of the house, and in all its departments only the most skillful services are rendered. Besides a large retail trade considerable jobbing operations are transacted, the trade of the house extending throughout Southern New York and Northern Pennsylvania and showing an annual increase in volume. Prudent people will do well to consult this establishment when requiring anything in the way of optical goods.

DARROW HAY COMPANY,
Manufacturers and Shippers of Short Cut Hay in Bales, Oak and Gaines Streets.

The facilities of the above named company embrace a series of large buildings used for storage and manufacturing purposes, the equipment including hay cutters, baling presses and other necessary appliances, which are operated by a 15-horse power steam engine. The company purchases hay from the adjoining section in large quantities, cuts it up into short-cut feed, packs in bales and ships it to the trade throughout the Eastern States, Pennslvania and as far south as Washington. From two to three thousand tons of hay are handled annually, which is sold by the carload only to large dealers. This enterprise was originally established by R. S. Darrow, the present proprietors, Messrs. Charles Davis and Fred L. Titchener, having assumed control of the business in 1889. The trade-mark of the company attached to all their bales is a guarantee of good, sweet and well-cured hay, which will be found economical to consumers from the fact that the animals to whom it is fed will not waste it as is the case with inferior qualities. We are pleased to chronicle the success and prosperity of this enterprise in this Board of Trade review, and it may be ranked as among the old established and permanent enterprises of Binghamton.

BARNES & CONGDON,
Binghamton Marble Works, 96 Chenango St.

The monumental industry is particularly well represented in Binghamton by the eminent house of Messrs. Barnes & Congdon, which besides being one of the oldest establishments of the kind in the interior of the state, is also one of the most notable and prominent. It was founded over half a century ago, in 1840, by Mr. J. N. Congdon, and since 1870 has been conducted by Messrs. Barnes & Congdon, Mr. J. H. Barnes having during all this time been its active business manager. Though the house has long been a prominent feature of the local monument trade, its business is by no means confined to this city, but extends generally throughout the United States as far west as the Pacific coast. The firm has always kept one traveling salesman on the road soliciting orders for monuments, and Mr. Barnes himself has done much traveling for the same purpose. The facilities of the house embrace a large show-room, shop and yard where a stock of marble and granite monuments and head-stones is shown. Monuments of all kinds and of the largest dimensions and most artistic character, are also designed and made to order, and this class of work is the special feature of their business. Monuments are set up in any part of the country and all contracts are invariably finished to the entire satisfaction of patrons. While the cemeteries of this and neighboring cities as well as those of other states are graced by many beautiful specimens of this firm's skill, they have also erected many notable public monuments in various localities. They designed and erected the Soldiers' Monument in this city at a cost of $10,000, and the Soldiers' Monument at Montrose, Pa., at a cost of $4,000, the Soldiers' Monument at New Berlin, at a cost of $5,000; they furnished the design for the Soldiers' Monument at Owego, N. Y., which cost $8,000, and designed the Soldiers' Monument at Sherburne, N. Y., which cost $3,500, as well as many others. Mr. Barnes is well equipped by long experience to fully meet the wants of the public in the matter of monumental work, and the enterprise of which he is the head is the most important of its kind in this section.

W. P. HOLBERT,

Manufacturer of and Wholesale and Retail Dealer in Lumber, Stone, Lime and Cement, 1, 3 and 5 George Street.

Mr. Holbert is an old experienced lumber manufacturer and dealer, having been established in the business at Equinunk, Pa., as long ago as 1860. He opened his business in this city in November, 1890, but still retains his interests at Equinunk, where he has two mills in operation getting out hardwood lumber and he also controls the product of another mill in Potter County, Pa., which produces hemlock. With these advantages of being a producer of two kinds of lumber, he enters the realm of the dealer so well equipped as to command the attention of buyers. His plant in this city embraces extensive yards located on the line of the D., L. & W., affording all facilities for receipt and shipment of stock. Commodious buildings for storage are provided and every modern facility is at hand, about twenty workmen being given employment about the yards and in making deliveries. The stock handled embraces hemlock, pine and hard-wood lumber, lath, shingles, etc., and the house is also a jobber in Glen's Falls lime, and Howe's Cave, Rosendale and Portland cement. Estimates are furnished on all kinds of cut stone work, blue and brown, and flag walk and curbing are also furnished at lowest prices. The trade of the house while being largely local with builders and manufacturers also extends in a wholesale way to all the towns along the several lines of railway centering here. The long experience of Mr. Holbert in the business, and his liberal and enterprising methods have secured for his establishment a high position in the esteem of this community.

ABEL BENNETT & Co.,

Merchant Tailors and Clothiers, Hotel Bennett Block.

A striking example of the recognition of merit is found in the extraordinary popularity and growth of the merchant tailoring and clothing house of Messrs. Abel Bennett & Co., which is not only a splendid monument to the intelligent enterprise of its management, but is one whose great success sheds lustre upon the name of the city. This important enterprise was established in 1876 and is located in the handsome Hotel Bennett, which was erected by the late Abel Bennett, who was one of the most public spirited of Binghamton's honored citizens, and was the head of the firm until his demise in 1890, since which time the management of the business has devolved upon his son and partner, Mr. Fred Bennett. The firm's salesrooms are large, well lighted and attractively appointed, with splendid glass show-windows, which display the goods to admirable advantage. The stock embraces everything in the way of men's, boys', youths' and children's clothing, the finer lines being in every respect equal to the best custom work in fit, finish, elegance and fashion. An important feature of the business is the merchant tailoring department, where is placed at the disposal of patrons a large and choice stock of cassimeres, tweeds, diagonals, fancy suitings, etc., and indeed the finest of imported and domestic fabrics of all kinds, from which fashionable and desirable clothing may be made to measure to suit the wants of the most exacting class of patrons. The business policy adopted is that of liberality, fair dealing and honest representation in every instance, and thus the name and fame of Abel Bennett & Co. has been widely spread abroad as the leading merchant tailors and clothiers of Binghamton.

THE ARLINGTON,
Kennedy & Tierney, Proprietors, Corner Chenango and Lewis Sts.

The Arlington, the leading hotel of Binghamton, was first opened to the public April 24, 1888, by its present proprietors and owners, who have since made it a favorite with tourists and travellers. The building, which is the most recently erected modern hotel edifice in the city, is a four-story brick structure, and it is an ornament to the city. It is provided with every modern convenience and comfort for its guests that experience could suggest or money procure. The office, reading room and dining room are located on the ground floor and are handsomely finished in oak and decorated in an attractive and cheerful manner. The hotel is heated by steam, lighted by gas and electricity, the rooms are connected by electric call-bells and a general fire-alarm system, and the sanitary conditions have been made as perfect as modern investigation has made possible. There are one hundred rooms for guests, all light, airy, and comfortable, and furnished in a luxurious manner. The culinary department is presided over by an accomplished chef and the table is remarkable for its lavish and selected fare. Special attention is given to commercial men, who will find here every inducement to make the Arlington the best hotel in the Southern Tier, in which to remain over Sunday. The proprietors, Messrs. J. W. Kennedy and E. M. Tierney, are both experienced hosts, accomplished caterers, and genial entertainers, and both do all in their power to make the Arlington a popular hostelry. The rates are $2.00, $2.50 and $3.00 per day, according to the location of rooms, and while the accommodations afforded are in every respect equal to those of any other hotel in the state, few even in the metropolitan centers offer greater inducements for a longer or shorter sojourn.

NELSON & LEGGE,
Wholesale Dealers in Foreign and Domestic Fruits and Produce, 219 Chenango Street.

An old established and well-known house, engaged in handling foreign and domestic fruits and produce in Binghamton is that now, and since October, 1890, known under the the title of Nelson & Legge, which was originally founded in 1870 by B. H. Nelson & Co., Mr. M. S. Nelson being the Co. It has a wide circle of patrons extending throughout Central and Southern New York and Northern Pennsylvania, to whom shipments are made daily by the roads diverging in seven directions from this city. In fact, the railroad facilities have been a powerful feature in building up the trade of this house, since country merchants can have orders filled from this city with greater promptness than any other market in the State. The firm's premises afford ample accommodations for storing goods and prompt shipments, and six assistants and one traveling salesman find occupation with the house. The goods handled embrace foreign fruits of all kinds, oranges, lemons, bananas, figs, prunes, grapes, nuts, raisins, etc., as well as domestic green fruits, berries and produce, clams, etc. During the season the firm are in daily receipt of fruits and produce by the car-load which is promptly distributed to their trade in quantities to suit. They also solicit consignments of anything in their line on commission, for which market prices and quick returns are assured. The individual members of the firm are M. S. Nelson and W. S. Legge, each of whom is thoroughly experienced in all the details of the business to which they give their close personal attention. In conclusion we may be permitted to add that the energy and enterprise shown in the conduct of the business of this house have resulted in a well merited and substantial success and the high esteem in which the firm is held for honorable character and fair and liberal dealing adds no little to the commercial supremacy of Binghamton.

STONE & GERMOND,
Manufacturers and Jobbers of Boots, Shoes and Rubbers, 183 and 185 Water St.

This house was originally established in 1865 by Messrs. J. M. Stone & Co., who were succeeded by Stone, Goff & Co. in 1872, the present firm coming into possession of the business in December, 1890. The plant of the firm is comprised in a handsome four-story and basement brick building, having an elegant and spacious salesroom on the first floor, and the manufacturing department on the upper floors. The latter is equipped with all the latest improved labor-saving machinery known to the trade, operated by steam power, and from ninety to one hundred skilled operatives are given steady employment. The products of the factory consist of a large line of medium grades of men's and boys' boots and shoes. All goods are made from serviceable materials and with the greatest care, while in style and finish they are fully equal to goods of a much more expensive character, and the result is a class of shoes that for durability and service cannot be excelled. Besides the goods of their own production the firm handle a general line of boots, shoes and rubbers for men, women and children suitable for the retail trade, which is procured from the most noted manufacturers of the country, and is not surpassed in the state for variety, extent and general desirability. The trade of the house is chiefly confined to the Middle and Western States, where the firm is represented by traveling salesmen. The members of the firm are Herbert E. Stone and Joseph S. Germond.

A. G. WILSON,
Fire and Accident Insurance, 6 McNamara Block.

The above named reliable insurance agency was established about twenty years ago, and it has long enjoyed the fullest confidence and consideration of a wide circle of clients in this city and vicinity. Mr. Wilson transacts a regular Fire Insurance business, and he represents a group of stable companies which stand at the very head in insurance circles. They are the Agricultural, of Watertown, N. Y., the Sun Fire of London, the Phœnix, of London, the Hanover, of New York, the Continental, of New York, and the American, of New York. The Sun Fire, of London, is the oldest insurance company in the world and a veritable rock of stability, and the Agricultural, of Watertown, which writes policies on farm and residential property only, is the most successful company of its kind in the country. The above list represents $27,000,000 of capital, and the standing and character of these organizations are such as to guarantee positive indemnity in case of loss. Mr. Wilson also writes accident policies and issues bonds of indemnity through the Fidelity and Casualty Co., of New York. Insurance effected through this agency is obtained at lowest rates consistent with safe methods and all losses are promptly and equitably adjusted and paid. Mr. Wilson is an experienced underwriter and an enterprising citizen, who enjoys the esteem of this community and his agency is an important adjunct to the business conveniences of the city.

BOSS, STOPPARD & HECOX,
General Insurance Agents, 82 Court Street.

The general insurance agency of Messrs. Boss, Stoppard & Hecox has long been recognized as the leading underwriting enterprise in Binghamton. It is the oldest and largest agency in the city and was founded in 1875 by Chittenden & Boss, who were succeeded in 1883 by Boss & Stoppard and by Boss, Stoppard & Hecox in 1890, and Mr. Boss has been actively engaged as an underwriter since 1868. The firm represents only the strongest and staunchest of companies, and to its credit it may be said that every just claim during its history has been promptly paid. They include such high class organizations as the Ætna, of Hartford; Buffalo German, of Buffalo; Firemens', of Newark; Firemans' Fund, of California; German American, of New York; Germania Fire, of New York; Guardian, of London; North British and Mercantile, of England; Insurance Company of North America, of Philadelphia; Merchants, of Newark; Phœnix, of Hartford; Pennsylvania Fire, of Philadelphia; Royal, of Liverpool; Western, of Toronto, Canada; Hartford Steam Boiler, of Hartford; Travelers Accident Co., of Hartford and Lloyd's Plate Glass Co., of New York, the latter being the pioneer and the most popular in its line in the country. The firm write policies on all classes of insurance except life, including fire, accident, plate glass, steam boiler, etc. Their clientage, while chiefly local, also comes from the neighboring localities and agricultural district. The members of the firm are Messrs. Homer B. Boss, Moses Stoppard and W. H. Hecox. The agency they control has long afforded great conveniences and manifest advantages to the residents of this city and country in assuring them certain and solid indemnity in case of loss and disaster by fire.

HATHAWAY & BERRY,
Millers' Agents and Dealers in Flour and Grain. Office: Room 2 Perry Block.

As an illustration of the facilities of the city in a commercial sense, reference is made to the enterprise of Messrs. Hathaway & Berry, who are sales agents for many principal Western millers, and thus bring direct to the doors of the flour and grain trade of Binghamton and its tributary territory all the advantages and trade accommodations afforded by the producing sections of the country. This enterprise was started here in 1888 by Mr. H. H. Hathaway, who continued it until November 2, 1891, when he associated with him Mr. I. L. Berry, under the above named firm style. The firm represents in this market the Humboldt Mill Company of Minneapolis, L. Christian & Co. of Minneapolis, L. M. Godley & Co. of Scottsville, N. Y., and R. P. Fish of Chicago, besides which they are in frequent and daily receipt of special communications from millers, producers and grain operators in all the great trade centers of the West and East. Their connections are such that they are enabled to supply the trade with the best brands of flour, grain and mill-feed in the largest quantities and at lowest market rates, and insure prompt dispatch in filling orders. Sales are made in car-load lots, or quantities to suit, both for shipment direct from the mills or in transit. Besides visiting the trade in person, daily quotations on grain by postal card are sent to all patrons within a radius of one hundred miles of Binghamton. Mr. Berry, the new member of the firm, has for the past eleven years been the sole representative of the Mosely & Motley Milling Company of Rochester, N. Y., and Mr. Hathaway has been engaged in the same line of trade for several years. It will pay the trade to investigate the methods of this firm, who offer advantages equal at least to those obtainable even in the metropolitan trade centers of the country.

THE BINGHAMTON BUTTER PACKAGE CO.,
24 Wall Street.

The Binghamton Butter Package Company, of which Mr. Henry C. Wood is the proprietor, was instituted in 1888, and came into his possession in August, 1891. The Company's manufacturing facilities embrace two floors, where all necessary tools and appliances are at hand and employment is given to about a dozen skilled workmen. The Binghamton Butter Package is made upon an entirely different principle from all others, and is, beyond question, the best and cheapest butter package of merit in the market. Briefly, it is a tin package with a movable non-metallic lining. This lining is not only capable of retaining the brine in the butter contained in the package, but also effectually guards against the butter becoming tainted or stained by coming in contact with the metal. The packages may be used repeatedly by simply changing the linings. In the Binghamton Butter Package the absorption of brine is obviated, the admission of air is prevented, with the result that butter contained in these packages is preserved sweet and pure for months. Another advantage this package has over all others is its weight, it being the lightest package in the market, and it is the lowest priced package of merit known. Dealers prefer this package on account of the facility with which the butter may be stripped by reason of the movable lining. The package is neatly painted and bound with wooden hoops, top and bottom which give it durability and strength. These packages are made in several sizes and are in active demand by dairies and buttermakers in all parts of the country.

NORTH & SHAW,
Wholesale Provision Dealers, 180 State St.

This house was founded in 1889, though this date by no means represents the experience of the firm in the business, since its senior member, Mr. G. S. North, has been actively engaged in the same line of trade in this city for the past twenty years, and may be said to be one of the pioneers in the provision trade of Binghamton, and Mr. Shaw has been in the trade for the past five years. The firm occupy, for the purposes of the business, a four-story and basement brick building, located as above indicated, where they carry a large and complete stock of provisions—flour, salt, beans, cheese, salt and dried fish, salt and smoked meats, bacon, hams, soap, matches and other specialties, which are offered to the trade at lowest market rates. The firm have their own smoke-house on the premises, where they smoke their own hams, which enjoy a high reputation in the trade and are much sought after by epicures. About five employes find occupation with the firm and two traveling salesmen represent them throughout the circuit of their trade, which extends throughout Southern New York, and Northern Pennsylvania. With excellent facilities for the transaction of a large business, receiving all goods direct from first hands and in large lots, and with a thorough knowledge of the trade, this firm is enabled to offer inducements to dealers which are equal, if not superior, to those obtainable from any other quarter.

THE BINGHAMTON STEAM AND HOT WATER WARMING CO.,
Gaylord and Eitapenc, Corner State and Henry Sts.

This now well known and leading establishment, the largest of its kind in the Southern Tier, was established in May, 1889, by Messrs. W. H. Gaylord and F. Eitapenc, its present proprietors, since which time it has built up a trade that extends throughout a large section of New York and Pennsylvania, as well as reaches into other more distant localities. The manufacturing department is equipped with a 60-horse power steam engine and all the latest improved machinery necessary for the business, including a pipe cutting and threading machine capable of cutting an 8-inch pipe, which is the largest machine of the kind between New York and Rochester. The firm give employment to from twenty to thirty skilled workmen. A full and complete line of steam fittings, boiler and steam packing and engineers' supplies is carried, including all kinds of iron pipe, valves, gauges, etc., which are offered to the trade at lowest market prices. The firm are contractors for the supply of all kinds of steam and hot water heating apparatus, and they also make a specialty in furnishing and setting up steam plants for mechanical purposes. They undertake the complete erection and construction of steam and hot water heating plants for public and private buildings, private residences and manufactories in any part of the country, and estimates are promptly furnished from specifications. They furnished the heating plants for the Binghamton Trust Co.'s building, Phelps Bank building, the Ackerman Block, the Ross building, Broome County Court House, the Westcott building, the Rogers flats, the Windemer flats, Judge Spaulding's flats, the Bronner Block, and many other buildings in this city and vicinity, and they are at the present writing about completing the work in the State Asylum at Binghamton. They also furnished all the apparatus for heating in the new factories of the Lestershire Boot and Shoe Co. at Lestershire, as well as the automatic sprinkling apparatus, and set the boilers of 300-horse power. In this city and vicinity innumerable private residences have also been supplied with the productions of this house. Their facilities are unsurpassed and the work executed has always been of superior excellence.

G. S. ACKLEY & CO.,
The Real Estate Sellers, Ackerman Building; Branch Office, Lestershire, N. Y.

The real estate enterprise of Messrs. G. S. Ackley & Co., who, though having conducted the business in this city only since September 1, 1891, have by reason of their energetic and progressive methods, already become among the most prominent representatives of the profession in Binghamton and their success fully entitles them to the title of The Real Estate Sellers of Binghamton. While the firm do a general real estate business, buying, selling and exchanging real property of all descriptions, they have recently devoted a greater part of their attention to the sale of the Lestershire lots, which are located in the beautiful and attractive suburban village of Lestershire, situated two and one-quarter miles west from the Court House Square of Binghamton. The firm are exclusive agents for these lots, and they have met with remarkable success in disposing of them. The village of Lestershire is accessible by both the Erie and D., L. & W. railroads and by street railway from this city. Although the village has been laid out only two years it now has two fine churches, a school house, handsome and convenient passenger stations, a variety of stores, a well organized fire department, a brick engine house and hall, a number of large manufacturing establishments and a large number of private residences. A weekly newspaper, *The Lestershire News*, one of the best looking, best edited and liveliest journals in the State is issued from its own plant, and every convenience and luxury may be obtained there that can in any way add to the comforts or pleasures of home life. Lots may be obtained here for from $150 up to $1,000 each and to those who wish to secure a really profitable investment or a desirable site for a home where pleasant surroundings and healthful locality contribute to make life happy and enjoyable, no location in the State offers so many and valuable inducements. Taking present value and certain future advancement into consideration, these lots are offered at prices lower than any others in this vicinity, and payments will be adjusted to suit the convenience of purchasers. We believe that no better opportunity ever was offered to obtain a home in a delightful neighborhood under the most favorable conditions, than is afforded by this firm at Lestershire. Mr. G. S. Ackley, the active manager of the business is a man of push and energy and is never satisfied with small results. He is thoroughly proficient and capable to advance and foster all interests with which he may be entrusted, and he is always ready and willing to give his time and attention to any who may wish to investigate the value of any of the properties he has for sale.

E. C. SMITH & CO.,
Manufacturers of Spokes and Hubs, 4 and 6 State Street.

An important adjunct to the carriage building trade of the country is the hub and spoke works of E. C. Smith & Co. This enterprise was founded about four years ago by J. F. Severson & Co., the present proprietors succeeding to the business in 1890. It is the only industry of the kind in the city and its products have attained a high reputation in the trade for excellence of quality, resulting in a demand for them that extends throughout a large part of the country. The plant is comprised in a part of the building located as above indicated and is fully equipped with all the necessary machinery of improved patterns, is operated by a 30-horse power engine and furnishes employment to a number of skilled workmen. All kinds of spokes and hubs are made, the woods used being chiefly oak and hickory for spokes and birch for hubs, which are first thoroughly seasoned and are procured direct from the original sources of supply, thus enabling the proprietors to put the finished products on the market, of a quality and at a price that commands the attention of the trade. In connection with the production of spokes and hubs, the firm are also prepared with all facilities to make to order for carpenters and builders, columns, newels, balusters, brackets, etc., and also execute all kinds of general and ornamental turning, planing, scroll and band sawing at reasonable prices. In every respect the house occupies an important position in the productive accommodations of Binghamton.

CHARLES WOODRUFF,
Manufacturer of Cigar Boxes, 4 South Street.

The extensive manufacture of cigars in Binghamton has created a correspondingly large demand for boxes in which to pack them, and this demand is largely supplied by the enterprise of Mr. Charles Woodruff, who annually turns out immense quantities of them. This, the chief enterprise of the kind in the city and one of the largest of the kind in the State, was instituted about sixteen years ago, by its present proprietor. The manufacturing plant is embraced in a two-story factory which is fully equipped with a large amount of late improved special machinery, operated by water power, and employment is here given to about sixty workmen. The wood for the cigar boxes comes to the factory in the log, and this house is the only one in the State outside of New York city, which saws up its own Spanish cedar from the logs. The products embrace Spanish cedar, veneer cedar and imitation cedar boxes, which are warranted strictly air dried and of the best quality. New and novel styles are continually being introduced, and the stock of cigar box labels, trimmings, edging and ribbons is a heavy one. Mr. Woodruff is a practical man at the business to which he gives his close personal attention. He enjoys special facilities for supplying this class of goods, and his steadily increasing business shows the estimation in which his house is held by the trade and indicates the enterprise and ability with which the industry is conducted.

WILLIS SHARPE KILMER,
Newspaper Advertising Agency, Office No. 376 Chenango Street.

A recent and important addition to the general business facilities of this city is the Newspaper Advertising Agency of Mr. Willis Sharpe Kilmer, which gives every promise of becoming a leading institution of its kind. Mr. Kilmer enters upon this enterprise fully equipped by practical experience, assisted by a competent corps of experts, and already has some twenty-five hundred of the prominent newspapers of the country under contract, and additions are constantly being made to this list. He is fully prepared to place advertisements in all newspapers at lowest possible rates, and furnish patrons with the most advanced facilities in the way of advertising that is possible to be obtained in any of the great metropolitan centers. The writing and preparation of matter for publication is one of the special features. The press of the country will also find it desirable to be represented by this agency, which is rated in highest credit by both Bradstreet's and Dun's Commercial Agencies, thus assuring publishers prompt settlements for all space used. Mr. Kilmer already numbers many prominent advertisers among his clients and estimates for any line of advertising will be promptly furnished upon application. As an enterprise greatly contributing to the completeness of the commercial accommodations of Binghamton this agency is fully entitled to the support of the business men of this city and vicinity.

W. C. FOWLER & CO.,
Manufacturers and Dealers in Confectionery, 92 Chenango St.

There are no people in the world that are such consumers of confectionery as the Americans, and the manufacture and sale of confectionery is therefore an important branch of industry. Actively and prominently engaged in this line of trade in Binghamton is the house of Messrs. W. C. Fowler & Co., whose factory and salesrooms are located as above indicated, and embrace a handsomely appointed store, the retail department being in the front and the wholesale department in the rear, a separate building being used for manufacturing purposes. The firm manufacture a general line of staple and fine candies and all their products are pure and unadulterated. In the retail department the goods handled are chiefly of the firm's own production and are made fresh daily, while in the wholesale department a full and complete line of machine made candies and penny goods is also carried for the trade. The firm employs three traveling salesmen and their trade extends throughout a large part of Southern New York and Northern Pennsylvania and is rapidly increasing in volume. The members of the firm are Messrs. W. C. and J. G. Fowler. The business was established in 1888 by Mr. W. C. Fowler, the present firm having been organized in 1890. The house is a growing one and enjoys the confidence of the business community both at home and abroad, of which it is in every respect worthy.

WHITE & CO.,
Wholesale Dealers in Wines and Liquors, 164 Court St.

A leading, enterprising and ably managed representative of the wholesale trade accommodations of Binghamton is the house of Messrs. White & Co., of which Mr. Charles White is the proprietor, the "Co." being nominal only. Mr. White began operations in this line in 1863 at New York and removed to this city in 1883, succeeding to the older established business of Conwell & Rockwell, since which time the scope of operations has been greatly extended and a trade has been built up that extends throughout a large section of New York, Pennsylvania, Western Connecticut, and Eastern Ohio, and is annually increasing in volume, requiring the services of two traveling salesmen. The firm offers the strongest inducements to the trade in the way of superior goods, reasonable prices, and the most advanced accommodations. The complete stock of goods carried embraces the best distillations and vintages of foreign countries and the United States, and all the leading brands of imported wines, gins, brandies and other liquors may be found in stock, while in domestic products, and especially fine Kentucky bourbon and rye whiskies, nothing is left to be desired. The endeavors of the management are directed to handling pure and reliable goods which are sold just as they come from the producers and are warranted exactly as represented, and whiskies are sold in bond or free as may be desired. A New York city office is maintained for the accommodations of the trade. Mr. White may be quoted as an honorable merchant and enterprising business man and his business is conducted upon a basis of strict commercial probity.

OTIS BROTHERS,
Pharmacists, 63 Court St., Corner State.

This enterprise was originally instituted in 1872, the present magnificent store having been first occupied but a few months ago, and it is probably the most elegantly appointed and furnished drug store in the state. It is 25x90 feet in dimensions and occupies a corner, thus being lighted on two sides. The entire fittings are of mahogany, richly and tastefully carved, while every line of the woodwork is one of beauty and symmetry, Bangs of Boston being the designer. The firm make a specialty of supplying the public with family medicines, filling physicians' prescriptions, and carrying in stock a full and complete line of drugs, pharmaceutical preparations, toilet articles and proprietary medicines. The prescription department is conducted with a due appreciation of its responsibilities, and only absolutely pure and high-class drugs are used. The firm are also manufacturers of Otis Brothers' Never Failing Corn Cure, and Camphorated Cream of Glycerine, Hodge's Dentifrice Powder, Cream and Fluid Dentifrice and Rogers' Throat Confections, all of which have been proved of superior excellence and are widely distributed to the trade throughout the country. The members of the firm are Messrs. Clark Z. Otis and F. D. Otis. The former, who is the resident partner and active manager of the business, is widely known as an accomplished pharmacist, and has served as president of the New York State Pharmaceutical Association and also on the State Board of Pharmacy. The latter is a resident of New York where he is engaged in the wholesale drug trade. The profession of the pharmacist has been elevated to a dignified position in late years, in no particular second to that of any other learned profession, and the enterprise of Messrs. Otis Brothers is conducted upon a policy in full sympathy with this high position.

GEORGE A. KENT & CO.,
Manufacturers of Cigars, 53 to 63 Chenango Street.

One of the leading cigar manufactories of Binghamton is the old-established and prominent house of Messrs. George A. Kent & Co., which was instituted in 1876 and has since been conducted with annually increasing success and influence. The plant is embraced in a three-story and basement brick building fronting on two streets and affording an abundance of light. The mechanical equipment embraces all the latest improved machinery known to the trade that has been found useful in decreasing the cost of production and at the same time maintaining the high standard of quality, operated by a 20-horse power steam engine, employment being afforded to about five hundred operatives. The products of the factory comprise a large number of brands of medium and fine grade cigars, and the output reaches from fifteen to twenty millions per annum. The cigars manufactured by the firm bear high favor in the trade for superior quality and are in demand by the jobbing trade in all parts of the United States. While the brands made are numerous, the "Red Star" and "Wishbone" five cent cigars and the "Commercial" ten cent cigars are particularly popular ones and are not excelled by any other goods of the kind in the market. In fact whenever the firm's brands are once introduced the demand for them continually increases and many of the first customers of the firm are still numbered among the most extensive buyers of their goods. The individual members of the firm are George A. Kent and William Rood, both prominent and influential members of the business community and closely allied to the growth and prosperity of Binghamton, and both are members of the Board of Trade. With an ample capital, honorably accumulated, and every facility afforded by experience and connections, Messrs. George A. Kent & Co., are certainly in a position to offer lasting and valuable inducements to the trade.

JOHN GUMBERG & CO.,
Cigar Manufacturers, 30, 32 and 34 Commercial Avenue.

The above named firm is a leading representative of the great cigar manufacturing industry of Binghamton. The business was founded in 1886 by Van Wormer, Gumberg & Co., the present firm, composed of Messrs. John Gumberg and Cyrus S. Clapp, having succeeded to the business in 1889. The manufacturing facilities of the firm embrace a four story and basement brick factory 60 x 80 feet in dimensions, which was erected for the purpose in 1887, and is fully supplied with the most perfect accommodations for the economical conduct of the business. The mechanical equipment embraces all the latest improved modern appliances and machinery, operated by a 50-horse power steam engine, and employment is furnished to an average force of about two hundred and fifty skilled operatives, the factory, however, having ample accommodations for the employment of at least five hundred hands, should the exigencies of the trade demand. The products of the house consist of fair and medium grade cigars, which are sold to the jobbing trade only, and the trade of the house extends throughout the United States generally, two traveling salesmen being constantly employed to visit the firm's customers, and the annual output of the factory averages about 8,000,000 cigars. Among the high grade cigars made by the firm we note the following popular and well-known brands which are in annually increasing demand: "El Brilliante," "El Solitario," "Chiquito," "U. S. Mutual," "La Perdita" and "Red Bat." These are particularly well made and fine cigars, which have an established reputation over a wide territory, and are popular alike with consumers and dealers. Every facility is possessed by the firm for the transaction of a large and growing business, and the greatest care is taken in all the processes of manufacture, so that the high standard of excellence already achieved in the product shall be scrupulously maintained. Mr. Gumberg is an experienced and practical manufacturer and gives his close personal attention to all the operations of the business, and Mr. Clapp is one of the prominent capitalists of this city, and is largely interested in other of this city's interests. The enterprise of the firm is deserving of every confidence, and is a leading factor in the growth and prosperity of Binghamton.

GEORGE BUCHANAN,
Dealer in Wines and Liquors, 114 Washington Street.

Among those houses which can claim a lengthened and honorable career and have been prominently identified with the commercial growth of this community, that conducted by Mr. George Buchanan is conspicuous. It was originally established in 1857 by Erastus Ross, the present proprietor succeeding in 1873. The house has always enjoyed the highest reputation for handling pure and reliable goods and this fact has been realized by dealers and the public and has contributed largely to its prosperity. The stock embraces American and imported wines and liquors, which are sold in five-gallon lots or less, for medicinal and family uses, and a specialty is also made of fine bottled goods which are received direct from first hands in original packages. All goods are sold on their merits and strictly as represented. Mr. Buchanan also handles at retail cigars and tobacco, offering the finest and most popular brands of these goods at the lowest prices. For over a third of a century the policy of this house has remained unchanged and it is still conducted with that conservative liberality and reliability which have always entitled it to the confidence and popularity of this community.

G. A. MATTHEWS,
Real Estate and Fire Insurance, 43 Court Street.

The real estate and insurance agency of Mr. George A. Matthews has long been recognized as one of the most prominent in Binghamton. Mr. Matthews has enjoyed a lengthened experience in the business, having been continuously engaged in it since 1878, formerly at Candor, N. Y., and in this city since 1887. Besides a general business knowledge and acute judgment he possesses in an eminent degree the essential qualifications for the successful prosecution of his enterprise. He devotes his energies to handling all kinds of real estate either on commission for clients or on his own account. He has upon his books a very large list of desirable property and his connections both with buyers and sellers are intimate and valuable. The great advancement that has been characteristic of Binghamton within the past few years is only the beginning of the tide of expansion that will reach its flood in the future and therefore now is the time to invest in real estate, which is sure to largely grow in value. Mr. Matthews is in a position to advise and help the investor, and under his representations the risk of a false move is reduced to a minimum. A special feature of the business is the sale of city lots upon easy terms, thus enabling those of small means to share in the profits that are sure to come. Fire insurance policies are also written in sound and safe companies and an important business is done in this line. The business policy of this agency is one of liberality and fair dealing and its standing is such as to require no commendation at our hands.

S. N. MITCHELL,
Real Estate and General Insurance Agency, I Ross Block.

The real estate agent has become a prominent factor in the resources of this city, and one of the leading and most reliable representatives of this profession is Mr. S. N. Mitchell, who for the past seven years in this city and for a dozen years previously at Susquehanna, Pa., has devoted himself to the study of real estate values, and his experience, knowledge and sound judgment are at the service of investors and capitalists who desire to take advantage of the large profits which are sure to follow the purchase of property in Binghamton and vicinity at the present time. Mr. Mitchell has a large list of business and residence property in all parts of the city for sale and he also transacts all other business relating to the purchase, sale, exchange and renting of real estate. An important division of his business is his general insurance agency. He represents in this locality the Imperial, of London; the Commercial Union, of London; the National, and Hartford, of Hartford; the City of London, of London; the Fire Association, and Franklin, of Philadelphia; the Springfield, of Springfield, Mass.; the Home, of New York; the Travelers' Life and Accident, of Hartford; the American Casualty and Security Steam Boiler Insurance Co., of Baltimore, and the Metropolitan Plate Glass, of New York, the latter being the largest and most noted company in its line in the world; and all of these guaranteeing positive indemnity in case of loss. The insurance department of the business enjoys the largest patronage from business men, manufacturers and individuals, and all losses that have been made have been promptly adjusted. This agency is also one of the oldest in the city, having been instituted in 1873 by Page, Chaffee & Babcock, who were succeeded by Babcock & Mitchell in 1885, the present proprietor having assumed sole control in 1888. Mr. Mitchell is an energetic and enterprising business man and is closely identified with the growth and commercial advancement of Binghamton.

BROWN & CO.,
Wholesalers of Foreign and Domestic Fruits and Produce, 219 Washington St.

Among the most important houses engaged in this line of trade in this city is that of Messrs. Brown & Co., which was established in 1887, since which time a large and annually increasing business has been built up, both direct and on commission, which extends throughout Central and Southern New York and Northern Pennsylvania. The premises of the firm, located as above indicated, are commodious and conveniently arranged for the receipt and shipment of goods, and contain, besides other facilities, a large banana ripening room, where by means of heat supplied by gas this luscious fruit is ripened ready for market. The firm handles every variety of foreign and domestic fruits in their season, including oranges, lemons, bananas, grapes, apples, pears, berries of all kinds, Bermuda potatoes and onions and Southern early vegetables and produce, as well as nuts, dried fruits, etc., and make a specialty of peaches and sweet potatoes. All goods are received direct from first hands and producers and are promptly distributed to the trade, and the firm are shippers and receivers of produce in car lots. The firm make liberal advances on consignments of country produce, guarantee quick sales and prompt returns, and offer shippers all other advantages which may accrue from the best modern methods of conducting the business. The members of the firm are Messrs. William R. and John A. Brown, both young and enterprising business men and closely allied to the promotion of the commercial relations of Binghamton.

THE RILEY BUSINESS COLLEGE,
Westcott Block.

The Riley Business College, Shorthand Institute and School of English Training is among the best-known and most celebrated educational institutions in this section of the country. It was established in 1886 by its present principal, Prof. J. F. Riley, A. M., and has since acquired a reputation for complete and systematic methods of instruction second to that of no other similar institution in the State. The college is pleasantly located in the attractive Westcott block on State street in the very heart of the city and is readily reached by all the principal street car lines of the city which pass the door. The school is perfectly appointed, its many windows afford an excellent light and in every respect it is a very pleasant and agreable place in which studies may be pursued under the most favorable conditions. The school is heated by steam, is lighted by electricity, is connected by telephone and is approached by a rapid elevator, and in all its interior arrangements is provided with the most modern facilities and conveniences and is on a par with the best in the land. Prof. Riley is assisted in his work by an efficient and experienced corps of assistant teachers, each an expert in his specialty, and the course of instruction includes both theoretical and practical business training in all its branches, embracing bookkeeping, commercial correspondence, business forms, commercial law, banking and exchange, penmanship, accounting, etc., which are taught by a system that achieves the best results in the shortest time. Special instruction is also given in shorthand and typewriting, which may be pursued separately or in connection with the business course. Besides the business course general instruction in all the English branches is given, so that the student is acquiring the rudiments of a liberal education while at the same time he is obtaining the practical benefits of actual business experience. Prof. Riley has earned the highest reputation as an instructor of youth and has turned out more proficients than has any similar institution of the same age. An average of about 300 students annually attend the sessions of the school and both sexes are provided for, evening classes being also held for the benefit of those unable to attend in the day. Many successful men and women owe no small measure of their prosperity to the accomplishments and culture they have acquired under the tuition of Prof. Riley, and his school gives every evidence of a continuance of the good work of the past in the future, thus further adding lustre to the reputation of its principal and fame to this city as a seat of learning.

W. S. SMITH & SONS,

Druggists, Grocers and Commission Merchants, 58 Court Street.

For many years the enterprise of W. S. Smith & Sons has been widely and familiarly known to this community as the Peoples' Store, and no other similar establishment in the city can lay claim to greater popularity. It is also one of long establishment, having been founded by W. S. Smith in 1845, and the present firm style was adopted in 1876, its individual members now being Messrs. Wm. T. and Edward C. Smith. The premises occupied are comprised in two floors each 30 x 125 feet in dimensions which form one of the most attractively arranged and commodious salesrooms on the main thoroughfare of the city. The stock carried embraces a full and complete line of drugs, medicines, chemicals, proprietary medicines, toilet articles, surgical instruments and appliances and physicians' supplies, as well as staple and fancy groceries of all kinds, imported and domestic wines and liquors, teas, coffees, spices, canned goods, etc. The trade of the house, while being largely local in character and at retail, also extends in a wholesale way among small dealers in the surrounding counties and is annually increasing in volume. Prompt deliveries are made in all parts of the city by the firm's own wagons, which are of the most modern construction and are equal to any in use in metropolitan cities. A special feature of the business is the sale of European steamship tickets. All facilities are offered tourists or others in this regard that are obtainable at the offices of the companies. For nearly half a century this house has occupied an honorable position in the commercial resources of Binghamton and its record of the past is but an evidence of its future usefulness and increased influence.

E. A. ABELL,

Manufacturer of Pie Preparations, 187 and 189 Water Street.

Mr. Abell inaugurated his enterprise June 1, 1890, and has since built up a trade for his preparations that already extends throughout New York, Pennsylvania and New Jersey, and they are gradually being introduced to the trade generally throughout the country, three traveling salesmen being employed in visiting the trade. The products embrace a variety of evaporated pie preparations, which, with the exception of mince meat of various kinds and qualities, are the only pie preparations on the market today which are all ready for use. So far, those made by the house, embrace mince, apple, plum, raisin, peach, currant and apricot, and this list is constantly being increased. These preparations are put up in an evaporated condition, are well dessicated, and contain all the ingredients necessary to make palatable and wholesome pies, requiring the addition of nothing but water, and are ready for immediate use. They are the most useful, cheapest and handiest articles of food that have ever been introduced, and a pie in five minutes is an absolute fact by the use of these preparations. The preparations are put up in half-pound cartoon boxes, each box being sufficient for two pies, and it is also put up in bulk in paper sacks and wooden pails for the convenience of large consumers, bakers, hotels and restaurants, by whom it is in large and increasing demand. All who have used any of the products of this house unite in extolling their virtues and desirability, while as a matter of economy, a single trial will prove that the same quality of pies cannot be made at the same cost in any other manner.

JOHNSON & LAMB,

Manufacturers of Ladies', Misses' and Children's Fine Shoes, 215 Washington St.

No house has achieved more celebrity in its line within the past few years than has that of Messrs. Johnson & Lamb, who instituted it in 1888. Since that time they have become widely known for the exclusive manufacture of a particularly high grade of ladies', misses' and children's fine shoes, and though not turning out such large quantities or covering so wide a territory with their trade as some other Binghamton houses, they may be said to equalize this in the high quality of the product. The premises occupied by the firm are commodious and well equipped with all the latest improved machinery, employment being given to about thirty hands, with a daily capacity averaging 200 pairs of shoes. Wherever introduced the shoes made by this house have become well known for high quality, style, fit and beauty of finish, and at the same time the prices will be found eminently reasonable, taking their excellence into consideration. The trade of the house extends throughout a large part of this state, Pennsylvania and New Jersey, and is with the leading retailers in the principal cities and towns. The members of the firm are Messrs. C. B. Johnson and George L. Lamb, both of whom possess a full and complete knowledge of all the details of the business to which they give their close personal attention, Mr. Lamb being the manufacturer, while Mr. Johnson markets the product.

BARRETT BROTHERS.
Dealers in Pianos and Organs, 98 and 100 Court Street.

Messrs. Barrett Bros.' extensive music and musical warerooms are the largest of the kind in this section of the State. This enterprise was originally instituted in 1872 by Mr. S. W. Barrett, who discontinued it for a time and re-established it in 1865, the present firm succeeding to the business in 1880. Their commodious and handsomely appointed warerooms are embraced in a double store and basement, each 40 x 90 feet in dimensions, where they display a magnificent and complete stock of pianos, organs and musical instruments of all kinds for amateurs, teachers and musical organizations, as well as all descriptions of the most popular American and foreign sheet music and music books. The firm handle chiefly the Steinway, Weber, Hardman, Knabe, Newby & Evans, Sterling and Peck & Sons' pianos, and the A. B. Chase, Estey and Chicago Cottage organs. They offer their instruments upon the most liberal terms, payments being accepted periodically in small amounts. All instruments are warranted, and pianos and organs are also rented. The trade of the house reaches throughout Southern New York and Northern Pennsylvania, and is annually increasing in volume. One traveling salesman is employed, and one local agent looks after the trade in a near-by village. Mr. S. W. Barrett is an artistic musician, and at one time was a teacher of music, and later, a publisher of music in New York. He spends his winters in California, where he owns a fine vineyard. Mr. V. P. Barrett devotes his attention and energies exclusively to the management of the business, and both are enterprising business men who take marked interest in the commercial and industrial advance of the city.

BABCOCK & STOWELL,
Wholesale and Retail Dealers in Iron, Steel, Metals, Heavy and Shelf Hardware, 174 Washington and 125 State Sts.

This concern, whose trade facilities and business ramifications are of a metropolitan order, was originally founded in 1874 by Carter, Porter & Johnson, the present firm succeeding in 1888, after several changes of title had intervened, the senior member of the present firm having been a partner in two of the preceding ones. The headquarters of the firm are embraced in a four-story and basement building extending through from Washington to State street, 30x165 feet in dimensions. The first floor is devoted to the salesrooms and office, and the remainder of the building for storage of the enormous stock carried. This includes every variety of articles comprised under the general heading of Heavy and Shelf Hardware, and embraces builders' hardware, cabinet hardware, locks and locksmiths' supplies, butchers' tools and supplies, merchant bar iron and steel, carpenters', mechanics' and machinists' tools, table and pocket cutlery, manufacturers' supplies, and a multitude of other articles the mere enumeration of which would require a volume greater than this. In every case their goods are procured direct from first hands, and they enjoy especially close and advantageous relations with large makers, which place them on a par, as far as prices are concerned, with the manufacturers themselves. The trade of the house is diffused throughout Southern New York and Pennsylvania, and entails the services of twenty-five assistants and four traveling salesmen. The members of the firm are Messrs. B. M. Babcock and J. E. Stowell, both gentlemen of long experience in the business, to which they devote their close personal attention. They are energetic, progressive and indefatigable in their efforts to reach the acme of perfection in their accommodations to the trade and also in the promotion of the industrial interests of Binghamton.

BINGHAMTON CHAIR COMPANY, Limited,
Manufacturers of Fancy Artistic Rockers, Etc., Montgomery Street.

This enterprise, of which Mr. R. J. Bump is the active manager, was instituted about ten years ago, but their present magnificent plant has been but recently erected, and is one of the most complete establishments of the kind in the country, and is as perfect in all details as the command of adequate capital and long experience and human contrivance could procure, and is far in advance of any similar establishment in this city. The location adjoins the tracks of the D., L. & W. R. R., affording the most complete facilities for the receipt of raw materials and the shipment of the finished products without rehandling, and large yards give ample room for storing lumber. The main buildings, two in number, are each three stories high, built of brick on the slow-burning principle. The larger one is 50 x 150 feet in dimensions, the other 50 x 75 feet, and they are connected at the upper stories by bridges. The floors are solid planks five inches in thickness, and are held in place by heavy timbers without joists. There are no openings in the floors, the stairways being on the outside of the buildings, and each floor is equipped with automatic sprinklers. The mechanical equipment embraces all the latest improved machinery known to the trade, which is operated by a 100-horse power steam engine, and one hundred and twenty-five skilled workmen are given employment. All oils, varnishes, and other specially inflammable materials are stored in a separate underground vault. The productions embrace a large variety of styles and designs in fancy rockers upholstered in silk plush, tapestries and other fine fabrics, and polished wood seat chairs for halls, reception rooms and alcoves. Many of these are fancifully and uniquely carved and ornamented, and fashioned after antique models. New styles and designs are constantly being introduced, each one, if possible, more beautiful and artistic than its predecessor. The company issues plates of their chairs as fast as new ones are introduced, in place of semi-annual catalogues, and hence they are always up to date.

MEAGLEY & BLANCHARD,
Dealers in Coal, 25 Prospect Avenue.

The coal trade forms a very important item in the list of industries of Binghamton, and there are a number of extensive dealers here who have availed themselves of all modern facilities for promptly supplying the demand for this staple, among whom Messrs. Meagley & Blanchard occupy a prominent position. This house was inaugurated in 1878, and has since built up a large trade with families and manufacturers throughout the city that involves the handling annually of upwards of twelve thousand tons. The facilities of the firm embrace a yard and coal pockets for storage which adjoin the Erie railroad main line and admits of the discharge of supplies of coal direct from the cars without rehandling. Telephonic communication insures prompt fulfillment of orders, and with an ample storage capacity, a full supply of the various varieties of coal is always kept on hand. The active management of the business devolves upon Mr. La Motte Blanchard, who is eminently qualified for its successful conduct. The firm has always been recognized as enterprising, liberal and fair dealing, and it is one of the most prominent of its kind in the city.

VICKERS & BROOKER,
Plumbers and Gas Fitters, Steam and Hot Water Heating,
136 State Street and 29 Commercial Avenue.

This firm commenced operations here in 1885, and have since executed a large amount of work in their line for the owners of public and private buildings in this city and vicinity, notably the Rich building and the Rogers apartment house. The firm occupy a commodious store and basement, with shop in rear, where they carry an extensive stock of plumbers' materials and steam and gas fittings, including the latest improved sanitary appliances, and in fact, everything necessary or requisite for the perfect execution of sanitary plumbing and gas fitting in all its branches. They also make steam and hot water heating a prominent feature of their business, and they are agents in this city for the celebrated Perfect hot water heaters and steam boilers manufactured by the Richardson & Boynton Co. These devices are widely recognized as being the most perfect before the public for the proper and economical heating and ventilating of public and private buildings. The firm promptly submits estimates for any work in their line, and the marked success they have met with, and the entire satisfaction they have given to their large number of patrons in the past fully entitles them to be numbered among the leaders in their line of trade.

THE BINGHAMTON SAFE DEPOSIT CO.,
151 Washington Street.

The vaults of the Binghamton Safe Deposit Co. are located on the ground floor of the building at 151 Washington St., and in the rear of and connected with the offices of the First National Bank, the management of the two institutions being practically the same, and as follows: Pres., F. T. Newell; Vice-Pres., Harper Dusenbury, and Sec'y and Treas. John Manier, to whose active and indefatigable efforts is largely due the credit for originating and successfully managing this important enterprise, which has proved so beneficial to the citizens of Binghamton and vicinity, and which was the pioneer in its field of accommodation. The company was organized to furnish an absolutely safe and convenient place of deposit for valuables of every description, under guarantee, including bonds, stocks, deeds, mortgages, specie, jewelry, diamonds, silver plate, etc. For this purpose a large vault has been provided which contains a large number of small safe deposit boxes, which are leased to individuals for any length of time at a small annual rental. These boxes are so arranged as to be easily accessible for their lessees, and absolutely safe from interference by anyone else. The vault is both fire and burglar proof, and is furthermore constantly watched by armed guardians. In fact, in the construction and charge of the vault every modern appliance that is in any way calculated to defy the ravages of fire or the attacks of burglars or a mob, has been provided, and the patron who confides his valuables to the safekeeping of the company may feel as secure as if they were locked up in the rock of Gibraltar.

THE HOFFMAN LUBRICATING OIL COMPANY,
Manufacturers of Lubricators and Lubricating Oils, Office and Works, South Street.

The Hoffman Lubricating Oil Company ranks, in the production of lubricating oils and lubricators, second to no other in this section. This company was originally established about ten years ago and was incorporated under the present title in May, 1890. The premises utilized for manufacturing purposes consist of a series of suitable buildings, which are equipped with all necessary appliances and afford ample room for storage purposes. The products of the company in the oil department embrace a variety of cylinder and machinery oils, which are highly commended by consumers for superior quality and economy in use. They are in active demand by the trade and consumers throughout the coal and iron regions of Pennsylvania as well as in this city and vicinity. A prominent specialty of the company is the manufacture of the Hoffman Automatic Lubricator for stationary engines. This lubricator has no equal for simplicity and reliability of work and is the only lubricator that does not chill or freeze up in cold weather, and stops and starts with the engine. It operates by the current of steam as it passes from the boiler to the engine, and by this method, when the engine labors hard and requires more oil, the current of steam is greater and the lubricator will feed faster. The company manufactures an oil especially adapted for use in automatic lubricators which is confidently recommended to all parties desiring a first-class article. These lubricators are in use in all parts of the country and are highly commended by all engineers who have used them. The officers of the company are Messrs. R. J. Hoffman, pres., and R. W. Lester, sec'y and treas.

L. I. WEED,
Engineer and Manufacturer of Artistic Cabinet Work, 25 and 26 Wall St.

"There is always room at the top" in every calling and acting upon this trueism Mr. L. I. Weed established himself in this city about two years ago as an interior and exterior decorator and designer and manufacturer of fine artistic cabinet work, since which time he has achieved a marked success and built up a demand for his services that extends troughout the trade radius of Binghamton. His facilities embrace a commodious and well-equipped workshop, where employment is furnished to a force of skilled workmen and where all necessary machinery is at hand. The products of the house consist mainly of hard-wood mantels made from original designs, store, office and bank fixtures, counters, railings, desks, church furniture and interior and exterior decorations of all kinds in wood and fine cabinet work. The most elaborate productions are made when desired, consisting of beautifully carved and polished wood-work, made from the most expensive hard woods, single mantels frequently being valued at many hundreds of dollars, being turned out from this establishment. Mr. Weed has furnished the interior hard-wood decorations for many of the most noted private mansions and public buildings in this city and vicinity, a list of which with privileges of reference may be obtained upon application. Drawings and estimates for any class of interior or exterior decorations or artistic cabinet work may be obtained, and while the high character of all work produced is guaranteed, the prices are made upon a liberal and fair-dealing basis, which is sure to prove satisfactory to all patrons. A specialty is also made of slate mantels, tiles and grates and in fact all work of this character.

MT. PROSPECT MEDICAL INSTITUTE,
80 to 90 Prospect Street.

The Mt. Prospect Medical Institute of Binghamton was recently established for the treatment of inebriety from whatever cause, whether from alcohol, opium or other narcotics. The institution, since its purchase by its present proprietors, has been extensively remodeled and improved and in its present condition is one of the best equipped private institutions in the country. It is admirably situated, in a most beautiful and healthful location, about half way up Mt. Prospect, overlooking from its windows and broad piazzas the city and valley —east, south and west— while the wooded slopes of Mt. Prospect in the rear protect it from the cold north winds and make it a delightful retreat for invalids. The building is three stories high, substantially constructed, with high walls and sunny windows. It is heated by a combination hot water and hot air system and the sanitary arrangements and safeguards for health are all that modern experience and scientific research have dictated. The famous Mt. Prospect spring supplies the institution with the purest water and the large and well-shaded grounds that surround the building afford ample space for exercise. The general aspect is such as has a soothing and quieting influence on the inmates, and as the number of patients is limited, each has the benefit of the constant personal care of the faculty, and the habits of each are thus critically observed and studied, with the result that permanent and speedy cure is effected in many instances. Turkish, electric and plunge baths are among the conveniences of the institution, and in fact everything is at hand for the comfort and cure of patients. All the latest and most successful methods are employed in the management of this inebriety. The system includes both moral and medical treatment, the family plan being adopted, which while giving each patient the advantage of a comfortable and attractive home at the same time insures his being continually under the eye of a trained and experienced specialist and capable nurses. The proprietors of the institute are Dr. E. A. Pierce and Dr. C. W. Ingraham, both well-known and famous practitioners of this city. The former visits the institute daily and the latter is the resident physician, while Dr. C. B. Richards is the medical superintendent, and five of the most prominent physicians in the Southern Tier, Drs. J. G. Orton, S. F. McFarland, J. H. Chittenden, L. D. Farnham and W. A. Moore are consultants. The management has already had the gratification of effecting some remarkable cures, and the institute gives every promise of continued success and prosperity.

THE MERCANTILE AGENCY, R. G. DUN & CO.,
Phelps Bank Building, Chenango Street.

The question of credits is of vital interest to the business community, and anything that aims to protect and help the business man in the extension of his credits is worthy of confidence. The more thorough the system the greater the protection, and the more offices and subscribers to the system the greater the benefit. At the head of the few organizations instituted with this object in view, stands the mercantile agency of R. G. Dun & Co., which was established in New York in 1841, eight years before any other agency, and is therefore the oldest concern of the kind in the world. This firm have in all one hundred and forty-one branch offices in the United States, Canada, London, Liverpool, Manchester, Glasgow, Birmingham, Berlin and Paris, and at Melbourne, Australia. In this city the business is conducted under the able management of Mr. William H. Parsons, who has become well and favorably known to almost every merchant and manufacturer in Binghamton and vicinity, since his location here. One of the great secrets of the success earned by this organization is the thorough and systematic manner in which its reports are completed. Each office sends out traveling reporters over its entire territory regularly twice each year. These men, trained to the business, visit every cross-road town and county seat in the whole country and ascertain on the ground by personal investigation the status and condition of traders. They have also in their employ thousands of the ablest authorities upon the financial standing of the business people in every community, who are giving them the benefit of their invaluable knowledge This systematic work entails large outlay, but is found to be the only true way to do the business, which so much depends upon the reliability and thoroughness of the information rendered. It is gratifying to learn that this mercantile agency is patronized by the majority of the banks, manufacturers and merchants in this city and all over the vicinity, and it certainly invites the support of those who transact a business where credit is given and obtained.

BERWIND-WHITE COAL MINING CO.,

Miners and Shippers of the Eureka Bituminous Coals. Geo. E. Green, Sales Agent, Rooms 3, 4 and 5 Perry Block.

No interest in the range of industrial and commercial activity of Binghamton is more important than that of coal, and both as regards capital invested and the direct benefits derived therefrom to all classes of the community, no branch of trade in the United States is of a more useful or necessary nature. Binghamton is the headquarters of a branch office of the Berwind-White Coal Mining Co., of Pennsylvania, under the management of Mr. Geo. E. Green. This company is the largest colliery proprietor and shipper of Bituminous coals in the United States, operating extensive collieries in Clearfield Centre, Jefferson and Westmoreland Counties, Penna., as well as other sections of the State, shipping their products via. rail to all parts of New England, the Middle and Western States and Canada, and by transhipment at Philadelphia, New York and Baltimore to coastwise and foreign ports. Their celebrated Eureka Bituminous coals have long been the most popular fuels in the market for steam generating and general manufacturing purposes, and are unexcelled as fuel for steamships, locomotives, manufactories, rolling mills, forges, glass works, brick and lime burning, and especially adapted for the manufacture of steel, iron, etc., and are largely in demand for these purposes. From the Binghamton branch office sales are made throughout New York state and Canada, at wholesale only, in car lots, to railroads, coal merchants and manufacturers, shipments being made direct to consumers from the mines without breaking bulk. This company's coal is perfect in combustion, producing little smoke compared with ordinary Bituminous coal. Eureka coals contain a high per centage of fixed carbon, and an exceptionally low per centage of ash and impurities, producing intense heat and plenty of steam on small consumption. It is largely used by the principal manufacturers of this State and Canada, and its employment is annually increasing in volume. This agency is regarded as one of the permanent and important resources of Binghamton. Mr. Green is a capable and experienced manager, and enjoys the esteem and consideration of a large clientage. Altogether the enterprise may be considered as one which largely enhances the manufacturing interests of the city and district, while the establishment and maintenance here of a branch of such an important concern as the Berwind-White Coal Mining Co. is an evidence of the commercial importance of Binghamton. It may be incidentally mentioned that Mr. Green is also a member of the firm of Ashley & Green, Haven Building, Buffalo, N. Y., who do a large wholesale business in both Anthracite and Bituminous coals.

RICH BROTHERS,

Fire Insurance and Real Estate Agency, 69 Court Street.

This firm transacts a real estate and fire insurance business, chiefly with relation to their own holdings, they being largely interested in and owners of central business property in Binghamton. The individual members of the firm are Messrs. T. G. Rich, Jr., and E. B. Rich, both gentlemen of standing and respectability in this community. Their efforts have been productive of much good and conduce greatly to the general resources of this city, and at all times they stand ready to accord all advantages to patrons.

BARLOW, ROGERS & SIMPSON,
Cigar Manufacturers, 6, 7, 8, 9 and 10 Wall Street.

Widely noted as Binghamton is as an important manufacturing centre, there are among her varied industries some which have attained great prominence throughout the country. Easily in the lead is that of the manufacture of cigars. In this industry Binghamton has forged to the front until, for some years past, and at present, she occupies a foremost position in the cigar world. This is a standing tribute to the skill, energy and business ability of the men who have controlled and directed the affairs of the numerous firms in this line. Of such as have attained a national reputation and importance, none is more notable than the firm of Barlow, Rogers & Simpson. This house, founded in 1885, from its inception became one of the leaders and in the third year of its existence, 1888, established the proud record of not only leading the home production, but of making and selling more five cent cigars than any firm in the United States for which we give the figures from the record. We quote here in its entirety a letter from the only recognized and absolute authority on which no shadow of a doubt can be thrown:

U. S. INTERNAL REVENUE, DEPUTY COLLECTOR'S OFFICE,
BINGHAMTON, N. Y., December 31, 1888.

Messrs. Barlow, Rogers & Simpson:

GENTLEMEN:—In reply to yours of today, the U. S. Internal Revenue Records in my office show, that during the calendar year of 1888 you have paid into this office Sixty-one Thousand Six Hundred Eighty-four Dollars and Fifty Cents, ($61,684.50) for Cigar Stamps, representing Twenty Millions, Five Hundred and Sixty-one Thousand Five Hundred Cigars, (20,561,500.)

On examining the Records of this office for past years, I find this to be the LARGEST NUMBER OF CIGARS EVER SENT OUT BY ANY ONE FIRM FROM THIS DISTRICT IN ANY CALENDAR YEAR. Very Respectfully,
A. J. INLOES,
Deputy Collector, 7th Division, 21st District.

Their factory occupies a block of buildings, five in number and four stories in height, with full basements. All of this space, some 40,000 square feet, is needed and utilized in the different departments of their manufacturing business, while the leaf tobacco or raw material, of which they at all times carry an immense stock, is stored in warehouses in other localities. The mechanical equipment embraces all the latest improved special machinery used in the trade, which is operated by a 25-horse power steam engine and 45-horse power boiler which furnishes power to drive the machinery, run two elevators and heat the building in every part. The firm manufactures an endless variety of medium grade and domestic cigars which are put up chiefly under their own registered brands and are sold to the jobbing trade only, in unbroken cases in all the trade centres of the United States. Five hundred operatives are kept busy within the walls of this mammoth "beehive" of the cigar business and such a thing as a "lay-off" on account of dull trade has never as yet occurred. While the number of brands produced are large and varied, the following have attained great prominence and unequalled popularity among the lovers of a good cigar at a moderate price, and may be said to be their leading brands: "Red Seal," "Dispatch," "Cow Boy," "Honey Suckle" and "Fire Brigade." Once placed where the consumer can test their merit, their success is a foregone conclusion and the fact of their large and increasing trade from year to year, shows of itself the reputation in which the products of this justly celebrated firm are held by those to whom they have been introduced. Their trade may well be said to be a permanent one, and careful selections and blending of tobaccos, never ending originality of designs in artistic labels, new and beautiful packages with choice advertising matter calling attention to the same all combine to make an outfit seldom equalled and never excelled. Add to this the fairest and most courteous treatment from its gentlemanly representatives and the house itself, and it is surely a pleasure to be numbered among its legion of friends and patrons. The individual members of the firm are Messrs. George H. Barlow, Richard J. Rogers and John B. Simpson, all of whom are experienced in the manufacture of cigars and progressive business men. The firm is represented in the Binghamton Board of Trade. They are universally popular and respected, their commercial relations are wide spread, their facilities are unsurpassed and the wise guidance of their business enterprise has been noteworthy, resulting in having reared a great establishment which is a lasting source of credit to Binghamton's fair name and a monument to their own industry, genius and enterprise.

THE SINGER MANUFACTURING COMPANY,
Sewing Machines, 90 Chenango Street.

The Singer sewing machines are everywhere recognized throughout the civilized world as the best for all purposes. From its inception the company has put upon the market over 10,000,000 machines, of which more than 7,000,000 are used exclusively for family sewing. The company's new Oscillating Shuttle machine for family use is the latest development in sewing machines, and is an entirely new style different from all other machines, and contains the most valuable principles ever put in a sewing machine. This machine excels all others in fine family work and in decorative art needle work stands beyond competition. It is the fastest speed, the least noisy and the easiest running machine ever made. Other popular machines made by this company are the Vibrating Shuttle No. 2, which is an ideal family sewing machine, and the Automatic Tension which is a single thread machine. At the company's branch office, in this city, a full assortment of their perfect sewing machines is shown, and full information with regard to their merits will be cheerfully furnished to all investigators. The office here is under the management of Mr. E. R. Hildreth, who has been with the company for a number of years. He controls the business in Broome, Tioga, Cortland and Tompkins counties and employs about twenty agents and has four branch offices. By his energy and push he has done much to create a large demand for Singer machines in this section.

BINGHAMTON CIGAR COMPANY,
Manufacturer of Cigars, 15 and 17 North Depot Street.

The manufacture of cigars is Binghamton's leading industry, and there is hardly a town in the Union where her goods are not sold, and in all sections their reputation stands high for quality and uniformity. The Binghamton Cigar Company is one of the leading houses in the trade, which, in its particular specialty of fine Havana filled cigars, has few successful rivals in the country. This house manufactures cigars ranging in price from $20.00 to $120.00 per thousand in case lots and makes a specialty of goods which retail for ten and fifteen cents each, and all their products rank with the very best of the kind known to the trade. The business was established in 1887 and has since built up a trade that extends from the Atlantic to the Pacific, and is annually increasing in volume. The manufacturing facilities of the firm embrace a five-story and basement building, which is equipped with improved machinery and all modern appliances, operated by steam power and furnishes employment to about one hundred and fifty skilled workmen. Two resident salesmen and two travelers represent the firm to the trade, sales being made to jobbers only. The cigars made by the firm are principally packed under their own brands, though special brands to suit customers are also used. Among the most popular of the firm's brands are: "Berwind," "Moonstone," "Leo Grande," "Board of Trade," "Berkeley," "El Venito," "Windsor Castle," "Sure Catch," "Our Treasures," "Us Two," "Great American," etc., all of which have a wide popularity among dealers and consumers and are esteemed for handsome appearance, fine flavor, excellent smoking qualities and invariable uniformity. The firm use nothing but the best domestic seed and Havana stock, Sumatra and fine Housatonic wrappers, and exercise the greatest care in manufacturing in all departments. They aim to be abreast of the times in all improved processes that will in any way benefit their customers and propagate trade, and they are everywhere recognized as enterprising and prosperous manufacturers and honorable business men. The members of the firm are Messrs. Hon. Rodney A. Ford and Geo. E. Green, Theo. P. Calkin being the business manager. Their success is a well-merited result of an intelligent application of system and enterprise in their business, while the extent and character of their trade is another evidence of the fact that Binghamton possesses advantages as a first-class manufacturing and distributing center, which must result in extending and increasing her relations with the outside world.

SHAPLEY & WELLS,
Builders of Engines, Boilers, Tannery Machinery, Etc., Washington, Hawley and State Streets.

The extensive engine building and machinery works of Messrs. Shapley & Wells, besides being the only one of any considerable importance in this section of the State, is one of the oldest established concerns of the kind. It was originally founded in 1850 by Messrs. Shapley & Dunk and after several changes of firm style the present one was adopted in 1870. No single fact better illustrates the high reputation the perfected products of these works bear among the users of power everywhere, than that the engines and boilers made by this firm have been shipped to all parts of the civilized globe, and are now in use by manufacturers in all the countries of Europe, in China, in South Africa, in the West Indies, in Central and South America, in Canada and in every State and Territory of the United States. The firm's plant covers about half a city block, and the various departments comprise the machine, boiler and pattern shops, foundry and storage buildings. A force of 85 to 100 skilled mechanics is given employment, all of whose operations are conducted with perfect system and order. The firm are builders of engines and boilers of all kinds, complete tannery outfits and general and special machinery and are also dealers in steam engine supplies, fittings, etc. The Shapley Portable Engines are made in sizes ranging from three to fifteen horse power each. The boiler is a rapid generator of steam, and is the only one in which all the heating surfaces are below the water line, which avoids all liability to burn out the boiler, therefore increasing its durability. A very important advantage in the use of this boiler is the absolute absence of sparks, which are overcome by having water standing in the base, into which the vertical tubes discharge all their contents of smoke, etc. Another important specialty of the firm is the manufacture of bark mills for tanneries and complete tannery outfits. The individual members of the firm are Messrs. J. S. Wells, J. E. Shapley and W. M. Shapley, who are among the most prominent and progressive business men of Binghamton.

HENNESSEY BROTHERS,
Manufacturers of Fine Cigars, 161 Washington Street.

The enterprise of Messrs. Hennessy Brothers was instituted in 1888. The premises occupied are supplied with all modern facilities for the economical production of the high-grade cigars for which the house has become widely noted, including the special brands "World's Enterprise" ten cent cigar, and "Liberal League," "Hennessey's Three Star," "Pharmacist" and "Co-Operative" five cent cigars. These goods are all strictly hand-made, are uniform in quality and made by a corps of skilled workmen from carefully selected leaf tobacco of the best obtainable quality and are in large demand by fine retail trade throughout this State and Pennsylvania, including a large and ever increasing local demand. The members of the firm are Messrs. John, Louis and Charles V. Hennessey, all of whom take an active and prominent part in the management of the business. They are practical manufacturers and pushing business men, who have built up a large and growing trade by the production of a superior line of cigars and the success they have met has been fully merited by their enterprising methods.

P. E. FIELD,
Fine Groceries, 99 Court Street.

A prominent exponent of the grocery trade of Binghamton is the popular establishment of Mr. P. E. Field, which he has conducted for the past six years, the business having been founded a number of years previously. The premises utilized are spacious and attractively appointed and are furnished with all conveniences for supplying a large trade. The stock carried is complete and carefully selected and includes everything pertaining to staple and fancy groceries, provisions, fruits, etc. Specialties are made of Pillsbury's Best flour, the finest coffees and teas, choice country butter, fresh eggs and table delicacies of all kinds. The lowest prices prevail and the best value for money is guaranteed. Goods are delivered promptly to all parts of the city, and in all cases the service is courteous and satisfactory. Mr. Field is untiring in his efforts to please those who favor him with their patronage, and a large number of the best people in Binghamton are his steady and daily customers.

STOW MANUFACTURING COMPANY,

Manufacturers of the Stow Flexible Shaft and Machinery, Office and Factory, 443 State Street.

This enterprise was instituted in 1875 and its facilities embrace a large and well-equipped plant, which is comprised in a three-story brick building erected for the purpose and a suitable structure adjoining which is utilized for the manufacture of wire cables of any desired diameter or length. A 20-horse power steam engine operates the mechanical equipment. The Stow Flexible Shaft and its appliances consist, in brief, of an enclosed wire cable firmly attached to a pulley or head piece at one end and holding a tool at the other, by the use of which the workman is enabled to carry the power to the work instead of being obliged to carry the work to the power. These flexible shafts are made in a variety of regular sizes and lengths and special lengths are made to order. They are applicable for a variety of uses, notably portable drilling, reaming, tapping, grinding, polishing, etc., and for wood-working they entirely replace the use of the bit and brace and heavy, cumbersome boring machines. For metal working or drilling heavy machinery which is too large or inconvenient to handle, the flexible shaft is invaluable, as it can be taken to the work in whatever position it may be. The company also manufacture a number of machines for special uses in connection with the flexible shafts, notably, flexible boring machines, portable drills capable of drilling over a wide extent of surface, center grinders, portable screw feed drill presses, pedestal drills, breast drills, tapping and reaming machines, radial boring machines, originally designed for sash, door and blind makers, but now in use by all kinds of wood-workers, for which it is particularly adapted, and wood carving machines by means of which the use of hand tools is almost entirely dispensed with. All the dental shafts used by the S. F. White Dental Manufacturing Company of Philadelphia in their machines, which are in use by dentists in all parts of the world, are made by this company. The Stow Flexible Shaft and its appliances meet all the requirements in the large field which they cover and they have no superiors anywhere. The management of the business is in the hands of Messrs. C. F. Hotchkiss and C. C. Warner. The company is to be congratulated upon the success which has attended its efforts in introducing upon the market such a valuable invention.

STICKLEY & BRANDT CHAIR COMPANY,

Manufacturers of Artistic Chairs, 194 Washington Street.

This enterprise was incorporated in 1891, and is the outgrowth of the modest business established in 1884 at Brandt, Pa., by Stickley Bros. It has since grown to be the largest fancy chair manufactory in the country, and it was the pioneer of this now great industry. The facilities of the company embrace two large factories in this city which are fully equipped and furnish employment to 125 workmen. The products consist of antique, artistic and fancy chairs finished in the highest style of the art, and upholstered in silk, plush, tapestry and other fine fabrics. These are shipped to the trade throughout all parts of the United States. The officers of the company are Messrs. Schuyler C. Brandt, President; C. C. Jackson, Vice-President; F. A. Blakslee, Secretary and Treasurer, and Charles Stickley, General Manager. The trade will find this company wide-awake and fully abreast of the times, and relations with it will be found advantageous.

THE CITY OF BINGHAMTON. 119

STOW MANUFACTURING COMPANY.

J. D. WHITE,
Awnings, Tents and Flags, 91 1-2 State Street.

The enterprise of Mr. J. D. White is one of great convenience and importance to Binghamton. It was founded in 1876, and has since enjoyed an annually increasing trade for its products, which extends throughout the city and surrounding towns. The premises occupied are in every way complete for the work in hand and afford ample conveniences for the prompt fulfillment of orders. Here are made awnings, tents, flags, horse, trunk and wagon covers, boat sails, net and canvas goods of every description, from the best materials by experienced workmen, and warranted to give satisfaction. A large stock of cotton duck of all widths is carried and is offered to patrons at low prices. A specialty of the business is the decoration of buildings and halls with flags and bunting for festivals or other public demonstrations, and tents and canopies for connecting house doors with the street curb on special occasions, are rented at reasonable prices. Mr. White also takes down awnings in the fall and replaces them in the spring. Probably no other imprint is so often seen as that of this house, which may be found upon hundreds of awnings on all the principal streets of Binghamton. Mr. White has, by his promptness, reliability, and perfection of product, achieved a distinction in his line of trade peculiarly his own and which renders his establishment the leading one of its kind in Binghamton.

JOHN J. MOSES,
Wholesale Dealer in Wines, Liquors and Cigars, 157 Water Street.

The wholesale establishment of Mr. John J. Moses is the headquarters for an important and constantly growing trade in wines and liquors, and the demand for fine and reliable goods is supplied by this house in a manner that has met with the highest commendation from the trade. This house was founded in 1883, and has since built up a trade that extends throughout a large section of Southern New York and Northern Pennsylvania. From its inception it has been the policy of its management to handle only the best goods, and in fact, there are no choicer wines and liquors to be obtained anywhere than those offered by Mr. Moses. In domestic goods the stock embraces fine Pennsylvania, Monongahela, Monogram, Old Saratoga, and Private Stock whiskies, produced by the well-known firm of Rosskam, Gerottey & Co., for whom he is sole agent in this section of the country, also Pepper, I. W. Harper, Keystone Malt, and other well-known brands of Bourbon, rye and wheat whiskies, as well as New York, Ohio and California wines and brandies. The stock of foreign goods of direct importation, embraces G. H. Mumm & Co.'s champagnes, Calvet & Co.'s clarets, Ivison sherries, Graham & Co.'s ports, and sweet and dry wines from the vintages of France, Germany, Spain, Italy and Holland, together with brandies, gins, Irish and Scotch whiskies, imported Bass and Alsopp's ale and Guinness' stout, etc., which are offered to the trade in original packages, or in quantities to suit. Mr. Moses is agent for Strontia mineral spring water and Hungarian blackberry juice, and many other choice goods are to be obtained at the establishment. A special feature of the business is the trade in cigars, the leading brands of "Monogram," "Espanola," "H. A.," "Walt. Whitman," and others being regularly handled, and extra inducements are offered in job lots of cigars, for which the house has special facilities for procuring. The reputation enjoyed by this house for the expeditious and discerning manner in which all orders are filled, merits the appreciation of the trade, and we commend the house to all who are fastidious in the selection of wines and liquors and cigars.

THE LOWELL BUSINESS COLLEGE AND INSTITUTE OF SHORT-HAND AND TELEGRAPHY,

J. E. Bloomer, Principal and Proprietor, Corner Court and Collier Streets.

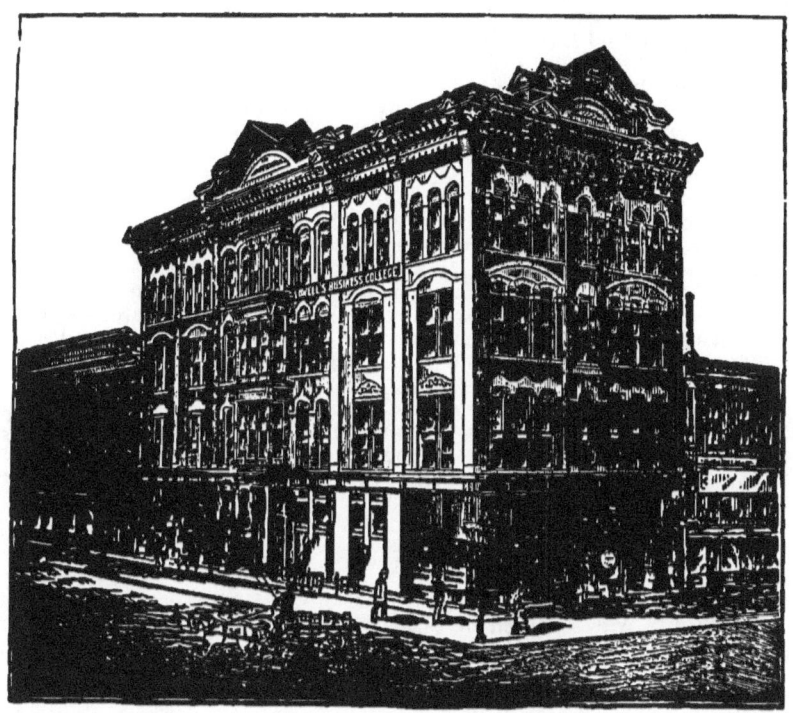

The Lowell Business College and Institute of Short Hand and Telegraphy is not only one of the oldest, but is also entitled to rank as one of the very best institutions of the kind in the country. Established in 1859 and conducted under its present proprietorship since 1888, it has during the period of its existence accomplished a great and good work and has become one of the steadfast educational institutions of the Empire State. Here students of both sexes have every advantage for obtaining a thorough business education and every modern facility is at hand for acquiring practical experience in the conduct of business matters and after the same methods that are in use in actual commercial establishments. The course of study embraces book-keeping, penmanship, business correspondence, commercial law, arithmetic, banking, commission, exchange, transportation, wholesaling, merchandising, shipping, real estate and insurance, and actual office drill in all business departments, and banks and business offices are located in the college with all the books, papers, desks, furniture, letter presses, etc., that would be in use in any regular business enterprise, and in the transaction of the business the student is taught to rely upon his own judgment and conduct all matters the same as if they were to be consummated by responsible parties. A marked advantage of this college lies in the fact that students of either sex may enter at any time and, as each student is given personal instruction, he is advanced as rapidly as his own abilities and perceptions admit, hence the brighter the student the more quickly will he acquire the coveted knowledge and experience. Special departments are also provided for teaching short hand, typewriting and telegraphy. The Graham system of phonography is taught and the use of five principal typewriters. A complete series of telegraph offices connected by wire is maintained and thorough instruction is given in this art by a competent and experienced operator, so that a graduate of this department is competent to at once enter upon the active duties of a commercial or railroad telegraph office. The corps of teachers is made up of specialists, and are among the most able in their departments to be found in the country. As regards the location of the school in this city no more healthful or advantageous point could have been selected and concerning the many advantages the Parlor City has to offer to students from a distance reference is made to the earlier portions of this volume where the many attractions of the city have been exhaustively treated. Mr. J. E. Bloomer, the principal and proprietor of the college, is a gentleman of large and varied experience as an instructor of youth; he was a teacher in the Binghamton public schools for two years and for seven years previous to his assuming control of the college was a member of its faculty. His scholarly abilities have gained for him a high reputation as one of the most successful teachers in the State. The Lowell Business College since its foundation has graduated hundreds who have since become shining lights in the commerce and manufactures of the country, and the institution is commended by many of the leading statesmen, professional and business men of the State.

STICKLEY & BRANDT,
Furniture Dealers, 194 Washington Street.

This house was founded in 1883 by Stickley Bros., the present firm having succeeded to the business in 1890. The warerooms of the firm have a floorage area of 37,000 square feet, two of the floors being each 120x70 feet, which form the largest furniture salesrooms in the State. The firm carry the largest stock of furniture in Binghamton and the finest goods in the market, and their facilities for procuring goods embrace the exclusive agency for the products of the principal manufacturers of Grand Rapids, Mich., as well as of other localities. In fine antique and artistic modern chairs and fancy rockers they offer the products of the Stickley & Brandt Chair Co. of this city. All upholstered furniture is manufactured on the premises, and a special and newly added department is that of fine draperies and upholstery, which is in charge of Mr. J. N. Piercy, who is an accomplished expert in this line. Among other specialties we note the Windsor folding beds and the Gunn combination beds. Though fine furniture is the specialty of this house the prices are very reasonable and no higher than inferior goods are sold for elsewhere. An important feature of the facilities of the firm is their ability to introduce customers to the most noted manufacturers of furniture in New York and elsewhere, where selections can be made and the goods delivered here the same as if purchased from the firms' own warerooms, thus virtually affording customers a selection from the stock of the entire country. Twenty-five assistants are employed in the warerooms and every courtesy is shown to customers that modern business methods have made possible or progressive ideas originated. The members of the firm are Charles Stickley and Schuyler C. Brandt, who are also respectively president and general manager of the Stickly & Brandt Chair Co., noticed elsewhere.

ACME OIL CO.,

William Mason, Manager. Office, 18 Wall Street. Works, Erie Street.

An important feature of the commercial facilities of this city is the enterprise of the Acme Oil Co., which is one of the largest producers of illuminating and lubricating oils in the country. The company's works in this city are located adjoining the tracks of the Erie railroad, which affords unsurpassed receiving and shipping facilities. The oils are received in bulk in tank cars from the company's refineries, located elsewhere, and are barreled here and supplied to the trade and large consumers. The accommodations for storing the products in this city are equal to the demands of a large trade, and in fact the company practically controls the supply of illuminating oils in this section, shipments being made to dealers throughout Southern New York and Northern Pennsylvania. Only the best grades of oils are handled, which are furnished at current market rates. The company is accomplishing a good work in providing the trade with the most advanced facilities for procuring oils at a minimum cost, and at the same time is adding to the prestige of the city as a leading market and source of supply for first-class products. Much of the success of the company in this market is attributable to the able and efficient services of Mr. William Mason, manager of the business here, and its future growth and development give every promise of being coeval with those of Binghamton.

SISSON BROS. & WELDEN,

Dry Goods, Carpets, Millinery, Cloaks, Etc., 59 and 61 Court Street.

There is always special interest attaching to old institutions, whether they be of national, municipal or mercantile character, and probably the most prominent of the latter class in Binghamton's business records is the old-established and extensive enterprise of Messrs. Sisson Bros. & Welden. This influential and well-known dry goods emporium, the largest enterprise of the kind in Binghamton, was founded over half a century ago by B. F. Sisson, the present firm having succeeded to the business in 1871. The premises occupied by the firm consist of a handsome four-story and basement stone front building, 50 x 100 feet in dimensions, which was erected with special reference for the business and is one of the architectural ornaments of the main thoroughfare of the city. The entire establishment is systematically divided into departments, the several floors being accessible by means of elevators. A particularly well supplied department is that of silks and dress fabrics, of which the firm carry the largest stock in this vicinity; no other firm in the Southern Tier being so large purchasers of all kinds of silks, velvets and fine dress goods. Other noteworthy departments are those devoted to laces and embroideries, cloaks, linens and housekeeping fabrics, domestic goods, ribbons, hosiery, ladies' and gentlemen's furnishings, millinery and trimmed hats, mourning goods, upholstery goods, carpets, rugs and floor cloths, etc. Every accommodation that modern business methods have rendered desirable has been provided patrons and goods are promptly delivered to all parts of the city and to trains for out-of-town customers. The patronage of the house is derived from this and the adjoining counties chiefly, and a considerable jobbing trade is also transacted with country merchants. Over one hundred clerks, salesmen and others find employment with the firm and this fact alone is an evidence of the extensive nature of the firm's business. The members of the firm are Messrs. C. F. and W. W. Sisson and J. K. Welden. The firm is represented in the Board of Trade and is always active in all matters pertaining to the growth and prosperity of the city.

HILLS, McLEAN & WILLIAMS,

Importers and Retailers of Dry Goods, Carpets, Millinery, etc., Corner Court and Chenango Streets.

An important feature of the dry goods trade of Binghamton is the house of Messrs. Hills, McLean & Williams, which in all that goes to make up a modern mercantile establishment, is surpassed either in extent of stock or quality of goods by few, if any, similar houses in the state outside of New York City. This great ladies' bazaar has been an important factor in the commercial resources of this city for the past ten years, and its facilities, resources, and trade have grown until to-day they are surpassed by those of none other in the city. Three floors of the handsome iron building at the corner of Court and Chenango streets, an illustration of which accompanies this article, are occupied. An elevator connects the several floors, and the whole is divided into numerous departments for the orderly display of the varied and comprehensive stock carried. About sixty employes here find constant occupation under the supervision of competent heads of departments, each of whom in turn is responsible to the members of the firm who personally direct all the operations of the enterprise. Visitors will find the salesrooms elegantly appointed and decorated and completely fitted up with every modern improvement that will in any way save time or facilitate the making of selections. In the retail transactions of the house the cash system is in vogue, as also the one price plan, which prove of mutual advantage to purchaser and salesman, as all goods are marked at lowest possible prices. The stock embraces a diversity simply impossible to describe in dry goods, fancy goods, carpets, draperies, lace curtains, millinery, cloaks, furs, notions, trimmings, linens and cottons, silks, velvets, ladies' and gents' furnishing goods, lingerie and bijouterie, hosiery and gloves, parasols and umbrellas, and in short every conceivable article of modern luxury, fashion and necessity that would properly be included under these general headings. The house caters to no particular class, but welcomes all and provides for all, and the establishment is truly a popular one, for it caters to the whole people. The late E. D. Hills was greatly esteemed in this community and no man in the city was more respected during life or mourned after death by those who knew his kindly heart, strict integrity and noble and true character, than was he. Since his demise his associates, Messrs. Wm. M. McLean and C. R. Williams, have actively managed the business, though his loss will be long felt both by them and the patrons of the house. The splendid success of this house may be attributed to a strict adherence to every representation made, an honest system of advertising and the provision for every want of the ladies at lowest possible prices.

THE BINGHAMTON OIL REFINING CO.,
Petroleum Products, Binghamton, N. Y. New York Office, 14 and 16 Desbrosses Street.

The Binghamton Oil Refining Co., instituted in 1872, forms an important feature of the diversified character of the industrial resources of this city, and is the only enterprise of the kind in this section. The plant is fortuitously located upon a plot of ground, triangular in shape, and surrounded on its three sides by the tracks of the railroad system of the city, which afford the most complete shipping and receiving facilities. The buildings, chiefly of brick, are several in number and are suitable for the processes of the industry, and equal to the demands of a large trade. The company are manufacturers of petroleum products, their specialties being lubricating oils and petrolina, or petroleum jelly. Illuminating oils are also produced. The crude petroleum is received by rail, in tank cars, direct from the oil wells, and is refined by what is known as the continuous process of distillation, the daily capacity of the works being about one hundred and sixty barrels of combined products. The leading feature of the products is their superior excellence, the management having never entered the race for producing low-priced goods. The result has been that their productions have become recognized as the best of their kind on the market and they are in active and growing demand by the trade throughout an annually increasing and widely extended territory. Their lubricating oils are shipped generally throughout the United States except to the Southern States, and their petrolina is in demand throughout the three Americas, Great Britain, European countries, Australia, the Sandwich Islands and South Africa. Petrolina, the name given to petroleum jelly by this company, is put up in packages of all sizes and shapes, from a two-ounce vial to a barrel. It is of particularly excellent quality and commands the appreciation of a discriminating trade. The management of the business is in the hands of Messrs. John S. Wells and Edward E. Kattell, the former being also a member of the firm of Shapley & Wells. Both gentlemen are prominently identified with the industrial progress of Binghamton, and their enterprise above briefly sketched, is creditable alike to this city and themselves.

ADDISON J. LYON,
Manufacturer and Dealer in Lumber, 16 South Street.

This enterprise was originally established about sixty years ago by Joshua Whitney and came into the proprietorship of Mr. Lyon in 1874, who is an experienced lumberman having formerly been engaged in the same business in Pennsylvania as early as 1856. The plant is located on the north bank of the Susquehanna river and covers an area of 675x170 feet, upon which are erected a series of suitable buildings used for the manufacture of lumber direct from the logs and also a complete line of planing-mill lumber. The works are equipped with all the latest improved machinery, including saws, planers, matchers, etc., are operated by water power and furnish employment to about thirty workmen. Logs are floated down the river direct from the forests and are cut up into lumber, and the products of the planing-mill embrace builders' finish, flooring, siding, etc. In connection with the mill products a full stock of all kinds of lumber is also handled, including lath, shingles, mouldings, etc., and Mr. Lyon is also agent for the sale of the celebrated Paragon plaster in this market. Adjoining the mills are large and improved dry-kilns, lumber yards, storage sheds, office building, etc. and the stock handled is such as to fill all the wants of the building trade. The products of the mill embrace hemlock, pine, oak and other kinds of lumber, and the capacity of the mill is about 10,000 feet per day.

THE BRADSTREET COMPANY,
Mercantile Agency.

The institution from which sprung the marvelous growth and prosperity of the Bradstreet Company had its origin during the remote and eventful year, 1849, its notable service to the mercantile community thus extending over this intervening period covering nearly half a century, and the lofty purposes of the organization, its practical uses, are broadly and fully comprehended and approved. Of one management, its innumerable force of employes and representatives acting in unison under a definite and effective discipline, the ramifications of the Bradstreet Company are world-wide, extending wherever within the bounds of civilization the conduct of trade is a factor, or the establishment of credit is recognized and adopted. Aside from the publication of the comprehensive volume of printed reports, the Mercantile Agency is the proprietor and publisher of "Bradstreet's", a journal devoted to the treatment and discussion of questions affecting trade, finance and political economy, whose authority in the industrial and commercial world is largely established. The Binghamton office of the Bradstreet Company is under the direction of Mr. Morris S. Lewis, Superintendent, through whose administration the office has earned its reputation for reliability and accuracy; also, the care and judgment with which it pursues the investigation of credits. Binghamton merchants largely appreciate the advantages of the Bradstreet Mercantile Agency, the majority of them subscribing for the books and reports of the company.

CORNWALL, REED & LANE,

Stock, Grain and Provision Brokers, Rooms 1 and 2 Hagaman Block.

Few people whose attention has not been called directly to the subject have any idea how extensive a business is transacted by residents of this city in the purchase and sale of stocks, bonds, grain, provisions, oil, etc., or how perfect are the facilities offered the public for this class of legitimate trading by the well known brokerage house of Cornwall, Reed & Lane. They established themselves in Binghamton March 1, 1891, and have a private wire connecting with their main offices in New York and Oil City, through means of which they are enabled to place orders for the purchase or sale of stocks, bonds, grain, provisions and oil, either on margin or for investment, with the same promptness obtainable were the customer on the floor of the several exchanges in person. To those wishing to make investments of this nature the firm offers their services, experience and judgment at the same rate of brokerage as is charged by all members of the exchanges. Full reports, quotations and information concerning and affecting home and foreign markets are received by telegraph constantly during business hours and are posted in the firm's offices for the benefit of patrons. Although so recently established in this city, the firm already enjoys the patronage of a large and constantly growing clientage, which embraces business men, capitalists and speculators. All their operations are conducted upon the most liberal and advantageous terms for patrons. Correspondence from out of town investors is solicited, to which the prompt and advanced methods of the house insure satisfaction. This enterprise has come to be recognized as a marked feature in the commercial facilities of the city, and is commended to the public as thoroughly reliable and fair dealing.

BINGHAMTON VENEER CO.,

Manufacturers of Perforated and Plain Chair Seats and Backs, 38 Commercial Avenue.

The Binghamton Veneer Co. is one of the latest additions to the manufacturing resources of this city, having been instituted in May, 1891. Notwithstanding its youth, however, it has been conducted with such energy and enterprise and upon such progressive methods as to have already acquired a large and growing trade for its products that extends generally throughout the United States. The company's facilities for manufacturing, which it is contemplated to soon increase, embrace the larger part of the building located as above indicated, which is fully equipped with all necessary tools and appliances operated by steam power, employment being given to about ten workmen. The products of the company consist of perforated and plain chair seats and backs made from veneers, and also all kinds of glued-up wood made of birch, maple, ash, oak and cherry veneers. The location of the city being in close proximity to the mills in this state and Pennsylvania, where the veneers are manufactured, enables this company to procure their raw materials upon most advantageous terms, while the central location of the city, its unexcelled shipping facilities and abundant supply of labor, combine in enabling the Binghamton Veneer Co. to offer the trade advantages in quality of goods and low prices difficult to procure elsewhere. The members of the firm are Messrs. S. Hammond, Jr., G. W. Stone, A. F. Mann and E. S. Everts, all of whom take an active interest in the management of the business. The success of the Binghamton Veneer Co. is fully assured and is well merited.

THE WHITNEY-NOYES SEED COMPANY,
Binghamton, N. Y.

Binghamton is the center of a very extensive trade in timothy and clover seeds, and is one of the leading markets of the country for both domestic and export business. This fact is largely due to the extensive enterprise of the Whitney-Noyes Seed Company. This company was incorporated in 1883, and besides dealing largely in field seeds at wholesale, conducts a special business of cleaning timothy and clover into uniform grades that in purity are unequalled. The complete separation of weed seeds involves processes so difficult, and machinery so original and various, that the grades produced by this company are properly called manufactured products, and in this view we represent this establishment among the manufacturing industries. The factory and warehouses erected by Mr. Joseph P. Noyes for the use of the company form one of the most extensive establishments in this city devoted to manufacturing purposes. The plant includes much special machinery and valuable inventions owned and used exclusively by this company. A well-equipped machine shop is maintained for the manufacture and repair of machinery, tools, etc. An excellent water privilege supplies cheaply an abundance of power (day and night when required), and this aids greatly to do the cleaning at moderate cost. The company handles great quantities of field grass seeds in carload lots, received directly from the principal growing sections of the country, and distributed to the trade in the Eastern and Middle States, and largely in Europe. Its chief specialty, however, is the production and sale of high grades of seeds, of unequalled purity and uniformity, under its own brands which have become known as indicating the highest possible excellence in field grass seeds, and are now so accepted by the trade and consumers. Until the institution of this company's business, it was not possible to procure in any market timothy or clover seed that was freed from weed seeds. All timothy and clover seeds, as generally sold, whether called "Prime," "Choice," or "Fancy Re-cleaned," are more or less foul with weed seeds and other waste. The use of impure seeds causes great loss to the farmer, not only in the cost of that which is of no value, but still more by the propagation of weeds which injure the value of his product and exhaust his land. The high grades of this company are not simply selections from occasional lots, but are special products upon which its extensive and annually increasing business has been established. These seeds are also sold at reasonable prices, and while of necessity they cost more than seeds containing a large proportion of weed seeds and waste, they are, in fact, much cheaper than usual qualities. The increased cost to the farmer in sowing the best seeds amounts to only about five cents per year per acre, while the value of the crop is increased from 25 to 50 per cent. This company's methods are the first and only ones that have ever secured the same results, and those who have used its grades of timothy and clover have in every instance experienced the advantages of pure seeds. This company believes that its products are absolutely unequalled in the world; that "the best goods are cheapest;" that "there is room at the top," and it proposes to earn its money and to command increasingly the patronage of the most intelligent buyers of seeds. Binghamton possesses great advantages as a favorable location for the prosecution of an enterprise of this character, and with its trunk line railways, reaching out into every part of the great West, the seeds of all producing sections are naturally shipped here and distributed to consumers in the most direct and favorable way. Dealers requiring carloads of assorted kinds can find no other market where equal advantages are obtainable. See map page 2.

B. H. NELSON & SON,
Private Bankers, Nelson Block.

Binghamton, highly favored in many ways, is no more so than in the number and high character of her financial institutions. One of the most recent additions to her banking interests is the private banking house of Messrs. B. H. Nelson & Son, which is the only bank located on the north side of the city and is the only enterprise in the city embracing all that the caption of this article implies. It was instituted January 1, 1890, by Mr. B. H. Nelson and his son, Mr. George R. Nelson, the senior member of the firm having been for a number of years previously actively engaged in the wholesale fruit business. The firm enjoys every facility for covering each branch of their business and they already enjoy the distinction of being among the most prominent private bankers, underwriters and real estate agents of the city. In the banking department a legitimate business is done. Deposits are received, payable on demand, commercial paper is discounted, collections are made at all points and foreign and domestic exchange is bought and sold. The principal correspondents of the bank are the Seaboard National Bank and the Western National Bank of New York City, and through these, banks in all parts of the Union are reached. In the insurance department fire policies only are issued and the risks covered by the most staple insurance companies doing business in this State; they include the North British and Mercantile Ins. Co. of London and Edinburgh, Eagle Fire Ins. Co. of New York, the Jersey City Insurance Co. and the United States Insurance Co. In real estate the firm buy, sell and exchange real property of all kinds, and now have on their books many choice central and suburban improved properties, as well as vacant lots for all purposes. Mr. B. H. Nelson is also a director of the Merchants' Bank of this city; he is an esteemed citizen, prominently identified with the growth and prosperity of Binghamton and a member of the Board of Trade. The enterprise the firm are conducting is an important convenience to its own immediate locality as well as prominent factor of the commercial and industrial advancement of the whole community. The handsomely appointed offices of the firm, located on the ground floor of the Nelson Block, are conveniently arranged for the business and the bank enjoys the esteem and consideration of a large and growing list of customers, who number many of the prominent manufacturers, merchants and capitalists of this thriving city.

SOMETHING FOR BOARDS OF TRADE, A USEFUL BOOK.
By F. Newell Gilbert.

Under the comprehensive title of "Forms and Laws for the Organization and Successful Management in every State and the Dominion of Canada, of Boards of Trade, Village Improvement Societies, Business Men's Associations and Chambers of Commerce," Mr. F. Newell Gilbert, Secretary of the Binghamton, N. Y. Board of Trade, and attorney-at-law, has published a most useful book with separate supplement, which contain a vast amount of information, which make the books invaluable for the organizations above named as well as for every business man. The books contain various forms and styles of attractive advertising matter used by associations in the East, West and South, a list of manufacturers who are considering a change of location, inducements offered by cities to manufacturers, plans for model factory, plans for opera house, lists of prominent architects, prominent manufacturers of fire department supplies, bridges, road machines, contractors for paving and sewerage, etc., and much other matter that will be found useful to all city and village associations of whatsoever character. The books are forwarded by mail to address upon receipt of one dollar, by the publisher, F. Newell Gilbert, Secretary Binghamton Board of Trade, Binghamton, N. Y.

HANRAHAN BROS.,
Wholesale Dealers in Wines and Liquors, 168 Washington St.

An important and growing factor of the wholesale trade of Binghamton is the enterprise of Messrs. Hanrahan Bros., which from its inception has been recognized as headquarters for fine wines and liquors. The firm occupy commodious premises where they carry a large and carefully selected stock of fine American and foreign wines and liquors, embracing brandies, rums, gins, whiskies, and sweet and dry wines from the most celebrated manufacturers of the old and new worlds. The firm are agents for H. H. Shufeldts & Co.'s standard gins and whiskies, the Hannis Distilling Co.'s Mount Vernon Distillery, and Moore & Sinnott's Gibson and Excelsior rye whiskies, which are well known to the trade and consumers as being the best in the market. American whiskies are also kept in store in the bonded warehouses in the states where manufactured, and are sold either free or in bond, and are withdrawn as the exigencies of the trade demand. All goods are procured direct from manufacturers and first hands and are offered to the trade at lowest prices compatible with quality. The trade of the house extends throughout a large part of New York and Pennsylvania and is annually increasing in volume. The members of the firm are Messrs. Edward M. and James L. Hanrahan, both progressive business men and closely identified with the growth of the commercial resources of Binghamton.

BUNDY MANUFACTURING COMPANY,
Manufacturers of Time Recorders and Watchmen's Clocks, 40 Commercial Avenue.

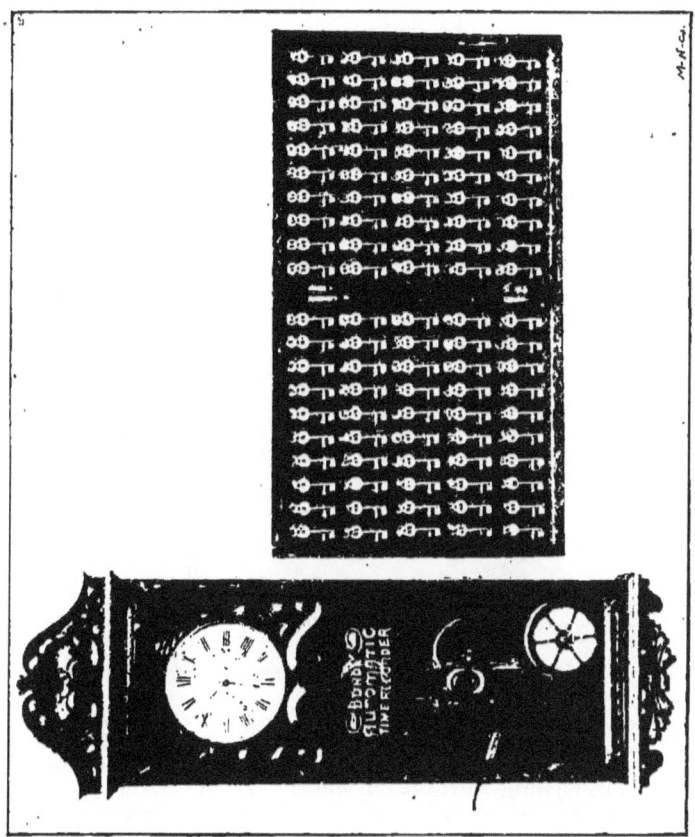

A recent acquisition to the manufacturing facilities of Binghamton and one altogether distinct from other industries here is that of the Bundy Manufacturing Company, which was incorporated in 1889 for the purpose of manufacturing the celebrated automatic workmen's time recorders, the Auburn watchmen's clock and fire alarm and other mechanical devices for automatically recording various matters. The officers of the company are Messrs. George E. Green, prest., J. P. Fiebig, vice-prest., Harlow E. Bundy, treas. and manager, A. Ward Ford, sec'y, and W. L. Bundy, supt. the latter also being the inventor of the company's specialties. The Bundy automatic time recorder is a simple, accurate and economical mechanical device by means of which a record is made, in a permanent printed form, of the hour and minute at which persons arrive and depart in the morning, at meal times, or at any time, day or night. It is invaluable in factories, shops, stores and, in fact, every establishment where men's time is required to be noted. By the use of the Bundy automatic recorder no time-keeper is required since every man is his own time-keeper, no errors can be made in booking time, no disputes can occurr as to accuracy, no jealousy is possible between time-keepers and employes, neither can there be collusion between them and there is no expense for time-keepers' salary. The machine is perfectly made, is durable, the number of times in which it will make the register being practicably illimitable. The machine has met with great favor both with employers and employes and is now in daily use by hundreds of prominent business houses in all parts of the country, a list of which, to whom reference is made, will be forwarded to anyone desiring to investigate the practical workings and advantages of the recorder. Another specialty of the company is the "Auburn" watchmen's register and fire alarm, which is indorsed by fire insurance companies and boards of underwriters and is the only system combining a watchman's detector, fire alarm, with and without the thermostat system and superintendent's alarm. This register besides showing on a paper dial whether the watchman has performed his duties, also is furnished with an attachment which will ring a bell in the house of the proprietor or superintendent, should the watchman neglect for any cause to start on his rounds at five, ten or any desired number of minutes after the hour. The company are also about introducing another new electrical watchman's clock, which will embody several new and desirable features. Their products are daily growing in demand in the United States where they are everywhere recognized as the perfection of simplicity, efficiency and economy, and they are also about introducing them into Australia.

HIRSCHMANN BROTHERS,

Importers and Dealers in Dry Goods, Millinery, Fancy Goods, Cloaks, Etc., 15 and 17 Court Street.

This enterprise was founded in 1858, and has occupied its present extensive premises since 1865. While exceeded in age by one other similar establishment in Binghamton, it may well lay claim to being the first to afford the public of this city and vicinity with those modern facilities and advantages which are now recognized as necessary by all progressive emporiums of this character. In 1865 the continued growth of their business necessitated more room than was then at their disposal and their present extensive quarters were arranged for their occupancy. The premises consist of three floors, each 66x200 feet in dimensions, affording a total floorage area of 40,000 square feet. The whole establishment is conveniently arranged, handsomely appointed and supplied with all modern improvements. The stock embraces literally everything in the way of ladies' goods, dry goods, fancy goods, underwear, hosiery, cloaks, men's furnishings, laces, lingueric, housekeeping linens and cottons, toilet articles, notions, millinery, etc. The patronage of the house is derived from the city and towns and villages in Southern New York and Northern Pennsylvania, and prompt attention is given to mail orders, inquiries answered and prices quoted. The magnificent show windows of the house, on the main thoroughfare of the city, are a most prominent feature of the business enterprise of the firm, and attract the attention of both residents and strangers. The firm is represented on the board of directors of the Board of Trade and is always active in all matters pertaining to the growth and prosperity of the city.

CALLAHAN & DOUGLAS,
Hardware, 55 Court St.

A prominent representative of the trade facilities of Binghamton is the hardware house of Messrs. Callahan & Douglas, which was established in 1889, and has since built up a large and annually increasing trade, which gives ample promise for greater growth in the future. The premises utilized are comprised in a commodious and centrally located store and basement, with an ample warehouse in the rear for storing surplus and heavy stock. The facilities possessed by the firm enable them to offer the best inducements to the public, and the experienced knowledge of the proprietors with the wants of the market insures the handling of a class of goods which gives general satisfaction. The firm enjoy intimate relations with manufacturers, importers and first hands, and the favorable terms secured, owing to large operations, combine to enable the firm to offer the best goods at the lowest prices. The stock includes everything in the way of builders' and shelf hardware, mechanics' tools, house furnishing goods, etc., and a specialty is made of fine cutlery and mechanics' tools in which departments the variety carried is unusually large and attractive. The business policy of the house is based upon enterprise, liberality and fair dealing, and relations formed with it are sure to prove advantageous. The members of the firm are Messrs. J. H. Callahan and J. J. Douglas, both young men who are determined to gain patronage by all honorable methods, and by conserving the interests of their customers in all available ways.

CORNELL, DAVIS & SHEAR,
Grocers, 250 Chenango Street.

The widely recognized leaders in the grocery trade of the North Side are Messrs. Cornell, Davis & Shear, whose handsomely appointed and attractively furnished establishment is a model of system and order and veritable gold mine of good things in the way of family table supplies and delicacies. That it pays to be enterprising and progressive is evidenced by the growth of this firm's business, which bids fair to distance those of all rivals in amount of sales, as it already has done in advanced methods. This house was founded in 1879 by Cornell & Davis, the present firm succeeding in April, 1891, at which date they first occupied the present commodious store, and since which time they have largely increased their trade as well as the scope of their operations. Their establishment now is in all respects the equal of the most advanced metropolitan groceries. The store and basement, each 100 feet deep, are completely filled with an endless variety of the best goods in the market, and embrace many articles which can be obtained in perfection here only. They make a specialty of fine teas and coffees, canned goods, flour, salt meats, sugar and molasses and fresh baker's supplies, while in staple and fancy goods they carry everything known to the trade and goods from every clime and every country. As for the prices, they are absolutely as low as it is possible to make them, and in many cases the best quality of goods are sold at a less price than inferior goods are furnished for by others. An inspection of the store and stock will be found advantageous to all, whether in search of value for money or choice goods. The aim of the firm has always been to merit patronage by giving customers the greatest inducements in prices, quality of goods and prompt service, and that they have succeeded none will doubt who once enter their attractive store.

BINGHAMTON CUTLERY CO.,
**Manufacturers of Pocket Cutlery, and Importers of Fine Razors,
Office, 215 Washington Street.**

This enterprise was originally instituted at Richmond, Ind., about eight years ago, and was removed to this city in 1888. The products of the company embrace an almost unlimited number of styles, sizes and kinds of pocket knives, which under the stamp, "The Very Best," fully vindicate the claims of the maker by their uniform high quality. The aim of the company has always been to produce the best goods in the market, goods for all purposes and for everybody. All their products are made throughout by experienced workmen, and the blades are hand-forged from Wardlow's English steel, which is everywhere recognized as the best steel produced in the world for cutlery. The knife blades are all finely edged and ready for use, and are warranted to be exactly as represented or money will be refunded. The company puts up everything in the way of pocket cutlery, and also handles at wholesale fine razors of their own importation. They are also headquarters for the Ohio Co-operative Shear Company, whose products they supply to the trade at manufacturers' prices. The trade of the house extends throughout a large section of New York and Pennsylvania, and in the Western States generally, and is annually increasing in volume. The Binghamton Cutlery Company is fully abreast of the times in all that could add to the high quality of, their products or tend to decrease the cost of production, and the trade will find upon entering into business relations with it that advantages will accrue difficult to procure elsewhere. Mr. J. M. Hanford, the enterprising proprietor of the establishment, is an expert in the production of fine cutlery, and is well and widely known to the trade as a progressive and fair dealing business man.

BENNETT MANUFACTURING CO.,
**Manufacturers of Overalls, Fine Woolen Shirts, Pants, Etc.,
174 and 176 Water Street.**

The Bennett Manufacturing Company was instituted in 1884, and since the death of its founder, Mr. Abel Bennett, in 1890, has been conducted under the active management of Mr. Fred. Bennett, the surviving partner. The manufacturing plant is comprised in a five-story brick building 44 x 100 feet in dimensions, and is equipped with about 150 sewing machines, and all other appliances for the economical production of superior goods. About two hundred operatives are furnished employment in the factory and an 80-horse power steam engine furnishes the motive force for the mechanical equipment. The products of the house consist of overalls, fine woolen shirts, pants, sack coats, etc., which are made from the best materials by careful workmen, and are everywhere recognized by the trade as being unsurpassed for quality, finish, style, durability and general excellence. The company's trade extends to all parts of the United States and is annually increasing in volume. About 1,000 dozen garments are produced weekly. The enterprise is a prominent factor in the general thrift of this community.

CHARLES W. SEARS,
Books, Stationery and Paper Hangings, 51 Court Street.

The oldest book-store, as well as the most prominent, in Binghamton, is that of Charles W. Sears, which was originally founded as long ago as 1840, the present proprietor having been connected with its management since 1855, and in sole control since 1863. The premises occupied are centrally located, commodious, and well adapted for the transaction of a very extensive business. The stock embraces all the new books from the leading American and English publishers, and covers every department of literature, history, science, biography, poetry, travel, fiction, theology, mechanics, agriculture, and in fact every subject to be found in a first-class book-store. Rare old books, French and German literature, are also to be found here, as well as school books, bibles, hymnals, blank books, fine stationery and periodical literature of all descriptions. A special department is devoted to paper hanging, and this stock includes a large variety of wall papers and mural decorations, from the cheapest grades to the most elaborate and expensive imported goods. In these days of rapid printing, no single establishment in the world could carry copies of all publications, but any book or periodical not in stock at this store will be promptly procured and supplied at publisher's price. Mr. Sears has always conducted the business with energy and discriminating judgment and the success he has attained is as well merited as it is prominent.

BINGHAMTON DAIRY ASSOCIATION,
Dealers in Dairy Products, 70 State St.

The Binghamton Dairy Association was incorporated April 1, 1891, with a capital stock of $25,000, for the purpose of supplying the residents of Binghamton and vicinity with pure and unadulterated dairy products of the best quality and at prices that would command attention for fairness and liberality. The stock of the association is taken by producers of milk in this vicinity, who thus find a steady and increasing outlet for their products at market prices, and the profits upon the sale direct to the consumer is thus returned to them instead of being monopolized by middlemen, while the public is benefitted by the assured high quality and purity of the milk obtained. The association now occupies the store and basement, located as above indicated, as the headquarters of the business. The equipment embraces an elevator for handling the milk cans, coolers for milk, separator for cream, churns, etc., which are operated by a 15-horse power steam engine, employment being furnished to seventeen assistants in the several departments as well as to a number of horses for delivery purposes. The association receives large quantities of milk daily from the stockholders, which is supplied to customers in all parts of the city, the surplus being made into fine dairy butter. The efforts of the association have met with prompt appreciation from the community and its success has been an assured one from its inception, so much so that already a plot of ground at 98 Washington street has been purchased, upon the rear of which has been built a brick barn two-story and basement, 95 feet long and 53 feet wide, and an ice-house adjoining large enough to supply an abundance of ice, and it is contemplated to soon erect a large block on the Washington street front suitable for the purposes of the business. The officers of the association are Messrs. P. H. Shafer, president; James D. Blakeslee, vice-president; J. E. Rogers, secretary and treasurer, and R. W. Wright, superintendent, to whose earnest efforts and able management the credit for the establishment and success of the enterprise is largely due.

EBBLIE & RIDER,
Jobbers of 5 and 10 Cent Goods, 84 Court and 105 Collier Streets.

Improvements in machinery and methods of manufacture of late years have resulted in the production of almost endless numbers of small and large articles of use, ornament and necessity in the household at such prices as place them within the reach of all, and great enterprises have grown up devoted to their collection and sale, which have come to be known as five and ten-cent stores. Binghamton is not behind her sister cities in the possession of a well equipped enterprise of this character. Messrs. Ebblie & Rider opened their five and ten-cent store here in August last, and have commodious premises fronting on two streets, where they carry a large and complete stock, embracing a multitudinous variety of articles, and covering nearly every line of goods manufactured. The chief specialties are household utensils and ornaments, and the housekeeper will find here many articles indispensable in the house at prices impossible to be obtained elsewhere. The firm enjoy a large and increasing patronage, and they also do a considerable jobbing trade. New goods and novelties are constantly being received, and it is really a wonder what handsome and useful things may be obtained here for the nominal prices of five or ten cents.

GEORGE L. PARKER,
Dealer in Lehigh Valley Coal. Office, 9 Ross Building; Yard 39 Liberty St.

This is one of the leading establishments in the city in the coal trade. The yard at Liberty street on the Erie railroad, has the best improved facilities for receiving, storing, handling and delivering the "black diamonds." Trains of cars are run onto the trestle under cover and the contents of the cars are dumped directly into pockets under each car, each size in the proper place; wagons are backed under the pockets, and the coal, passing over screens, is ready for the consumer. Mr. Parker is the only dealer in the city who is supplied by the Lehigh Valley Coal Company, or to whom their product is shipped, so he controls the sale of the famous "L. V.," and is assured that the rapidly increasing business he has is because he sells only "the Brightest, the Cleanest, the Best." He introduced, and has, the only coal yard in Binghamton that delivers with the Eureka wagon, which unloads without shoveling, thereby saving time and avoiding much of the usual noise and breakage. Those who deal with Mr. Parker always find that he takes the greatest care to deliver orders promptly and in good order, and furnishes the best coal in quality, size and preparation. His office in the Ross building is very central, and with his telephone, 305 there, and 252 at the yard office, those wishing to purchase coal of him will find it a very convenient matter.

C. M. CLAPP,
Wholesale and Retail Dealer in Boots, Shoes and Rubbers, 37 Court Street.

The most prominent retail shoe store in Binghamton is that of Mr. C. M. Clapp, which also transacts an extensive wholesale trade that extends throughout a considerable part of New York and Massachusetts. This house was founded in 1879, and at one time combined manufacturing with the other departments of the business; this, however, has been discontinued of late. The stock carried is the largest of the kind in the city, and embraces the very finest grades of shoes for men, women and children that are manufactured, as well as a general line of serviceable goods for the masses. All goods are procured direct from the manufacturers and in large quantities, many lines being made to order expressly for the trade of the house, and by reason of its large transactions the lowest possible prices prevail in all cases. Equal inducements are also afforded dealers, chief among which may be mentioned the fact that from this stock sizes may be sorted up without waiting for goods to be made, and orders are filled with promptness, whether for large or small quantities. The house is well known to retail buyers as a leader in fashions, and its success is as well merited as it is pronounced.

MORGAN, AINSWORTH & CARROLL,
Real Estate and Insurance, 120 State St. Room 16.

The recently organized firm of Morgan, Ainsworth & Carroll is the direct successor of the old-established insurance agency founded in 1846 by S. H. Hall. Mr. Julius P. Morgan, the head of the firm, has been engaged in the business since 1861, and the other two members were formerly in partnership together in a similar enterprise. The combination of the two agencies brings to the new firm a list of insurance organizations that cannot be excelled for strength, reliability and honorable dealing. The transactions of the office also cover all branches of the real estate business, including purchase, sale, lease and exchange of business and residence properties, vacant city lots, tracts, farms, etc. They control the sale of the J. E. Ely tract, situated in the East End, and also have a number of choice lots in a tract at Rossville, as well as others in various sections of the city. The companies represented embrace the Home of New York, Connecticut of Hartford, Lancashire of Manchester, British American of Toronto, Phœnix of Brooklyn, Niagara of New York, Queen of Liverpool, Northern of London, Scottish Union & National of Edinburgh, Lion Fire of London, Orient of Hartford, Dutchess County Mutual of Poughkeepsie, Williamsburgh City of Brooklyn, Traders' of Chicago, Westchester of New York, New York Bowery of New York and Fidelity & Casualty of New York. The above list may be said to represent many millions of dollars which stand ready to indemnify the firm's clients from loss, and the prompt adjustment of every honest claim is characteristic of their business policy. The members of the firm are Messrs. Julius P. Morgan, Albert A. Ainsworth and Louis A. Carroll, all pushing business men and well qualified for the successful maintenance of their enterprise.

JUDSON S. NEWING,
Manufacturing Jeweler and Optician, 138 Court Street.

Ever since the inception of this enterprise, in 1881, it has enjoyed a high reputation for artistic work, and acquired a trade that extends throughout Southern New York and Northern Pennsylvania, and is annually increasing in volume. A commodious and handsomely appointed store is occupied as salesroom, with another floor for manufacturing purposes. The latter is fully equipped with all necessary tools, machinery and appliances and furnishes employment for from six to ten skilled workmen. In the salesroom a department for optical goods is an important feature, and Mr. Newing is an expert and skillful optician. He also carries a fine and well selected stock of jewelry, watches and clocks which are offered to the public at lowest prices. In the manufacturing department, the products consist chiefly of badges, emblems, jewels for societies and secret orders, presentation medals and memorials and jewelry of special design to order, mounting and setting diamonds, and other precious stones and general repairing. A most enviable reputation for high-class and artistic work, promptness and reliability has been attained, which bids fair to continue to expand with the growth of the industrial resources of this city.

LOWELL HARDING & SON,
Buyers of Hides, Skins, Raw Furs and Tallow, 200 Water St.

One of the commercial landmarks of this city is the above mentioned enterprise, which for over half a century has contributed greatly to the wealth and reputation of Binghamton. It was founded in 1836 at Albion, Mich., Mr. Harding, Sr., removing to this city in May, 1839, since which time it has been continuously conducted by Mr. Harding and his sons, Theodore and George L. Harding, the former having been associated with his father from 1868 to 1876, the latter having been admitted to an interest in the business during the present year. The premises occupied for the business are embraced in one of the most complete and convenient establishments of its kind in the country. It is a handsome four-story and basement building 22x100 feet in dimensions, erected in 1891 and owned by Mr. L. Harding. The operations of the house embrace the collection and purchase of hides and skins of all kinds, raw furs and tallow, which are procured from the producing centers of the country and are shipped to the trade in Boston, New York, Philadelphia, Buffalo and Trenton chiefly. The highest market cash prices are paid for anything in these lines and consignments from merchants and others are solicited. Mr. George L. Harding attends to all buying of goods on the road and covers a large territory, transacting an annual business that would do credit to much larger cities. In the buying and handling of raw furs, this house stands among the largest and best known in the state.

WILLIAM H. MOSHER,
Fine Family Groceries, 42 Court Street.

A visit to the popular and centrally located grocery store of Mr. William H. Mosher will develop the fact that the residents of Binghamton and vicinity are here provided with advantages for procuring the choicest food supplies, equal to those offered the public in metropolitan centers. This house was founded in 1863 and has always been recognized as a leader in its line. The stock is particularly desirable, choice and varied, and a specialty is made of handling fine and rare goods. It includes the finest delicacies from all parts of the United States and many foreign lands, such as olives from Spain, sardines from France, cheese from Holland and England, condiments and sauces from Great Britain, and in fact all sorts and descriptions of delicious and tempting delicacies, pickled and potted meats, canned goods, mustards, curries, preserves, etc., that will tempt a sated appetite or please a normal one. In domestic products, the stock embraces everything in the way of staple and fancy groceries demanded by a first-class trade, and it will be found that if the best goods and reasonable prices are wanted, they can be obtained of this old-established and well-known house in perfection. The trade of the house is among the best families of the city and is constantly increasing in volume. The house has attained a high rank in the trade conveniences of the city, and its success and prominence is well merited.

A. S. PATTEN & BROTHER,
Dealers in Provisions, 158 and 160 Washington Street.

The enterprise of Messrs. A. S. Patten & Brother was established in 1868 by A. S. Patten; the present firm, composed of the founder and Mr. W. E. Patten, having been organized in 1875. The premises occupied as headquarters for the business are embraced in a four-story building 32x70 feet in dimensions. The ground floor is used as the retail salesroom and is attractively and handsomely fitted up and furnished, forming a marked and agreeable contrast to many other places used for a similar purpose. Here everything has been provided that could in any way add to the high character of the food supplies handled or would tend to absolute cleanliness in handling them. A ten-ton Hendrick Pontifex refrigerating machine, which gives an absolute cold, dry air to all their cooling rooms, is one of the conveniences, and every part of the establishment has an air of complete neatness and orderly system. The upper floors are used for storage and packing purposes and for curing hams. The firm deal in all kinds of fresh and salt meats, beef, pork, lamb, mutton, hams, lard, sausages, poultry and game in season. Only the best qualities of provisions are furnished patrons and the high reputation of the firm has resulted in a large and important trade, embracing the principal hotels and restaurants and largely with private families in all parts of the city, prompt deliveries being a feature of the business.

W. J. CARVER,
Dairy Products, 7 Main Street.

An important feature of the trade accommodations of this city is the milk depot of W. J. Carver, which he instituted in 1885, and has since conducted with annually increasing trade and influence. The headquarters of the business are embraced in two floors, each 25x75 feet in dimensions, which are fully equipped with late improved appliances and apparatus for the successful conduct of the business, and the equipment includes creameries, separators, churns, etc. The business is both wholesale and retail in character, and four wagons are kept constantly in commission, three of which supply retail customers and one supplies the wholesale trade. The products handled consist of pure milk and cream, buttermilk and creamery butter, which are furnished to customers fresh daily. Only absolutely pure milk is handled, and the relations of the house with producers are such that an almost unlimited demand can be supplied. The surplus stock is made into butter, of which about twelve tons annually are manufactured, six tons being supplied to city customers, and the balance being disposed of in New York. No articles of food are so universally appreciated when fresh and pure as milk and butter, and the public may feel certain that those procured at this establishment are up to the highest possible standard.

HUMES & SMITH,
Fine Groceries, Main Street.

Wilkinson Brothers' Block, Corner Main and Front Streets.

This enterprise was founded in 1886, and so great, indeed, is its trade as to make its operations wholesale in character though supplying the trade at retail. The premises now occupied by the firm are at the southeast corner of Main and Front street, but upon the completion of the new Wilkinson block on the opposite corner, the business will be removed there, where increased room and accommodations will be afforded. The stock is of the finest selection and includes choice teas, coffees, spices, condiments and sauces, table delicacies, domestic and imported canned goods, pickles, preserves, potted meats and game, and in fact, everything in these lines of the best and most celebrated manufacture. A specialty is made in the firm's Delmonico blend coffee, which is in increasing and popular demand, and all their coffees are warranted the very best that money can buy, and they are fresh roasted every week. Other specialties are Maud S. flour, which is confidently recommended as unsurpassed, Miss Larrabee's celebrated home-made cookies, fresh every day, and C. P. Ball's celebrated Excelsior creamery butter in five pound packages. The trade of the house extends throughout the county, and so marked and steady has been its growth that it is entitled to be numbered among the leading concerns of the kind in the State. The members of the firm, Messrs. E. M. Humes and M. S. Smith are both progressive merchants and popular citizens.

LEWIS HOUSE,
William Shanley, Proprietor, Prospect Ave. cor. Lewis St.

The Lewis House has long been recognized as one of the best two-dollar-a-day hotels in New York state, and in fact it is not surpassed in any essential characteristic by any other hotel wheresoever located. It is conveniently and pleasantly situated but a few steps distant from the passenger stations of the railroads centering here, and is in close proximity to the business center of the city. Having a frontage on three streets, every room in the building is light and airy, and its spacious piazzas become a favorite resting place during the summer months, for the guests of the house in the cool of the evening at the close of a hot day. The hotel is heated by steam and lighted by gas and electricity, and the sanitary arrangements are constructed after the most modern and improved methods, making the hotel one of the best drained and most healthful in the city. The office and dining room are on the ground floor, and the rooms for guests, of which there are about one hundred, are tastefully and handsomely furnished and are comfortable and cheerful sleeping apartments. As regards the cuisine, we can only say that it is fully up to the standard of modern first-class hotels, along with the additional advantages often unattainable in great cities—of an abundance of pure dairy products and fresh fruits and vegetables, which are obtained from the near-by farms and dairies, for which Broome county is widely noted. For accommodation of commercial travelers who prefer it, a large and light room on the main street of the city is provided for use as a sample room. Mr. William Shanley, the proprietor, has a large and pleasant acquaintance with the traveling public, and his hotel is always full during the season.

GEORGE W. BEARDSLEY,
Dealer in Leather and Findings, Etc., 150 State Street.

A leading and recently instituted accession to the general trade conveniences of Binghamton is the enterprise of Mr. George W. Beardsley. This house is conveniently located and well arranged for supplying the trade with everything required in leather and shoe findings, and the stock which is large, complete and well selected, embraces cut stock, boot and shoe uppers, harness leather, shoe-makers' and harness maker's tools, etc. All goods are procured direct from manufacturers and first hands, and are offered to the trade at lowest prices. The trade of the house extends throughout Southern New York and Northern Pennsylvania and gives every promise of continued and rapid increase. Mr. Beardsley is an experienced man at the business, is progressive and enterprising, and is providing his customers with the most advanced facilities for procuring the best goods at lowest prices. The enterprise is an important one and we commend it to the trade with the assurance that relations with it will prove advantageous in all respects.

FOLSOM & HUNGERFORD,
Stoves, Ranges and Furnaces, 125 Washington Street.

Among the large, well-conducted and prosperous mercantile enterprises of Binghamton will be found that of Messrs. Folsom & Hungerford, which was originally founded in 1884 by F. P. Costello, the present firm, composed of Messrs. R. W. Folsom and A. E. Hungerford, having been organized in 1890. The commodious premises are comprised in a store and basement, each 25x125 feet in dimensions, which afford ample accommodations for the display of a large and complete stock, which embraces the latest improved stoves, ranges and a full line of Carton furnaces, and tinware and kitchen furnishing goods generally. The firm furnish estimates for furnace work, and execute all contracts in a first-class manner. They also do a general jobbing business in tin, sheet-iron and copper work, tin roofing, etc., for which they are fully prepared with all necessary facilities, skilled workmen and materials. All goods are procured direct and are offered at bottom prices. The trade of the house extends throughout the neighboring country and is annually increasing in volume, and the business policy and reliability of the firm are such as to insure satisfaction to all who may require their services or goods.

GOLDSTEIN BROS.,
Clothiers and Custom Tailors, 43 Court St., Branch Store, 215 Chenango St.

The above named house is fully entitled to be classed among the most enterprising and the most reliable of the retail establishments of Binghamton. The business was originally instituted in 1886, upon a modest scale, and from its inception it grew and expanded until enlarged quarters were demanded, and the present handsomely appointed and commodious store was occupied, which has already come to be recognized as headquarters for fine tailor-made clothing in Binghamton. The firm carry a large stock of ready-made clothing, hats, caps, and gents' furnishing goods, and they also make fine clothing to order, for which they display foreign and domestic suitings in large variety. Only such garments are handled as will withstand legitimate wear and will, after lengthened use, still appear as when new. In fact, the clothing handled by the firm is strictly tailor-made, and is really different from custom made in nothing except the price, which is very much less. From their stock a gentleman can procure garments perfect in style, quality of material, fit and finish, and as such they are guaranteed. To those who are more notional, they offer their services in their custom tailoring department, guaranteeing perfection and reasonable prices. The members of the firm, Messrs. Jacob and Samuel Goldstein, are both progressive business men and esteemed citizens, and the success they have attained is both creditable to themselves and gratifying to this community of which they are honorable members.

O. B. MARSH,
Jewelry, Watches, Diamonds, Etc., 56 Court Street.

An important feature of the trade accommodations of Binghamton is the jewelry establishment of Mr. O. B. Marsh, which is representative of the highest skill in the art, and its reputation for fair dealing and honorable methods stands on no lower plane than that of the first in the land. Mr. Marsh is probably the oldest practical jeweler and watchmaker in Binghamton and is one of the most skillful in the country. He was the first man in the Waltham Watch Company at Roxbury, Mass., and still possesses the first watch made at that factory.

He carried on the jewelry business at Newark, N. J., for thirty years and established his enterprise in this city in 1876. The elaborately ornamented and perfectly finished marble clock which attracts the attention of all who pass the show windows of his store was entirely made by him and is as perfect an example of horological skill as was ever produced either in this country or abroad. At the handsomely appointed salesrooms is shown a magnificent collection of fine watches, clocks, jewelry, diamonds and precious stones, silverware, etc., all of which are offered at reasonable prices and are warranted exactly as represented. A specialty is made of fine watch repairing as well as other services incident to the trade, and watches are adjusted to heat and cold and rated in position and warranted. The house enjoys a wide spread patronage among the most discriminating of this community.

J. C. CORNELL & SON,
Furnishing Funeral Directors, Office and Warerooms, 240 Chenango Street.

It is only within a comparatively few years that any apparent progress has been made in the custom for the burial of the dead, and it is wholly due to the refinement of the present age that the occupation of the funeral director has risen from a trade to the dignity of a profession. In connection with these facts special attention is directed to the prominent funeral furnishing house of Messrs. J. C. Cornell & Son. This firm occupy well appointed premises, comprising office, ware-rooms and work-shop, and here may be seen samples of the latest designs in caskets and burial cases, as well as all other necessary goods to meet with the requirements of all classes of patrons. The firm are prepared to take full charge of funerals and the burial of the dead, furnishing everything that may be required, casket, shroud, hearse, carriages, mourning for pall-bearers, etc., and to conduct the funeral with decorum, and thus entirely relieve friends of any responsibility. The peculiar calling of the funeral director requires a sympathetic nature and a due regard and respect for its difficult duties. Both members of this firm, Messrs. J. C. and W. T. Cornell are endowed with all the traits needed in this vocation, and have ever given the greatest satisfaction to patrons. The relatives of the dead can safely leave everything to their care at a time when of a surety, their minds could not be troubled with sad details.

F. H. ROGERS,
Stationery, Wall Paper, Periodicals, Etc., 213 Chenango Street.

This enterprise, which is the only one of any considerable importance of its kind on the North Side, was instituted in 1884 by W. L. Mudge, the present proprietor having succeeded to the business September 1, 1891. The premises occupied are embraced in a commodious and attractively appointed corner store and contain a large and complete stock of fine stationery for all purposes, blank books, autograph and photograph albums, periodicals, newspapers, etc., as well as wall paper, window shades and fixtures, etc. In paper hangings the house does both a wholesale and retail business and the stock is particularly large and varied. It includes all kinds from the cheapest to the most expensive and of both foreign and American production, and the prices named are as low as goods of equal quality can be procured anywhere. The trade of the house is not confined to its immediate locality, but extends throughout the city and surrounding country and is annually increasing in volume. Mr. Rogers brings to the enterprise a complete knowledge and experience of all its details and the well-established representation of the house for honorable methods will not only be maintained in the future but augmented in every available manner.

MATTHEW O'NEIL,
Stoves, Furnaces and Ranges, Etc., 18 Ferry Street.

This enterprise was instituted in 1869 and occupies commodious premises, consisting of a two-story and basement building 18x70 feet in dimensions, where is displayed one of the largest and most attractive stocks of stoves and ranges to be found in the State. Mr. O'Neil is sole agent in this market for Rathbone, Sard & Co.'s Acme square parlor stoves and ranges, which are everywhere recognized as the most beautiful and most improved stoves in the market. A general jobbing and repairing business is also transacted in tin, copper and sheet iron work, for which all necessary facilities are available. The stock also embraces a general line of kitchen tinware and utensils, all of which are offered at lowest prices. The house offers customers the advantages of a large stock to select from and low prices, by reason of smaller expenses of selling than is possible for similar establishments located on the main streets, while the high-class goods are the best in the world.

J. F. BISHOP,
Cabinet Maker, 20 Lewis Street.

The wood-working enterprise of Mr. J. F. Bishop is an important feature of the manufacturing facilities of Binghamton, and ever since its inception has enjoyed a growing patronage. The plant is embraced in a two-story building which is equipped with a steam engine and all necessary wood-working machinery, employment being furnished to a force of skilled workmen. The products consist of a general line of fine and fancy cabinet work, hard-wood mantels, store fixtures, stair-work, newels, balusters, railings, and all kinds of wood-turning. Mr. Bishop undertakes the manufacture of all kinds of hard-wood interior finishing and decorations for private residences and buildings from architects' drawings and original designs, and all work is accomplished in the most artistic manner. Hard-wood mantels and sideboards are specialties of the house, and much of the work of this character found in the houses of Binghamton and vicinity is the product of this establishment. Mr. Bishop is a thoroughly practical and experienced cabinet maker, and gives his close personal attention to all the details of his business in the interest of superior products.

CONGDON HOUSE,
Thomas Congdon, Prop., 80 Lewis Street.

The Congdon House, located directly opposite the D., L. & W. R. R. passenger station, offers the traveling public a pleasant and comfortable sojourning place while in Binghamton. The hotel is heated throughout by steam and lighted with gas, and the rooms, both single and en suite, are handsomely furnished and appointed, far in advance even of many hotels of greater pretensions. The table is well supplied with both substantials and delicacies and the attention and service are first-class. In all its apartments the most thorough cleanliness pervades, and guests are given the same attention that may be looked for in any well regulated hotel, while the homelike character of the house is a grateful change from that of larger hostelries. The location of the house, contiguous to both railway stations, makes it a convenient one to travelers, who will receive such treatment here as will insure many returns. The rates are but $1.50 per day and special rates are made for large parties, according to location of rooms, and for weekly guests. The hotel is well patronized by travelers and tourists and has always enjoyed a high reputation for the accommodation of the public.

A. WINKLER,
**Pattern and Model Maker and Dealer In Engines, Boilers and Machinery,
196 State Street.**

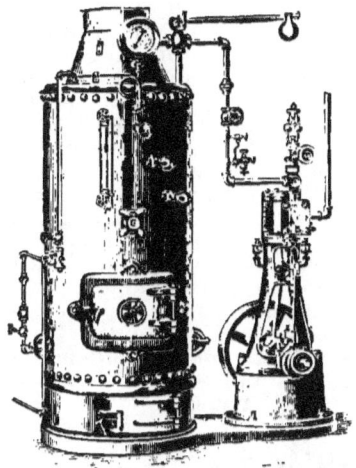

This city is fortunate in the possession of such an enterprise as that of Mr. A. Winkler, a gentleman of long and valuable experience, who removed here from Catskill, N. Y., in 1888 and has since established a large demand for his services among local and nearby manufacturers, besides whom he numbers among his customers manufacturers all over the United States. He is prepared with all facilities to execute all work in his line not only promptly but with that intelligent appreciation of design that is only found in an expert. As a maker of patterns for all kinds of brass and iron castings, as well as designing and drafting complicated machinery in sections or otherwise, he has acquired a most enviable reputation. Original designing of machinery is his specialty and any work of difficult construction is specially solicited. The carding and fitting of patterns for malleable iron and brass castings is also accomplished with great nicety. Special attention is also given to making models and drawings for experimental machinery and for the Patent Office. In connection with the above he deals in engines, boilers, shafting, hangers, pulleys and machinery, both new and second-hand, and the trade can frequently find second-hand machinery here at a great saving in price that will fully answer their requirements.

DELMONICO CAFE,
J. K. Marsh, Proprietor, Strong Block.

One of the finest public buildings in the "Parlor City" is the Strong block, a substantial brick structure recently erected and containing all modern improvements. In this beautiful building is found a fitting home for Mr. J. K. Marsh's splendid restaurant, which is without exception the finest restaurant in Southern New York, and is in all respects equal to many of the noted ones in the metropolis. It has been appropriately named Binghamton's Delmonico Cafe. The cafe occupies one-half of the front of the building on the ground floor. It is handsomely fitted up and appointed in hard-wood fixtures, the walls being relieved with mirrors and rich portieres divide the general dining-room from the ice cream parlor. The table furnishings are of the most elegant character, handsome china and glassware, silverware and napery of Damask linen. The cuisine is excellent and the service first-class in every respect, while the bill-of-fare includes every delicacy of the season and the market. Regular meals at stated hours are served to patrons, and orders a la carte are served at all hours day and night at reasonable prices. A specialty is made of ice cream with choice natural fruit flavors and of after-theatre suppers. No wines or liquors are served. Mr. Marsh also conducts another restaurant at 47 Court street which is also open at all hours day and night. He is an experienced caterer and an esteemed host.

JAMES O'NEIL,
Manufacturer of Light Carriages and Wagons, 255, 257 and 259 Water St.

This enterprise was founded in 1877, and the present commodious plant was erected in 1880. It is a two-story brick building 60x100 feet in dimensions, which is fully equipped with all modern conveniences for rapid and perfect production, and employment is given to a force of skilled workmen, all of whose operations are conducted under the close personal supervision of the proprietor. The products of the factory consist of but one quality of work, and that is the very best. Light carriages for business or pleasure are made in all the leading and fashionable styles, and also light and heavy business wagons of all kinds. While most of the vehicles are made to order, a considerable stock is also carried from which selections may be made. In addition to the manufacture of vehicles, Mr. O'Neil devotes particular attention to repairing of all kinds. The trade of the house extends throughout the city and vicinity, and many of the carriages and wagons in use in Binghamton are the products of this enterprising house.

GLEAZEN & KINGMAN,
Fine Boots, Shoes and Rubbers, 21 Court Street.

This house is a representative of the better class of retail establishments in this city, and while it caters to the masses, the goods handled are of a far superior character to those frequently offered as bargains but which are more often bad bargains in the end. It was instituted in the spring of 1887 and at once took a leading position in the trade. The store is centrally located and attractively appointed and contains a large and well selected stock of the very best goods in the market. While the goods are superior, the prices are governed by a commendable spirit of moderation and are quite as low as those of any competitor. The stock embraces boots, shoes and rubbers for men, women and children, in great variety of style and shape and in all sizes and widths, which have been chosen with experienced judgment and great care as to quality. The firm guarantee the quality of every pair of shoes they sell. The members of the firm, Messrs. W. H. Gleazen and Jefferson Kingman, are both progressive merchants and enterprising in all that relates to their business. Their establishment is a striking exponent of the attractive retail trade conveniences of this thriving city and is the parlor shoe store of the Parlor City.

PARLOR CITY BAKERY AND CONFECTIONERY,
G. G. Kaeppel, Prop., 22 Court Street.

The Parlor City Bakery and Confectionery, of which Mr. G. G. Kaeppel is the founder and proprietor, has long been recognized as a leading representative of the trade accommodations of the city. It was founded in 1880, and has since built up a large and growing trade, both at wholesale and retail, which extends throughout the city and surrounding towns. The premises occupied are commodious and well adapted to the business and are embraced in two floors, each 23x70 feet in dimensions, besides which two storage rooms are occupied elsewhere. The equipment of the plant embraces all the latest improved appliances known to the trade, operated by an eight-horse power steam engine, and employment is furnished to ten assistants, three wagons also being utilized for delivering the products to the trade and consumers. All kinds of bakery products are manufactured and with chemical uniformity. Only the best materials are used and the result is a high quality of product that is fully appreciated by the trade. Specialties are made of fine cakes, fancy wedding cakes and handsomely decorated cakes for entertainments, in which branch of the business this house has no successful competitor in the city. A full line of fine confectionery is also handled and the display of fine goods in this line, made in handsomely appointed salesrooms, is a most attractive one. Mr. Kaeppel is a native of Germany and is an expert and practical baker, and gives his personal attention to all details of the business in the interest of excellence of product. He is an esteemed citizen and progressive merchant and his success is as well merited as it is prominent.

CRANE & PARKER,
Dealer in Stoves and Ranges, 12 and 14 Court Street.

This leading and representative house was founded in 1881, the present firm, composed of Messrs. W. H. Crane and T. H. Parker, having been organized in 1886. The firm's salesrooms are embraced in a double store 35x60 feet in dimensions, where the stock shown is the most complete and comprehensive in all departments that can be found in this section. The line of stoves, ranges and furnaces comprises those whose superior heating and cooking qualities are familiar to every housekeeper, and includes the Sterling stoves and ranges made by the Sill Stove Co. of Rochester, N. Y. The firm also make a specialty of the wrought steel ranges for hotels, restaurants and private families, made by Sherman S. Jewett & Co., of Buffalo, N. Y., which are beyond question the acme of perfection in cooking apparatus. In the manufacture of tin, sheet iron and copper work, as well as general jobbing, the house occupies an unquestioned position at the head of the trade. The business of the house is active in this city and throughout the country and is constantly increasing under the stimulating effects of enterprising, reliable and progressive management.

R. REUBEN,
Merchant Tailor, 233 Chenango St.

A recent accession to the trade accommodations of that section of the city known as the North side is the merchant tailoring establishment of Mr. R. Reuben, which was instituted so late as October, 1891. This date, however, by no means represents the experience of the proprietor in the business, since he is an expert and practical cutter and custom tailor, and formerly conducted a similar enterprise at Elmira, N. Y. He occupies commodious and well arranged salesrooms, where he displays a carefully selected stock of fine imported and domestic woolens, suitings and cloths suitable for the production of fine garments for a discriminating and first-class trade. Notwithstanding the high quality of all garments produced the prices have been regulated by a commendable spirit of moderation and fair dealing, and are but little greater than is demanded for ready-made clothing while the garments are far superior. Mr. Reuben also carries in stock a variety of ready-made clothing of his own manufacture which is made up in exactly the same elegant manner as his custom made garments. Gents' furnishings goods are also carried in stock and a specialty is made in the manufacture of uniforms for all uses.

LYMAN CLOCK, SON & CO.,

Manufacturers of Tobacco and Cigars, 18 and 19 Wall Street.

The tobacco and cigar manufactory of Messrs. Lyman Clock, Son & Co. was founded in 1868. The premises occupied for the business are comprised in a handsome new four-story brick building 44x125 feet in dimensions which was erected in 1889 and is an architectural ornament to that part of the city in which it is located, not being dwarfed even by the Government building, which it adjoins. It is by far the best lighted and best fitted-up factory building in the city and was erected according to the experienced ideas and under the personal supervision of the head of the firm. The mechanical equipment embraces the latest improved tobacco cutting and cigar making machinery known to the trade, which is operated by a 50-horse power steam engine and employment is furnished to one hundred skilled workmen. The products embrace a full line of fine cut smoking and chewing tobacco, which is attractively put up and is in wide demand by the trade and consumers throughout Southern New York and Northern Pennsylvania, the chief brands of "Purity" and "Legal Tender" being especially popular and in demand by all dealers in this section. In cigars the firm manufacture a large number of grades which are sold to the jobbing trade only and are shipped to the Western States chiefly, as far as the Pacific slope. The members of the firm are Messrs. Lyman Clock, who has been connected with the business since its inception, and his son, W. A. Clock.

HOTCHKIN'S REAL ESTATE EXCHANGE,
163 Washington Street.

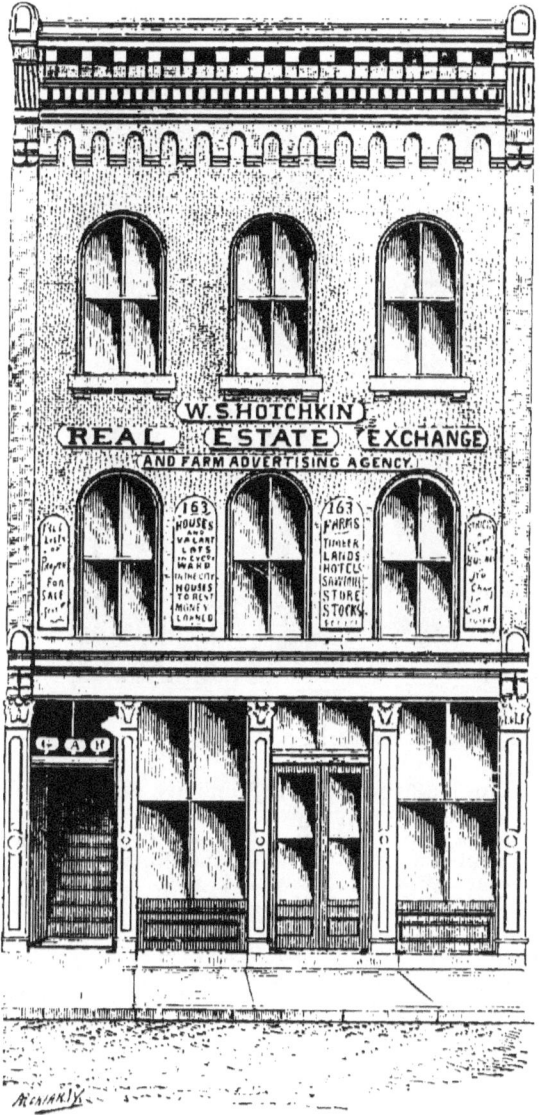

With the bright outlook that Binghamton enjoys for the future, investments in city property at the present time cannot but prove a most valuable medium for investors. Prominently engaged in providing favorable opportunities for persons in all walks of life, to acquire real estate upon the most favorable terms, is Mr. W. S. Hotchkin, who has particularly desirable plots of land and improved properties in all parts of the city, which he offers to investors at prices which are sure to give a wide margin of profit within a very short time. During the past five years over 600 vacant lots have been sold through this agency, besides several hundred thousand dollars worth of improved city property. Mr. Hotchkin makes a specialty of outside property, selling and exchanging, and his mammoth list which he sends free contains over 700 exchanges besides hundreds of city houses, vacant lots, farms, mills, hotels, stores, stocks of goods, village property, etc. for sale. He advertises largely and probably negotiates the sale and exchange of more outside property than any other agency in the State of New York. He also rents and takes charge of the property of non-residents, places loans, negotiates mortgages and serves patrons and investors in every available manner. He is well and widely known in connection with real estate matters and is a man in whom the utmost confidence may be reposed. He will be pleased to give callers full particulars with regard to Binghamton and outside real estate and all representations will be found based upon fair and honorable dealing.

STEPHENS & MILLER,

Wholesale and Retail Dealers in Stationery, Paper, Etc., 85 and 87 State St.

GEORGE A. KENT'S BLOCK.

This house was founded in 1881 though Mr. Stephens the head of the firm has been actively engaged in business in Binghamton since 1862. The firm deals in paper of every description including wrapping, writing, building, printing and wall papers, and also stationery and blank books, paper bags, twines, stationers' supplies, pens, inks, fancy articles and an infinite variety of goods much too numerous to particularize. They are the only firm in the city handling the same variety of goods and are the only jobbing paper warehouse here. They are by far the largest dealers in wall papers in the Southern tier and their stock in this line both for the wholesale and retail trade is complete in variety and high character. The premises occupied by the firm are embraced in a large double store 40x100 feet in dimensions, having three floors, which give them every facility to advantageously display their goods and to carry a very large stock. The trade of the house extends throughout Southern New York and Northern Pennsylvania chiefly, in which territory they are represented by traveling salesmen. A special feature of the business is the manufacture to order of blank books for banks, insurance and railroad companies and manufacturing corporations and firms. The members of the firm are Messrs. F. H. Stephens and Walter R. Miller. Mr. Stephens was at one time Mayor of Binghamton, and both gentlemen are closely identified with the commercial advancement of the city.

OTTO A. MALLES,

House, Sign and Fresco Painter and Dealers in Paints, Oils, Glass, Etc., 89 State Street.

The paint, oil and glass store of Mr. Otto A. Malles, though founded so recently as November 1, 1890, has, by reason of its enterprising and progressive management, a'ready placed itself in a leading position in the trade in this city and is enjoying a large and annually increasing trade. A commodious store and basement 22x80 feet in dimensions is occupied, which is filled with a large and complete stock of paints, oils, glass, varnishes, brushes and painters' supplies generally, as well as artists' materials. A full line of ready mixed paints is carried in all the leading and fashionable tints and colors, and the whole is offered to the trade and consumers at lowest possible prices. Mr. Malles also undertakes contracts for all kinds of house, sign and fresco painting which is executed in the highest style of the art. Employment is furnished to from fifteen to twenty skilled workmen and the facilities for the fulfillment of all orders with promptness are unexcelled. The work of this character in many of the newly erected buildings in Binghamton and vicinity has been performed by this house and with invariable satisfaction to all patrons. Mr. Malles is an enterprising merchant and a pushing business man, and his enterprise is a prominent feature of the trade facilities of the Parlor City.

ALONZO ROBERSON,

Manufacturer of Sash, Doors and Blinds, Main Office, 313 Chenango Street, Works, West End.

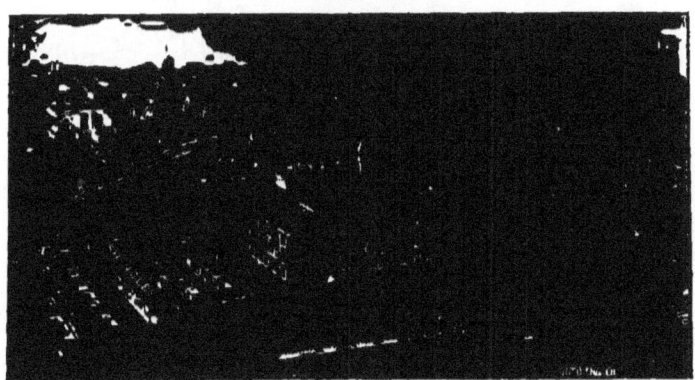

The extensive wood-working enterprise of Mr. Alonzo Roberson is the largest and most important establishment of its kind in the state, and one of the oldest industrial enterprises of Binghamton. It was founded in 1848 by Newman Marsh, the present proprietor having been at the head of its affairs since 1856, and in the management of the present extensive business, he has for the last few years been ably assisted by his son, Mr. Alonzo Roberson, Jr. The newly erected plant at the West End, which has been recently completed and occupied, covers ten and one-half acres and adjoins both the Erie and D., L. & W. railroads, affording with the network of side-tracks which gridiron the premises, the most perfect receiving and shipping facilities, which place the concern far in advance of any other house in this vicinity and on a par with the most extensive concerns of the kind in the country. The establishment in operation presents an interesting spectacle and is a perfect bee-hive of mechanical industry, employment being given to one hundred and fifty workmen. The products are shipped to all parts of the Eastern, Middle and Southern states, and are also exported through New York shipping houses to many foreign countries. They embrace sash, doors, blinds, builders' woodwork and planing mill lumber, hardwood doors, mantels and other hardwood finish for buildings, both for the trade in regular sizes, as well as special goods from architects' drawings, and many of the finest modern commercial and office buildings, hotels and apartment houses in the great cities of the East have been supplied with doors, sash, blinds and other interior woodwork by this house. The facilities of the house for production are unsurpassed in the state. The lumber is received direct from the original sources of supply and an enormous stock is constantly kept on hand maturing, as well as to supply the trade in this vicinity, the stock carried being by far the largest of any concern in Binghamton. Aside from manufacturing for the wholesale trade, a large business is done in planing, re-sawing and general wood-working for builders and others in this city, and although the manufacturing operations have all been removed to the new plant, the old lumber yards on Chenango street are still maintained for the accommodation of the public.

Binghamton has long enjoyed a high reputation as a source of supply for the best qualities of working men's clothing, and it is but just to state that this high reputation has been largely due to the efforts and enterprise of Mr. Reed B. Freeman, President and Manager of the Binghamton Overall Co. Mr. Freeman was the founder of the Freeman Overall Co. of this city, about ten years ago, and until recently one of its managers. On September 1, 1891, he organized the Binghamton Overall Co., and he is also interested in the proprietorship of the Freeman Manufacturing Co., of Scranton, Pa., which company is engaged in the production of a similar class of goods. The Binghamton Overall Co.'s plant occupies a considerable part of the five-story "Republican" building, with offices and cutting rooms on the first floor and manufacturing department on the upper floors. The company is in the possession of every modern facility for the production of superior goods, sewing machines being operated by steam power, and employment is furnished to a large number of skilled operatives. The products embrace the celebrated Freeman pant overalls and sack coats, also lumbermen's and hunters' flannel-lined duck coats, which have long enjoyed being the best goods of the kind in the market and are so recognized by the trade. In addition to the above they manufacture a large line of pantaloons, made from kerseys, jeans, cottons, worsteds, etc. The goods are all distinguished for the quality of the material, careful workmanship, high wearing properties and general excellence. At the same time the price is as low as goods of similar quality can be produced anywhere. This, indeed, may be said to be the corner-stone upon which the business has been founded, viz: the production of a line of goods which are at the same time both cheap and serviceable. The trade of the house is well spread over the Middle and Western States as far west as the Mississippi, and having been instituted under the most favorable auspices, gives every promise of long continued success and prosperity. Mr. Freeman is closely allied to the progress of Binghamton and is highly esteemed both by the trade and this community.

THE WILKINSON MANUFACTURING COMPANY,

Manufacturers of Children's Express Wagons and Sleighs, Dining Chairs, Etc., Foot Sanford Street.

This house, originally founded in 1860 by Winton & Doolittle, passed through several changes of proprietorship; the immediate predecessor of the present incorporated company was the Winton Manufacturing Company, The Wilkinson Manufacturing Company having succeeded in April, 1890. The plant covers several city lots and embraces a series of buildings, fully equipped with wood-working machinery, operated by water power with a 75-horse power auxiliary steam engine. Large yards are also utilized for storing lumber. The company employs about 125 skilled workmen and others, and the products embrace childrens' express wagons and sleighs of many designs, styles and sizes. The last year the company have also added to the above named specialties, the production of dining chairs, folding tables and other articles of furniture and their success in this department has been quite equal to the other. The trade of the house extends throughout the United States generally and their goods are also exported abroad. The officers of the company are Messrs. W. H. Wilkinson, prest., Charles Davis, vice-prest., W. H. Eastwood, sec'y, and C. E. Edgerton, treas. Mr. Wilkinson is also the senior member of the firm of Wilkinson, Son & Co., tanners, and Mr. Eastwood is of the firm of Wilkinson & Eastwood, chair manufacturers. The enterprise is one of the most prominent features of Binghamton's industrial activity and its success is creditable alike to the city and to its management.

ALEX. E. ANDREWS,
Real Estate and Insurance, 56 Court St.

Among the leading representatives of the real estate and insurance business of Binghamton is the agency of Mr. Alex. E. Andrews, who has been a prominent member of the fraternity for about twenty years, during which time he has developed great success in conducting a large business in both departments of real estate and insurance. He represents a first-class line of fire insurance companies, and the well known reliable Massachusetts Mutual Life Insurance Company, of Springfield, whose liberal and honorable business methods for over forty years have won the public confidence and are guarantees of its future stability. In real estate matters Mr. Andrews transacts a general agency business, buying, selling, and exchanging real property of all kinds. He has a large number of valuable and desirable central and suburban properties for sale, among which is the valuable Moeller estate of ninety acres within the city limits, and the certain advance of prices in the early spring will insure investors a handsome profit if bought at the present time, while to those who desire permanent investment of capital or are looking for home sites, the opportunities now offered were never excelled in the history of this city. Mr. Andrews also has the Lombard Investment Co.'s guaranteed mortgages and debenture bonds for sale, which will be found a safe and desirable form of investment for those of small or large means. Mr. Andrews is a highly respected citizen of Binghamton; he was twice elected as the representative of Broome county in the State Assembly, in 1878 and 1880, and he is closely identified with the progress and development of this city.

CASPER & CRITTENDEN,
Wholesale and Retail Dealers in Crockery, Glassware, Etc., 209 Chenango and 24 Eldredge Street.

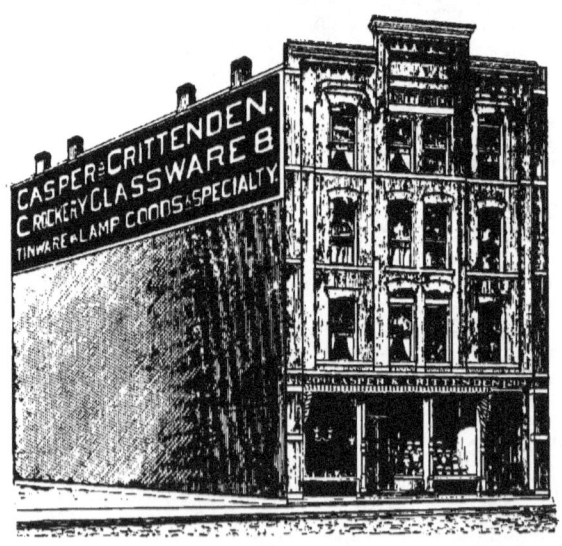

The extensive wholesale and retail establishment of Messrs. Casper & Crittenden has long been a leader in its line of trade in the Southern

Tier. The house was founded in 1883 by Casper & Honan, who were succeeded in 1887 by Casper & Wood, and they in turn by the present firm in 1890. The members of the firm are Messrs. B. Casper and H. A. Crittenden, the former having been at the head of its affairs from the inception of the business. The premises occupied for the business are commodious and well arranged for the display of a large and varied stock, and no house in the State outside of the great metropolitan centers is better prepared to meet the wants of the general trade than this one. The stock carried embraces a large and well selected line of crockery, glassware, tinware, lamps, kerosene goods, china, bric-a-brac, fancy goods, porcelain, etc., much of which is imported direct, and when of domestic production is procured from the factories in large lots. The variety of goods is large and the prices will be found as low as may be obtained in New York or elsewhere. The trade of the house extends throughout Southern New York and Pennsylvania, and traveling salesmen visit dealers within the territory at frequent intervals, thus affording them the best advantages to promptly and expeditiously sort up their stocks and have their orders filled with greater dispatch than would be possible from more distant sources of supply. The enterprise is a prominent feature of the retail and jobbing trade of Binghamton.

J. W. BROWN,
Laundry and Custom Shirts, 215 Washington Street.

The Binghamton Steam Laundry and the Otseningo Shirt Factory, of which Mr. J. W. Brown is the founder and proprietor, together form the chief enterprise of the kind in Binghamton. It is also one of old establishment, the laundry department having been instituted about twenty years ago, and the shirt factory was added in 1874. The premises occupied are comprised in the first floor and basement of the handsome four-story brick building, which was erected in 1888 by Mr. Brown. The equipment embraces all that has been found useful in modern laundry machinery and is operated by a 25-horse power engine, employment being given to about twenty operatives. From the inception of the business, the aim of the management has been to do thoroughly first-class work only, and every operation and detail of the business is carefully supervised by the proprietor in person. The result has been the establishment of a trade which is annually increasing and which includes all the discriminating members of this community. Branch agencies have been established in the surrounding towns and cities, and also in this city, and wagons also call for and deliver work to all parts of the city. Fine shirts are made to measure, which are perfect in fit and finish, and this department is well patronized by those who are fastidious in their wearing apparel. Mr. Brown is an enterprising and progressive man and has succeeded in building up a notable success in his chosen vocation.

L. L. & V. B. CANOLL,
Stoves, Heaters, Ranges, Etc., 101 Court Street.

This enterprise, which is one of the leading houses of its kind in Binghamton, was originally founded twenty-one years ago, by W. P. Canoll, and it has long been recognized as a prominent representative of the trade accommodations of the city. The premises occupied are commodious, centrally located and well adapted to the business, and ample accommodations are at hand for carrying a large and complete stock of stoves, ranges, heaters, house furnishing goods, tinware, etc. Altogether the stock is of an essentially superior character, is well selected with experienced judgment and covers a wide variety. The stoves and ranges are the best and latest improved appliances of the kind on the market and embody all the really desirable features that have been introduced together with peculiar excellencies exclusively their own, and they are confidently recommended to the public as economical of fuel, easy of management, and of high class efficiency. In house furnishing goods including the multitude of useful articles for lightening the labor of the house-wife, this house is headquarters, and a specialty is made of fancy moulds for culinary purposes, which cannot be obtained in so great a variety elsewhere in Binghamton, and no house in the city carries so many repairs for all kinds of stoves, ranges and furnaces, those not in stock being promptly procured. The established reputation of the house for reliability and liberal and fair dealing methods has resulted in an annually increasing trade and fully entitles it to the success it enjoys.

WILLIAMS & ROSENKRANS,
Pharmacists, Chemists and Perfumers, 23 Court St.

The elegant and tastefully appointed pharmacy of Messrs. Williams & Rosenkrans is one of the most attractively furnished establishments of the kind in the state, and is fully entitled to be recorded as a work of art. It was originally founded in 1874 by James E. Brown, the present firm having been organized April 1, 1891, at which date the present newly fitted up place of business was first opened to the public. The firm carry in stock a full and complete line of drugs, medicines, pharmaceutical preparations, physicians' supplies and proprietary medicines, as well as toilet requisites, fancy goods, druggists' sundries and perfumery. They make a chief specialty in compounding physicians' prescriptions and family recipes, with due regard to the responsibilities of the department. The pharmacy enjoys the patronage and esteem of a wide circle of customers, which is gradually extending as its reputation for reliability becomes more widely known. In the purchase of no other class of goods should greater discrimination be used than in procuring medicines, and bearing this fact in mind we take pleasure in commending the pharmacy of Messrs. Williams & Rosenkrans to the public as thoroughly reliable in all respects.

EZRA L. OSTROM,

Druggist, 246 Chenango Street.

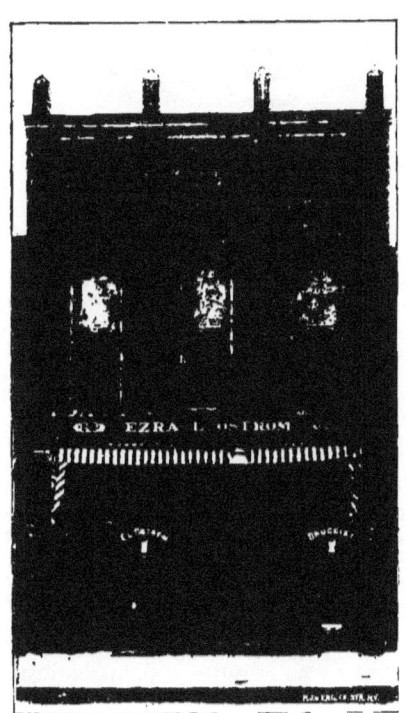

The pharmacy of which Mr. Ezra L. Ostrom is the enterprising proprietor, was founded by him about fifteen years ago, and is recognized as being a most popular adjunct to the trade facilities of the North side. The store is handsomely appointed, and the stock is large and complete, embracing a full line of drugs and medicines of every description, together with a complete assortment of all standard proprietary medicines, toilet articles and requisites, perfumes, fancy goods, druggists' sundries, etc. Special attention is paid to the accurate compounding of physicians' prescriptions and this department is a distinguishing feature of the business. The store presents that attractive appearance always associated with a thoroughly equipped establishment of this character and is also headquarters for the medical profession in the locality in which it is situated. Mr. Ostrom is practically conversant and skilled in all relating to his profession and enjoys the esteem and consideration of a large circle of patrons. He is courteous and liberal in all transactions with patrons and we are safe in predicting for him a continued expansion of operations in the future.

THE BINGHAMTON TRUST COMPANY,
Corner State and Henry Streets.

The latest accession to the financial and fiduciary institutions of Binghamton and one that occupies an important field is The Binghamton Trust Company, which was incorporated September 8, 1890, with a capital stock of $400,000, the stockholders also being personally liable for $400,000. Thus $800,000 stand between a depositor in this company and any possible loss. This company is the only one of the kind in the southern section of the State between New York and Buffalo and a large portion of Pennsylvania contiguous to Binghamton is unsupplied with a similar institution. Its field of operations is therefore wide-spread and it has already attracted a large and growing business. The capital of the company is required by law to be invested in securities of undoubted safety, of fixed value and of a kind unaffected by stock manipulations. By its charter the company has authority and is prepared to loan money on real or personal security; to act as fiscal or transfer agent, as trustee, guardian or receiver, as executor or administrator, as committee of the estate of persons of unsound mind; to act as agent in the collection of income or rents; to accept and execute trusts of married women in respect to their separate property; to take, accept and execute any and all trusts that may be committed to it; to receive deposits in trust; to receive deposits of money, in active account, subject to check at sight without notice; to receive deposits, and issue therefor certificates transferable and payable on demand, with interest at the rate of four per cent. per annum, if left three months, and special rates for other definite periods. Interest is paid at the rate of four per cent. on all deposits left three months, and compounded semi-annually and entered on the book of the depositor when presented. Interest is paid at a fixed rate and is not dependent upon earnings. There being no stated dividend period, deposits can be withdrawn at any time after three months and full interest will be paid to date of withdrawal. The company differs from a Savings Bank in that it has a large capital, safely invested, that is pledged as security to its depositors. It differs from a National Bank in that it can loan money on real estate security as well as personal, and is not restricted in the amount of its loans. The trustees are well-known business men. Successful in their personal affairs, they bring to the management of the Trust company experience and sound judgment, that are sufficient guarantees that any trust committed to the company will be faithfully and honestly executed. The Trust Company is free from the contingency of death, which is so often a disastrous feature in the selection and appointment of an individual as trustee. When a person selects it to act as his trustee, he has the assurance that it will be in continuance as long as the trust lasts. The officers of the company are C. J. Knapp, prest., H. H. Crary, vice-prest., J. B. Landfield, treas., Stoddard Hammond, Jr., secretary, Jacob Wiser, cashier, and W. J. Welsh, attorney, and the trustees are C. J. Knapp, J. S. Wells, S. Hammond, Jr., W. J. Welsh, M. Birdsall, H. S. Jarvis, J. B. Landfield, G. T. Rogers, J. B. Bowen, J. B. Simpson, A. J. Schlager, W. E. Taylor, Cyrus Strong, H. H. Crary and Frank Gould, and the list of stockholders is a directory of the wealth of Binghamton. The offices of the company are in the new Strong block and are attractively and handsomely fitted up and appointed and form a fitting home for so substantial and solid an institution.

INDEX.

Abell, E. A., Pie Preparations........ Page 106
Ackley, G. S. & Co., Real Estate............ 96
Acme Oil Co.,................................. 128
Adams, E. & Sons, Brass and Iron Works... 79
Alden, H. T., Cigar M'f'r................... 47
Andrews, Alex. E., Real Estate............ 154
Arlington, The.............................. 90
Babcock & Stowell, Hardware............... 107
Barlow, Rogers & Simpson, Cigar M'f'rs,... 114
Barnes & Congdon, Marble Works............. 88
Barrett Bros., Pianos and Organs.......... 107
Bartlett & Co., Planing Mill............... 74
Bates Steam Laundry........Opposite title page
Bayless Paper Co.,.......................... 71
Beach Electrical Supply, The Clarence E.... 41
Bean & Co., Wholesale Grocers.............. 77
Beardsley, Geo. W., Leather and Findings..141
Beman & Bayless, M'f'rs Barrel Heads....... 49
Bennett, Abel & Co., Clothiers............. 89
Bennett Bros., Cigar Box M'f'rs............ 70
Bennett M'f'g Co., M'f'rs of Overalls......134
Berwind-White Coal Mining Co..............113
Binghamton Blackboard Co................... 71
Binghamton Butter Package Co., The......... 94
Binghamton Chair Co., L'd.................108
Binghamton Cigar Co........................116
Binghamton Cutlery Co......................134
Binghamton Dairy Association..............135
Binghamton Glass Works..................... 38
Binghamton Glove and Mitten M'f'g Co....... 46
Binghamton M'f'g Co., Outing Garments...... 81
Binghamton Oil Refining Co................125
Binghamton Overall Co......................152
Binghamton Produce Co...................... 59
Binghamton Safe Deposit Co................110
Binghamton Trust Co........................158
Binghamton Veneer Co......................127
Binghamton Wire Goods Co., The............. 54
Binghamton Wire Works...................... 74
Binghamton Woolen Co....................... 57
Bishop, J. F., Cabinet Maker..............144
Bolles Hoe and Tool Co., The L., Hoe M'f'rs 69
Boss, Stoppard & Hecox, Insurance.......... 93
Bradstreet Company, The, Mercantile Agency.126
Bronson, W. C. & Co., Cigar M'f'rs......... 78
Brown, Dexter D., Furniture................ 86
Brown, J. W., Laundry.....................155
Brown & Co., Wholesale Fruits.............103
Buchanan Geo., Wines and Liquors..........102
Bundy M'f'g Co., Time Recorders...........131
Burhans & Barnes, Insurance Agents......... 50
Bush, H. L. & Co., Cigar M'f's............. 63
Callahan & Douglas, Hardware..............133
Canoll, L. & V. B., Stoves................156
Carver, W. J., Dairy Products.............140
Casper & Crittenden, China and Crockery, etc.154
Chubbuck, H. W. & Co., Spice Mills......... 80
Clapp, C. M., Boots and Shoes.............136
Clarke Co., John Ray, Wholesale Hatters... 68
Clock, L., Son & Co., Cigar M'f'rs........148
Congdon House..............................144
Conklin & Mersereau, Grass Seeds........... 83
Corbin A., Son & Co., Wholesale Drugs...... 36
Corbin, C. A., Egg Shipper................. 64
Cornell, Davis & Shear, Grocers...........133
Cornell, J. C. & Son, Funeral Directors...143
Cornwall, Reed & Lane, Brokers............127
Crandall, Stone & Co., Carriage Trimmings.. 72
Crane & Parker, Stoves....................147
Darling, C. S., Chicago Beef............... 47
Darrow Hay Co.............................. 88
Delmonico Cafe............................145
Doolittle, L., Custom Miller............... 56
Dun, R. G. & Co., The Mercantile Agency...112
Ebblie & Rider, 5 and 10 cent Goods.......136
Ely, S. Mills & Co., Wholesale Grocers..... 40
Empire Grain & Elevator Co.............60 61
Eureka Advertising Agency.................. 60
Field, P. E., Grocer......................117
Folmsbee & Ives, Cigar M'f'rs.............. 54
Folsom & Hungerford, Stoves...............142
Ford, G. H. & E. A., Coal Dealers.......... 49
Fowler, W. C. & Co., M'f'rs Confectionery.. 98
Freeman, Reed B., Overall M'f'r...........152
Gaylord, H. J., Real Estate................ 70
Gaylord's Storage Warehouse................ 63
Gaylord & Eitapenc, Steam Heating.......... 95
Gleazen & Kingman, Boots and Shoes........146
Gilbert, F. H.,...........................130
Goldstein Bros., Clothiers................142
Green, Geo. E., Coal Wholesale............113
Gumberg, John & Co., Cigar M'f'rs.........101
Hanrahan Bros., Wholesale Liquors.........130
Harding, Lowell & Son, Hides and Furs.....138

INDEX.

Hathaway & Berry, Flour and Grain............ 93
Heath & Harris, Machinists.................... 66
Hemingway, W. W., Stoves, etc................ 56
Hennessey Bros., Cigar M'fr's................117
Hills, McLean & Williams, Dry Goods..........124
Hirschmann Bros., Dry Goods..................132
Hoffmann Lubricating Oil Co..................110
Holbert, W. P., Lumber, etc................... 89
Hotchkin, W. S., Real Estate..................149
Hull, Grummond & Co., Cigar M'fr's............ 66
Humes & Smith, Grocers.......................110
Johnson & Lamb, Shoe M'fr's...................106
Jones of Binghamton, Scales................... 44
Kaeppel, G. G., Bakery........................146
Kent, Geo. A. & Co., Cigar M'fr's.............100
Kilmer, Dr. & Co., Proprietary Medicines..33-34
Kilmer, Willis Sharpe, Advertising Agency..... 98
Knapp & Son, Machinists....................... 67
Lacey, J. W., Cigar Box M'fr.................. 80
Lauder, I. & Son, Marble Works................ 41
Lee, Charles E., Lumber, Lime, etc............ 57
Lewis House..................................141
Lloyd & Gardiner, Wholesale Confectioners..... 62
Lowell Business College.......................121
Lynch & Christie, Grates and Mantels.......... 46
Lyon, Addison J., Lumber......................126
Malane, D. J., Plumber........................ 77
Malles, Otto A., Paints and Oils..............151
Marsh, J. K., Cafe............................145
Marsh, O. B., Jeweler.........................142
Mason, Edward R., Optician.................... 87
Mason, O. R., Agt., Plumber................... 51
Matthews, G. A., Real Estate..................102
McKinney, Everts & Co., Spice Mills........... 52
McMahon, M., Carriage M'fr.................... 76
Meagley & Blanchard, Coal.....................109
Middlebrook, C. D. & Co., Lumber.............. 73
M. I. S. T.................................... 48
Mitchell, S. N., Insurance....................108
Moon, Geo. Q. & Co., Flour Mills.............. 40
Morgan, Ainsworth & Carroll, Insurance........137
Morgan, Julius P., Cigar M'fr................. 68
Moses, John J., Wholesale Liquors.............120
Mosher, Wm. H., Grocer........................139
Mount Prospect Medical Institute..............111
Nelson, B. H. & Son, Bankers..................129
Nelson & Legge, Wholesale Fruits.............. 91
Newing, Judson S., Jewelry M'fr...............134
North & Shaw, Wholesale Provisions............ 94
Nowlan, John, Boiler Works.................... 79
Noyes, Jos. P. & Co., M'fr's Combs and Buttons. 42
Offenheiser, S. E., Wholesale Fruits.......... 72
Ogden, Wm. H. & Co., Cigar M'fr's............. 55
O'Neil, James, Carriage M'fr..................146
O'Neill, Matthew, Stoves......................144
Osgood & Thompson, Scale M'fr's............... 86

Ostrom, E. L., Pharmacist.....................157
Ostrom, Barnes & Co., Cigar M'fr's............ 37
Otis Bros., Pharmacists....................... 99
Parker, Geo. L., Coal.........................136
Patten, A. S. & Bro., Provisions..............139
Persels & Mack, Harness M'fr's................ 58
Rahilly, W. F. & Co., Wholesale Wines......... 67
Reuben, R., Tailor............................147
Reynolds, Rogers & Co., Cigar M'f'rs.......... 38
Rich Bros., Insurance.........................113
Richards, F. B. & Co., Cigar M'fr's........... 73
Riley Business College, The...................104
Roberson, Alonzo, Planing Mill................151
Rogers, F. H., Stationery.....................143
Russell, John M., Cigar M'fr.................. 85
Saunders, C. L. & Son, Dressed Beef........... 39
Searles, J. E., Tobacconist................... 48
Sears, Chas. W., Bookseller...................135
Sears, O. W., Coal Dealer..................... 35
Sec'ty Mutual Life Asso'tn, Binghamton, N. Y.. 81
Shapley & Wells, Machinists...................116
Singer M'f'g Co., The, Sewing Machines........115
Sisson Bros. & Welden, Dry Goods..............123
Smith, C. A., Cigar M'fr...................... 65
Smith, C. B., Jr., & Co., M'fr's of Cigars.... 35
Smith, E. C. & Co., Spokes and Hubs........... 97
Smith, W. S. & Sons, Druggists and Grocers....105
Star Electric Co.............................. 76
Stephens & Miller, Paper Warehouse............150
Stevens, W. D., Contractor.................... 64
Stickley & Brandt, Furniture..................122
Stickley & Brandt, Chair Co...................118
Stone & Germond, Shoe Mfrs.................... 92
Stone & Sanders, Paints and Oils.............. 58
Stow Manufacturing Co., Flexible Shafts..118-119
Sturtevant-Larrabee Co., The, Carriage Mfrs... 75
Talbot, J. B. & Co., Hides and Pelts.......... 36
U. S. Baking Co............................... 50
Vandebogart's Paper Box Factory............... 80
Vickers & Brooker, Plumbers...................109
Weed, J. B. & Co., Tanners.................... 42
Weed, L. I., Cabinet Work.....................111
Wells, Chas. C. & Co., Cigar Mfrs............. 82
White, J. D., Awnings.........................130
White & Co., Wholesale Liquors................ 98
Whitney-Noyes Seed Co., The, Grass Seeds......128
Wiedman Shoe Co............................... 52
Wilkinson Manufacturing Co., Sleds and Chairs.153
Wilkinson, Son & Co, Tanners.................. 87
Wilkinson & Eastwood, Mfrs. of Chairs......... 53
Williams & Rosenkrans, Pharmacists............156
Wilson, A. G., Insurance...................... 92
Winkler, A., Paper Maker......................145
Winton & Harroun, Brass Finishers............. 78
Woodruff, Charles, Cigar Box Mfr.............. 97
Young, Wm. F., Cooper......................... 43

www.ingramcontent.com/pod-product-compliance
Lightning Source LLC
Chambersburg PA
CBHW030301170426
43202CB00009B/836